LABOR IN INTERNATIONAL TRADE THEORY

Labor in International Trade Theory

A New Perspective on Japanese-American Issues

Junichi Goto

The Johns Hopkins University Press
Baltimore and London

The Johns Hopkins University Press
701 West 40th Street
Baltimore, Maryland 21211
The Johns Hopkins Press Ltd., London

∞ The paper used in this book meets the minimum requirements
of American National Standard for Information Sciences — Permanence
of Paper for Printed Library Materials, ANSI Z39.48-1984.

Library of Congress Cataloging-in-Publication Data
Goto, Junichi.
 Labor in international trade theory : a new perspective on
Japanese-American issues / Junichi Goto.
  p.   cm.
 Includes bibliographical references (p.   ).
 ISBN 0-8018-4005-8 (alk. paper)
 1. Foreign trade and employment — Mathematical models. 2. Japan —
Commerce — United States. 3. United States — Commerce — Japan.
I. Title.
HD5710.7.G68   1990
331.12′0973— dc20

89-13880
CIP

CONTENTS

PREFACE

THIS BOOK IS intended to serve three major purposes: (*a*) to develop a formal general equilibrium trade model under imperfect competition in both product and labor markets, which has a firm microeconomic foundation and yet is based upon new, realistic assumptions; (*b*) to demonstrate that such a rigorous framework can be readily used for practical applications; and (*c*) to analyze theoretically and empirically the U.S.-Japan economic relationship.

A careful look at U.S.-Japan trade reveals that international trade and domestic labor problems are closely related and that they strongly affect each other. For example, international trade affects the domestic unemployment situation through a change in domestic production. On the other hand, domestic labor situations may strongly influence the trade policy of a country through the lobbying activities of labor unions. Therefore, in order to understand the economic relationship in the real world, it is important to have an integrated analysis of the two issues.

Unfortunately, however, very few economic theories are available to make such an integrated analysis, mainly because international economics (especially international trade theory) and labor economics have been developed separately. Because of the lack of an integrated theory, discussions of the relationship between the trade problem and domestic labor problem often become emotional. For example, protectionists sometimes argue that while the United States is suffering from a huge trade deficit and a high unemployment rate, Japan is enjoying a huge trade surplus and low unemployment; *therefore*, Japanese exports of its unemployment are responsible for the unemployment problem in the United States.

In view of the above, one of the major purposes of this book is to establish a new rigorous theory of "trade-labor" problems, which might be called the labor-oriented international trade theory. Using the new model, trade conflicts in the real world, especially trade conflicts between Japan and the United States, are examined.

The idea of the labor-oriented trade theory has emerged from my work experiences at various institutions, including the Japanese Ministry of Labor, Yale University, and the World Bank, and I am deeply indebted to numerous people in these institutions. Although the number of people to whom I am indebted is too large to permit individual mention, I wish to thank, among others, the people at the Japanese Ministry of Labor, Yale University, and the World Bank whose insights, guidance, and comments were invaluable to the completion of this book. Also, I wish to thank my family who encouraged me greatly to continue the demanding task of preparing this book.

LABOR IN INTERNATIONAL
TRADE THEORY

CHAPTER ONE

Introduction

GROWING TENDENCY TOWARD PROTECTIONISM

While most industrialized countries have been struggling with economic difficulties after the first and second oil crises, Japan has been enjoying sustained economic growth supported by the dramatic increase in its exports. Such a remarkable performance has brought about growing trade conflicts with major countries, most notably with the United States and the EC. In fact, exports have led Japanese economic development ever since the Meiji era, and there is a long history of trade conflicts between Japan and the major countries. As early as the 1930s, Japan was forced to announce a voluntary export restraint (VER) on its cotton shipments to the United States after rather hostile negotiations between the two countries. Since then, Japan has experienced uninterrupted trade conflicts with many industrialized countries, although the product categories at issue have changed from labor-intensive goods such as textiles and clothing, to color television sets, and to capital- and technology-intensive products such as automobiles and personal computers.

Faced with rapidly growing imports from Japan, many countries have imposed restrictions on the inflow of various products made in Japan. For example, these days most countries impose import restrictions on Japanese automobiles. In addition to automobiles, various products, including textiles, steel, and VCRs, are subject to restrictions by many countries, and such restrictions seem to be expanded and strengthened every year. Restriction methods used by the importing countries are diversifying, from conventional tariffs to various nontariff barriers (NTBs), such as quotas and VERs. As examined in detail later in this book, NTBs tend to be more harmful to importing countries than tariffs because they bring about more serious market distortions. But, in many cases, the competitiveness of the Japanese industry is so strong that tariff alone (unless it is an extraordinarily high rate) cannot restrict imports to the level desired by the importing country. Therefore, more and more countries have resorted to nontariff measures in an attempt to protect their domestic industries.

FIGURE 1.1 Japanese Trade with the United States

Source: United Nations, *Statistical Yearbook*.

These restrictive measures, however, seem to be unsuccessful in curbing imports from Japan. As becomes clearer when we examine several
examples of trade conflicts (e.g., textiles, color television sets, and automobiles) between Japan and the United States, Japan has made various concessions to demands from the importing countries, often in the
form of the "voluntary" export restraint. In spite of such concessions,
the Japanese trade surplus has been increasing over time.

Figure 1.1 shows that the Japanese trade surplus over the United
States, the largest trading partner of Japan, has been increasing at an
alarming rate every year. In 1976 the value of Japanese exports to the
United States was $16 billion, which exceeded the U.S. exports to Japan
by 30 percent. Although the 30 percent gap is large, the trade gap in
the 1980s far exceeds it. During 1980–85 Japanese exports to the United
States doubled from $32 billion to $66 billion, but U.S. exports to Japan
did not grow very much (they increased slightly from $25 billion in 1980
to $26 billion in 1985). In 1986 U.S. exports to Japan increased by 13
percent to $29 billion, probably because of the dramatic depreciation
of the U.S. dollar after the Plaza agreement by finance ministers of five
major economies (G5) in September 1985. But, in spite of the weakening

of the U.S. dollar, Japanese exports to the United States increased by 23 percent to $81 billion. As a result, the Japanese trade surplus over the U.S. in 1986 was as large as $52 billion. In other words, the value of Japanese exports to the United States is three times higher than United States exports to Japan. Such trade imbalance seems alarming even to casual observers. Although various attempts were made by the two countries to reduce the trade gap, the huge surplus of Japan over the United States has not disappeared.

Faced with this alarming trade imbalance, protectionism has gained strong support in the United States, especially in the U.S. Congress. The U.S. government put ever-stronger pressure upon Japan to reduce Japanese exports and to open up the Japanese market. In 1989 the United States condemned Japan, Brazil, and India for unfair trade practices under "super 301." The trade imbalance is so large that desperate (short-term) measures have been taken to restrict Japanese imports, and foreign exchange has adjusted in the direction of weaker dollar.

Unfortunately, however, few attempts have been made to discuss the fundamental reasons for the huge difference in international competitiveness between the industries in the two countries and to establish long-term measures for structural adjustment. It is important to discuss why the international competitiveness of certain industries in the two countries is so different, in spite of the fact that Japan and the United States are similar in many respects, such as technological level and relative factor endowments. Emotional protectionism seems to prevail in the United States, without concern for fundamental issues. In view of this, one of the major purposes of this book is to objectively analyze the Japan-U.S. economic relationship. After a detailed theoretical analysis based on a newly developed general equilibrium model, it will be shown that imperfect competition in the product and labor markets is one of the major reasons for a weaker position in international competitiveness of certain industries, for example, automobiles and steel, in the United States. In the estimation part of the book, an attempt will be made to measure the losses to the U.S. economy when the United States imposes various import restrictions as a remedy for the trade imbalances without rectifying imperfect competition in certain industries that exhibit weak competitiveness in the international economy.

DOMESTIC LABOR PROBLEMS UNDERLYING TRADE CONFLICT

As examined in detail in later chapters, trade conflicts are greatly influenced by the domestic labor problems in the importing country. A

FIGURE 1.2 American Automobile Market

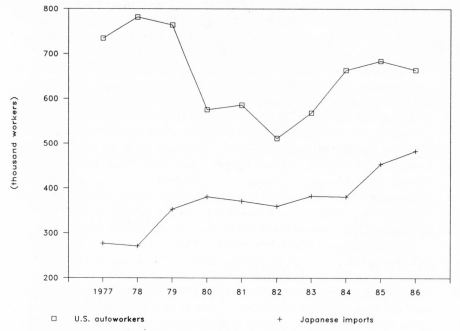

Source: U.S. Department of Labor, *Monthly Labor Review;* U.S. Department
of Commerce, *Survey of Current Business.*

careful look at Japan-U.S. trade, for example, reveals that international
trade and domestic labor problems are closely related and strongly affect
each other. For example, international trade affects domestic unemployment through changed production in domestic industries. At the
same time, domestic labor situations strongly influence the country's
trade policy through the lobbying activities of labor unions.

The American automobile industry after the second oil crisis gives
an example of the interrelationship between international trade and
domestic labor problems. When the sales of American automobiles drastically dropped after 1979, protectionism became very strong in the
United States. While the decline of sales of American automobiles resulted from various other reasons, such as a general decline in personal
consumption due to a recession, many protectionists argued that Japanese competition was the most important (or sole) reason for the difficulty of the American automobile industry and that Japan exported
her unemployment problems to the United States.

Figure 1.2 shows the number of American autoworkers and the number of Japanese automobiles imported since the middle of the 1970s.

The figure reveals how serious the unemployment problem in the American auto industry was after the second oil crisis and how rapidly imports of Japanese automobiles increased before the introduction of the Japanese VER in 1981. In 1978, the year immediately before the second oil crisis, the number of production workers in the American automobile industry was more than 780,000. But the number of workers declined to 760,000 in the next year, and in 1980, when the adverse effect of the crisis spread to the whole economy, the number of autoworkers in the United States decreased by 25 percent to 570,000. In other words, in the American auto industry, one in every four workers lost a job during the year after the second oil crisis.

In spite of the decline in automobile sales in the United States and the resulting difficulties of the American autoworkers, the number of Japanese automobiles imported rapidly increased. As examined in detail in chapter 2, when the price of gasoline exceeded a dollar and long lines were formed at many gas stations due to the shortage created by the Middle East crisis, car buyers moved away from domestic "gas-guzzlers" to small and fuel-efficient Japanese imports. While the sales of American-made automobiles plunged to the lowest level since the early 1960s during 1978–80, the number of Japanese passenger cars imported increased by 41 percent to 1.9 million vehicles.

As analyzed in detail below, the dramatic increase in Japanese imports was not necessarily responsible for the huge unemployment in the American auto industry. But, protectionists in the U.S. Congress insisted that the Japanese imports were directly and solely responsible for the misfortune of the American autoworkers. They argued that Japan exported its unemployment problems to the United States, and various protectionist measures were introduced in the U.S. Congress. Faced with such pressure from the United States, in May 1981 Japan was forced to announce the voluntary export restraint on its shipments of automobiles to the United States. As a result of this, Japanese exports of automobiles to the United States were severely restricted. As the U.S. economy began to show signs of recovery, the number of American autoworkers increased in 1983. Thus, international trade and domestic employment have a strong relationship, as this example shows.

International trade also affects wage level and labor-management relations through a change in the unemployment situation in the importing country. Such a relationship is easily found in the union-management negotiations in the American steel and automobile industries after the second oil crisis. As examined in detail in chapters 3 and 4, the wage rates in these industries were well above the U.S. average because the labor unions in these industries had strong bargaining power, and because the firms could easily transfer the increased labor cost to consumers through price increases under the oligopolistic market structure. The wage gap between these industries and other industries had been widening. But, in the 1980s, as unemployment became a serious problem and as Japanese competition became more and more intensified, both workers and management emphasized "job security with less wage hike." As a result, in the early 1980s, American autoworkers accepted a labor contract that froze their wages in order to secure their jobs. Further, in 1986, many steel workers in the United States accepted wage cuts to avoid unemployment. Thus, American workers in the industries that experienced fierce international competition accepted lower wages in exchange for secure jobs.

In the 1980s the union-management relationship is also changing from confrontation to cooperation. As examined in detail in chapter 3, more and more firms consider it important to consult with workers on production decisions in order to enhance labor productivity, which is necessary to successfully compete with foreign (high productivity) firms. In some cases, the firms allow workers to participate even in high-level decision making. As is well known, Chrysler appointed a union leader to its board of directors.

Just as international trade affects domestic labor problems, the domestic labor problems strongly influence a nation's trade policy through lobbying by labor unions. This is especially the case in the United States where the lobbying power of unions is very strong. As will be examined in chapter 2, when imports from Japan dramatically increased in many industries, including textiles, color television sets, and automobiles, the labor unions, along with management, submitted petitions for import relief to the International Trade Commission and requested that Congress enact protectionist legislation. Thus, international trade problems and domestic labor problems are closely related, and it is important to conduct an integrated analysis of the two issues.

INTERNATIONAL ECONOMICS AND LABOR ECONOMICS

As the volume of world trade rapidly expanded since the beginning of the 1970s, international economic relations have become more and more important in many countries. In the past, the United States did not attach much importance to the international economic relationship due to the large scale of its domestic market and its abundant natural resources. But, as the U.S. trade deficit became alarmingly large, heated debates have occurred on international trade. The trade deficit and the budget deficit have recently become the two most important problems in the U.S. economy. These days it is realized that international economic relations strongly influence the domestic labor problems, such as unemployment, wages, and labor-management relations, and vice versa. As trade frictions between the United States and Japan intensify, various arguments are being made on the relationship between trade and labor problems, which might be called *trade-labor* problems.

Unfortunately, however, very few economic theories allow an integrated analysis of trade-labor problems. Needless to say, a major role of economic theory is to abstract an essence from complicated phenomena in the real world economy which permits an orderly presentation of them. For example, when someone discusses the fiscal and monetary policies of the government, some economic theory, whether of Keynesian or monetarist framework, underlies such discussions. Even if the speaker is unaware of rigorous mathematical models, the discussion is often based on a theory derived from such models. In other words, there is a common framework for discussion of most economic phenomena. But, it seems that discussions of the relationship between the trade problem and the domestic labor problem often tend to be emotional. For example, protectionists sometimes make the following argument: While the United States is suffering from a huge trade deficit and a high unemployment rate, Japan is enjoying a huge trade surplus and low unemployment. *Therefore*, Japanese exports of its unemployment are responsible for the unemployment problem in the United States.

One of the reasons for emotional argument on trade-labor problems seems to be a lack of firm integrated economic theory, which might be called labor-oriented international economics. Traditionally, international economics (especially international trade theory) and labor economics have been two independent and very different disciplines. Although international problems and domestic labor problems are more and more interrelated in the real world, very few attempts have been made to integrate the two disciplines.

Generally speaking, orthodox trade theories are based on rather unrealistic assumptions, such as: (*a*) perfect competition both in product and labor markets, (*b*) constant returns to scale (CRS), and (*c*) homogeneous product. Based on such assumptions, these theories try to explain why countries exchange goods: the difference in production technologies in the Ricardian theory and the difference in relative factor endowments in the Heckscher-Ohlin framework.

Using the same assumptions, they analyze how countries gain from an international division of labor. Since the orthodox theories assume that the labor market, as well as the product market, is perfectly competitive, they fail to incorporate the possibility of wage markup by labor unions. They assume that the competitive wage rate is always achieved. In their framework, there is no unemployment because the demand for labor is always equated with the supply of labor through a change in wage rate. In other words, according to the orthodox trade theories, neither labor unions nor unemployment exist in the economy.

On the other hand, theories of labor economics have examined various problems of labor demand and labor supply within the framework of macroeconomics *in the closed economy.* Elasticities of labor demand have been widely studied within the framework of the Hicks-Marshall's derived demand. Determinants of labor supply have also been studied from a viewpoint of either demography or the tradeoff between wage and leisure as developed by Gary Becker. Recently, union-wage effects have attracted strong professional interest, too. In spite of a variety of topics, studies of labor economics have been confined to macroeconomic phenomena in the closed economy. Labor economists have not presented rigorous theories either on how international trade affects domestic labor problems such as the wage and labor-management relationship or on how domestic labor problems affect a country's trade policies. In other words, the relationship between international trade and domestic labor problems has eluded rigorous analysis.

While trade problems and the labor problems have become more and more interrelated in the real world economy, the two areas have been treated as totally separate phenomena in the world of the rigorous economic theory. Therefore, orthodox economic theories have no common framework of analysis for them. This lack of integration seems to be partly responsible for the often emotional debate of the trade-labor problems.

TOWARD LABOR-ORIENTED INTERNATIONAL ECONOMICS

This book establishes a new, rigorous theory of trade-labor problems, which might be called the labor-oriented international trade theory. Using the new model, trade conflicts in the real world, especially trade conflicts between Japan and the United States, will be examined.

Currently, analytical tools for trade-labor problems are insufficient because very few attempts have been made to integrate international economics with labor economics. The analysis in this book is intended to link these two fields of economics. Of course, it is not an easy task to integrate two fields that have been developed separately by many prominent economists, but the existing framework is sometimes not very useful for the analysis of trade conflicts in the real world. Generally speaking, international trade theory fails to incorporate trade unions or unemployment, while labor economics deals with macroeconomic phenomena in the closed economy. In view of this gap between the two disciplines, this book tries to establish a general equilibrium trade theory that incorporates labor unions and unemployment, to examine the U.S.-Japan trade conflicts, and to give a common framework to trade-labor problems.

Chapters 2 through 6 constitute the core of the book, where a new general equilibrium trade theory is established that incorporates imperfect competition in both product and labor markets. Such a framework is very different from orthodox trade theories. After the general equilibrium model is established, it is applied to recent U.S.-Japan automobile trade in order to demonstrate that a rigorous model can be easily applied to real world phenomena.

In chapters 2 and 3, important facts underlying trade conflicts are discussed. Trade conflicts about textiles, color television sets, and automobiles are discussed in chapter 2 as examples of trade conflicts between Japan and the United States. How industrialized countries imposed various restrictions on Japanese products to protect their domestic industries and how Japan often conceded with voluntary export restraints on her exports are examined.

Chapter 3 discusses the recent labor market situation and labor-management relations in the United States to show how domestic labor problems affect international trade conflicts. Various data show that strong unions achieved a big wage markup in many industries where trade conflicts are observed, and the high production costs due to this wage markup contributes heavily to the weak competitiveness of these industries in the international setting.

At the end of chapter 3, the recent trend of labor-management cooperation, rather than confrontation, in the United States is discussed. This cooperative trend appeared in the industries distressed by foreign competition, such as the steel and automobile industries. Faced with a large decline in production and high unemployment, both unions and management realized that cooperation is necessary to compete successfully with more efficient foreign firms.

In chapters 4 and 5, a rigorous framework is established for the analysis, based on labor-oriented international economics. In chapter 4, a general equilibrium trade model is developed to analyze what impact international trade—or its restrictions—has in the real world economy. The model developed in chapter 4 is a variant of the new trade theories that are generally called the theory of international trade under imperfect competition. International trade under imperfect competition has recently attracted intense academic interest in the United States, because the orthodox trade theories do not seem to be realistic when applied to the intraindustry trade of manufactured goods, which has become more and more important in the real world economy since World War II. The new trade theory is based on more realistic assumptions than orthodox theories: (a) imperfect competition in the product market; (b) increasing returns to scale; and (c) differentiated products.

While these new theories of international trade under imperfect competition incorporate the three realistic assumptions, the labor market is still assumed to be perfectly competitive, and therefore they fail to analyze important phenomena in the real world such as the impact of foreign competition on labor unions and unemployment. In view of this, the book attempts to establish a rigorous general equilibrium trade model that incorporates imperfect competition in both the labor market and the product market, although its starting point is the same as these theories of international trade under imperfect competition.

Various aspects of the trade conflict in the real world will be analyzed with this new model. It will be rigorously demonstrated that weakness in international competition often results from high production costs due to the price markup and wage markup produced by the imperfectly competitive structure in the product and labor markets, so that trade restriction is far from strengthening the international competitiveness of the domestic industries. Rather, such restrictions often contribute to an increase in market imperfections, and all parties concerned will lose in the long run.

While chapter 4 is intended to establish a general theory, chapter 5 presents a more specific model for the analysis of a specific problem, the U.S.-Japan automobile trade. A rigorous mathematical model is developed and applied to the U.S.-Japan automobile trade in order to get insights on (a) why Japan has a clear advantage over the United States in the production of automobiles in spite of the fact that the stages of development of the two economies are very similar; and (b) how consumers, producers, and workers in the two countries are affected by the trade restrictions in the short run.

After the theoretical analyses in chapters 4 and 5, estimations are made in chapter 6, where the model is applied to the automobile trade. Based on the rigorous mathematical model, the effects of trade (and its restrictions) on various economic variables (e.g., prices, production quantities, profits, wages, and employment) are estimated. The estimation suggests that when both product and labor markets are imperfectly competitive (as is the case in the U.S. automobile industry), trade restrictions are all the more harmful to the domestic economy, and since the restrictions further encourage market imperfections, both consumers and workers, even in the importing country, are worse off in the long run.

In chapter 7 the impact of foreign direct investment on the domestic labor market is discussed, because Japan's huge trade surplus has encouraged a dramatic outflow of Japanese capital in recent years. The possible deindustrialization resulting from an outflow of production capacity is also considered. Chapter 7 starts with a discussion of how Japanese foreign direct investments are accelerated by the sharp appreciation of the Japanese yen and by the import restrictions of many industrialized countries. Since the possibility of deindustrialization has become a hot issue in Japan recently, the experience of the United States and various theories on the topic are briefly summarized. At the end of the chapter, an estimation is given of how many Japanese workers have been displaced by the recent outflow of the Japanese firms and how many workers will be displaced by future outflow of Japanese capital.

The theoretical chapters (i.e., chapters 4 and 5) contain some complicated mathematics, because the book presents a rigorous framework for the analysis of trade-labor problems. But, after the mathematical proofs, intuitive explanations in plain language are given, so that the rigorous analysis becomes useful for the understanding of the real world economy. The essence of the analysis can be followed without interruption even if one skips the mathematical presentation. Since both rigor and usefulness are emphasized, practical application shares importance with establishing a rigorous theory of trade-labor problems.

CHAPTER TWO

History and Current Situation of Trade Conflicts

JAPAN-U.S. TEXTILE NEGOTIATIONS AND THE MULTIFIBRE ARRANGEMENT (MFA)

Voluntary Export Restraint (VER) in the Early Years

The early history of U.S.-Japan textile negotiations helps our understanding of the voluntary export restraint (VER), which has recently become a leading method of restriction on Japanese export of various products, including steel and automobiles. The production and export of textile products have played a very important role in the history of the economic development of many countries, from industrialized countries like the United Kingdom to developing countries like Hong Kong and Korea.

In Japan, raw silk and cotton products were the two most important export items in the early stage of her export-led industrialization (in the *Meiji* era). In the beginning of the Meiji era, Japanese textile exports consisted almost exclusively of raw silk, but the emphasis moved toward cotton textiles. In 1887 Japan began to export cotton textiles to the United States, and since then Japanese cotton exports have rapidly increased. In 1909 the Japanese export of cotton textiles exceeded import of the same products, and Japan became a net exporter. The Japanese textile exports continued to increase dramatically, and Japan became the largest exporter of cotton textiles in the world during the decade before World War II.

Figure 2.1 shows the levels of Japanese export of cotton textiles to the United States since the 1930s. Although the amount of Japanese cotton shipped to the United States was 1.6 million square yards in 1932, it achieved a fivefold increase to 7.5 million square yards in the next year, partly because of depreciation of the Japanese yen. It further doubled to become 17.4 million square yards in 1934. In 1937, when the amount of the Japanese cotton shipped to the United States was the

FIGURE 2.1 Japan's Textile Exports to the United States

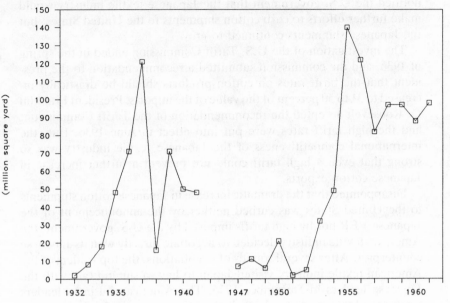

Source: Hunsberger 1964.

largest in the years before World War II, the shipment amounted to 124 million square yards, which was 80 times greater than the 1932 level.

Faced with a dramatic increase in imports of Japanese cotton textiles and the resulting decline in domestic production, the textile industry in the United States reiterated its complaints to the government. The U.S. goverment responded quickly, and it repeatedly requested that the Japanese government and Japanese industry impose a voluntary export restraint on cotton shipment to the United States. The Japanese textile industry conceded to U.S. pressure in late 1934, and it announced a VER on its cotton shipments to the United States and the Philippines, then a U.S. colony.

The VER turned out to be ineffective, because it did not stipulate a clear upper limit to Japanese cotton shipments to the United States. As shown in figure 2.1, Japanese cotton shipments increased dramatically after 1934 in spite of the VER. As a result, the protectionist power in the United States became even stronger. In 1935, the U.S. Senate adopted a resolution deploring the dramatic increase in the Japanese cotton shipments, and the U.S. Tariff Commission initiated an investigation into the impact of the massive shipments of cotton products from Japan and possible measures to rescue the domestic textile industry.

At the end of the year, the Japanese ambassador to the United States notified the U.S. government that the Japanese textile industry would make further efforts to curb cotton shipments to the United States, but the Japanese shipments continued to grow.

The investigation of the U.S. Tariff Commission ended in the spring of 1936, and the commission submitted a recommendation to the president that the tariff rates on cotton products should be drastically increased to 31 to 50 percent of the value of the imports. President Franklin D. Roosevelt accepted the recommendation of the Tariff Commission, and the high tariff rates were put into effect in June 1936. But, the international competitiveness of the Japanese textile industry was so strong that even a high tariff could not prevent a further increase in Japanese cotton exports.

Disappointed that the dramatic increase in Japanese cotton shipments to the United States was curbed neither by the announcement of the Japanese VER nor by high tariffs imposed by the U.S. government, the American textile industry decided to negotiate directly with its Japanese counterpart. After several rounds of negotiations, the top leaders of the American textile industry visited Japan to have a summit talk with the Japanese leaders in December 1936. The American business leaders briefed the Japanese press about the serious damage the Japanese cotton imports were doing to the U.S. textile industry. They reiterated that, unless the Japanese textile industry agreed on an effective VER on its cotton shipment, the United States would be obliged to take more direct measures, like import quotas, and therefore it was beneficial to Japan, as well as to the United States, to reach an agreement on a VER. After a month-long, intensive negotiation, the textile industries in the two countries reached an agreement. Although it was a gentleman's agreement, in which neither side signed a contract, agreement was reached on details of Japanese cotton shipments to the United States. It was agreed that the VER would be in force for two years (1937–38) and that Japanese cotton shipments to the United States in 1937 and 1938 should not exceed 155 million square yards and 100 million square yards, respectively. In return for the Japanese concessions, the U.S. textile industry agreed, in principle, that there was no need for further import restrictions on Japanese cotton textiles.

As shown in figure 2.1, Japanese shipment of cotton products to the United States was curbed after the agreement. Japanese shipments in 1938 declined dramatically from the levels of previous years. Although shipments recovered a little in 1939, it was only to half of the peak level. In 1938 the textile industries of the two countries agreed again, and the VER was extended for two more years (1939–40). When World II broke out in 1939, hostility toward Japanese products became very strong in the United States. As a result, Japanese cotton shipments to the United States remained stagnant.

The Japan-U.S. textile negotiations before World War II set a pattern for the trade negotiations between the two countries since then. Generally speaking, the Japan-U.S. trade conflicts seem to have been following the course shown below.

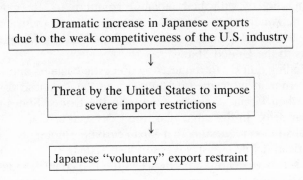

This pattern of Japan-U.S. trade conflicts was established more than half a century ago when the textile industries of the two countries negotiated intensively to agree on the Japanese VER. In this sense, textile negotiations in the early years has an important historical implication.

VERs after World War II and Their Effectiveness

Due to the destruction of production capabilities by World War II, Japanese export of textile products was close to zero for a few years after the war. But, as the Japanese economy began to recover from the war, Japanese export of textiles to the United States quickly took off. As shown in figure 2.1, Japanese cotton shipments to the United States in 1951 and in 1952 were 2 million square yards and 7 million square yards, respectively. These amounts were far below the peak in the prewar years (123 million square yards in 1937), but, since then, the increase in Japanese cotton exports was dramatic. In 1953 and in 1954, shipments increased to 33 million square yards and to 50 million square yards, respectively. In 1955 Japanese cotton shipments to the United States increased to 140 square yards, which exceeded the prewar peak.

Faced with the dramatic recovery of Japanese exports, strong protectionism reappeared in the United States. Since unemployment was a serious problem in the United States then, both workers and firms strongly pushed the government to restrict cotton products from Japan. As discussed in detail below, Japan gave in again and announced a voluntary export restraint, but there was a remarkable difference between the textile negotiation in 1950s and its predecessors. In the 1930s a direct agreement was reached between the textile industries in the two countries. But, as antitrust policies became more severe after World War II, the U.S. textile industry feared that direct negotiation by the private sectors to restrict trade, which was very likely to cause price increases, might be a violation of antitrust laws. Therefore, instead of negotiating directly with their Japanese counterparts, the workers and firms in the American textile industry requested that their government negotiate with the Japanese government for a VER on Japanese cotton shipments to the United States.

Responding quickly to requests by domestic business and labor, the U.S. government intensified its pressure on the Japanese government in 1955, when Japanese cotton exports to the United States exceeded the prewar peak. In the same year, the U.S. secretary of state gave an emotional address requesting that Japan curb her shipments, saying that the American textile industry was seriously damaged by Japanese competition. Intensive negotiations between the two countries followed the address, resulting in the Japanese government announcing a voluntary export restraint on her cotton shipments to the United States in December 1955. Partly because of strong resistance from the Japanese textile industry, the VER was not very restrictive; the limit on Japanese shipment of cotton products to the United States for the year 1956 was above the actual shipment in 1955. Offended by the ineffective VER, labor and business in the United States submitted petitions to the U.S. Tariff Commission which requested severe restrictions on the import of the Japanese products. It became increasingly likely that the Tariff Commission would accept these petitions and impose a severe restriction on Japanese imports.

An interesting event suggests how serious hostilities toward the Japanese textiles were in the southern states of the U.S. in those years. The state assemblies of South Carolina and Alabama passed a law stipulating that stores carrying Japanese textile products had to display a big sign saying "Japanese Textiles on Sale Here." Similar legislation was prepared in Georgia, too. Although objections by the Japanese government and the U.S. secretary of state prevented the legislation from being enforced, such expressions of hostility toward Japanese products were very shocking news to the Japanese government and the Japanese textile industry. Faced with growing pressures, the Japanese ambassador to the United States offered to renegotiate the ceiling on Japanese cotton shipments for the next year with the U.S. government. As a result of these negotiations, in January 1957 the two governments agreed on a limit on Japanese cotton shipments for 1957–61. The agreed limit was well below the actual shipments in 1955 and 1956.

TABLE 2.1.
Cotton Shipments to the United States (in Millions of Dollars)

Source	1956	1957	1958	1959	1960	1961
Total	154.3	136.2	150.0	201.3	248.3	203.3
Japan	84.1	65.8	71.7	76.7	74.1	69.4
Asia	16.0	18.8	31.7	69.8	97.5	72.0
(Hong Kong)	(0.7)	(5.8)	(17.4)	(45.8)	(63.5)	(47.0)
Other	54.2	51.6	46.6	54.8	76.7	61.9

Source: Hunsberger 1964.

Although protectionists in the United States argued that Japanese competition was responsible for the misfortune of the U.S. textile industry and they succeeded in obtaining protection from foreign competition, many problems in the U.S. textile industry (e.g., plant closures and unemployment) were considered to result from domestic factors rather than from foreign competition. First of all, the demand for cotton products in the United States was generally declining. For example, during 1940–60, the annual per capita consumption of cotton textiles by Americans decreased by 30 percent from 30 pounds in 1940 to 22 pounds in 1961. Second, production facilities in the U.S. textile industry were much older than their Japanese counterparts. Most Japanese textile plants were new because World War II destroyed its production facilities, while those in the United States were dated and their productivity was lower. This difference in productivity between the two countries was partly responsible for the massive inflow of Japanese cotton products to the United States. Third, frequent plant closures in the U.S. textile industry were caused not so much by foreign competition but by the general movement of textile firms from northern to southern states. Traditionally, there had been a division of labor between the North and the South; firms in the northeastern states produced fabrics and clothing from cotton fiber produced on southern plantations. But, as unions became powerful in the North and the wage differential between the North and the South widened, textile firms in the northeastern states moved south to seek lower wages and less intervention by the labor unions. The plant closures in the northern textile firms often resulted from this general trend rather than from foreign competition.

While Japanese shipment of cotton to the United States was successfully curbed by the Japanese VER of 1957, the United States could not reduce its total imports because imports from other countries increased sharply. Table 2.1 shows the U.S. import of cotton textiles by source countries. As the table shows, while Japanese cotton shipments stopped increasing, other Asian countries (especially Hong Kong) increased shipments to fill the gap. In 1956 (before imposition of the Japanese VER) the value of cotton shipments from Asian countries to the United States was $16 million, which was about one-fifth of the Japanese shipments ($84 million). When the Japanese VER came into effect, shipments from other Asian countries jumped to $100 million in 1960, which far exceeded the Japanese shipment ($74 million). Thus, the international competitiveness of the U.S. textile industry was so weak that the Japanese VER could not contain the total value of U.S. cotton imports.

Restrictions on one country often result in an increase in imports from other countries. For example, since the middle 1980s a Korean automaker, Hyundai, dramatically increased exports of automobiles to the United States to fill the gap created by the Japanese voluntary export restraint. Since the number of countries supplying textile products was so large, the United States pushed for a multilateral restriction in an attempt to curb total imports of textile and clothing products (discussed in detail below).

Japan-U.S. Textile Negotiations in Difficult Years

Due to the Japanese VER of 1957 and the following multilateral agreement, called the Long-Term Arrangement Regarding International Trade in Cotton Textiles (LTA), Japanese cotton shipments to the United States were contained, and the Japanese share of U.S. imports of cotton products continued to decline. But, U.S. imports of wool and man-made fiber rapidly increased. As a result, the emphasis has shifted from cotton to wool and man-made fiber since the middle 1960s, and active multilateral negotiations concerned these new products.

After the adoption of a multilateral agreement to restrict international trade of cotton products, the LTA, the United States took an initiative to restrict world trade of other fibers, such as wool and man-made fiber. In those days, the major exporters of woolen textile products to the United States were Italy, Japan, Hong Kong, and the United Kingdom. Therefore, the United States tried to conclude a multilateral agreement on restriction of woolen textile products with the four countries and invited these countries to negotiate a restrictive agreement. The two European countries refused the U.S. invitation.

Faced with a hard line from the European exporters, the United States decided to win concessions first from an easier partner, and it began bilateral negotiations with Japan, because Japan had often conceded easily to U.S. pressure before. The United States raised the issue at the Japan-U.S. summit talks in 1965, and Japan agreed that representatives of U.S. government and industry would visit Japan to discuss the matter. Active negotiations began in Japan in June of the next year. These negotiations sometimes involved a rather unfriendly atmosphere, partly because industry representatives, with a direct interest in the result of the negotiations, were included. The representatives of the U.S. textile industry took a very hard line, and they threatened their Japanese counterpart with possible legislation by the U.S. Congress to severely restrict Japanese imports. But, unlike the negotiations in the 1950s, the representatives of the Japanese textile industry did not give in easily, insisting that a unilateral political threat was inimical to a mutually agreeable solution. As a result, the U.S. representatives left Japan without reaching an agreement. After these unsuccessful negotiations, further negotiations on woolen products were interrupted for a few years, because the emphasis of textile negotiation shifted to the renewal of the LTA.

As soon as the LTA was renewed in 1967, restrictions on noncotton textiles again became a big political issue. The renewal of the LTA coincided with a dramatic increase in U.S. imports of noncotton textiles. In 1967, U.S. imports of man-made fibers exceeded exports for the first time. In 1968, imports of woolen textile products and man-made fiber products combined exceeded imports of cotton textile products. Under these circumstances, import restrictions on man-made fiber products became an important political issue. The U.S. House Ways and Means Committee requested that the U.S. Tariff Commission investigate the impact of man-made fiber imports on the domestic textile industry. In 1968 after the investigation, the Tariff Commission concluded that, although imports had increased dramatically, the domestic textile industry had not been seriously injured.

The Tariff Commission's report came in a presidential election year, and most candidates reiterated the importance of protective measures in order to attract voters in the southern states. As soon as the U.S. voters elected President Nixon, who had strongly advocated restrictions on textile imports, the U.S. government initiated negotiations with major exporting countries on trade restrictions on man-made fibers. As with the earlier restrictive measures on woolen textiles, the United States began bilateral negotiations with Japan, since European exporting countries refused to negotiate restrictions on their exports. In an attempt to request comprehensive restrictive measures on a wide range of textile products, the U.S. secretary of commerce visited Japan. Due to pressure from the Japanese textile industry, the Japanese government did not concede to the U.S. pressure.

Faced with Japan's refusal, the U.S. textile industry initiated a hard approach in 1970. Instead of waiting for the Japanese concession, the labor unions and textile firms begged the U.S. Congress to enact legislation to unilaterally restrict Japanese textile products. Responding to this request, the chairman of the House Ways and Means Committee submitted a bill to limit the textile imports in 1970 below the levels of 1967–68. In the fall of 1970, the bill passed the U.S. House. In 1971 President Nixon announced various measures to restrict imports, including imports of textile and clothing products, in order to defend the weakened U.S. dollar. In these circumstances, Japan was obliged to make concessions, and in October 1971 it announced a comprehensive voluntary export restraint on textile products, which was to be in effect for three years.

Although the Japanese VER was announced after the rather hostile negotiations, it turned out to be unnecessary. In the 1970s the comparative advantage of (man-made fiber) clothing products shifted from Japan to developing countries. The United States clothing imports from Japan declined, and the import ceiling set by the VER was never achieved. While Japanese exports of man-made fiber products to the United States in 1971 were 1.3 billion square yard equivalents (SYE, a widely used unit of imports of textile products), by 1973 the amount halved to 0.7 billion SYE. This dramatic decline in Japanese exports of man-made fiber products resulted from various reasons: after the Nixon shock in 1971 the Japanese yen appreciated dramatically (therefore, Japanese products in the United States became more expensive); some developing countries, including Korea and Hong Kong, emerged as newly industrialized countries (NICs), and they increased their exports of textile products. Thus, the imports of textile products from Japan declined dramatically in the early years of 1970s, while imports from NICs increased consistently.

This shift in comparative advantage from Japan to NICs is typically observed with clothing products, which are more labor-intensive than textile products (in the narrower sense). Figure 2.2 shows the change in major exporters of clothing to the U.S. market. As the diagram shows, in the 1970s the share of Japanese clothing in the U.S. market declined dramatically, while that of Hong Kong and Korea increased sharply. The Japanese share in the 1960s was 25–30 percent, but it fell below 10 percent in 1974. It further declined in the 1980s to a mere 2–3 percent. On the other hand, the combined share of Hong Kong and Korea increased sharply, and has held around 40 percent since the end of the 1970s, which far exceeds the Japanese share.

Thus, trade conflicts involving textile products have a long history. Although the Japan-U.S. trade conflicts in recent years involve more sophisticated products, such as consumer electronics and automobiles, the textile negotiation is very important as a pattern-setter for the trade negotiations thereafter.

FIGURE 2.2 U.S. Clothing Imports, by Sources

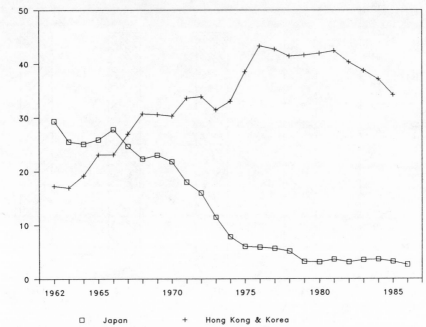

Source: United Nations, *Statistical Yearbook*.

Further Restrictions on World Textile Trade under the MFA

As discussed above, by the end of the 1960s, Japan was the largest textile exporter in the world, and textile negotiations involved primarily Japan and the United States. As Asian NICs (including Hong Kong, Korea, and Taiwan) dramatically increased their exports of textile and clothing products, multilateral negotiations have become more and more important.

Figure 2.3 shows the geographical shares of the world clothing trade since the 1950s. As shown in the figure, the share of developing countries, including Hong Kong and Korea, consistently and rapidly increased, while developed countries lost their shares. In 1955 the combined export share of developed countries in world clothing exports amounted to 71 percent, and the share of developing exporting countries remained a mere 10 percent. Since then, the share of developing countries has consistently increased, to 15 percent in 1963 and to 35 percent in 1973. In 1982 the share of developing countries amounted to almost half of the world exports of clothing (48 percent), and it exceeded by a wide margin the share of developed countries as a whole (38 percent).

FIGURE 2.3 Clothing Exports, by Regions

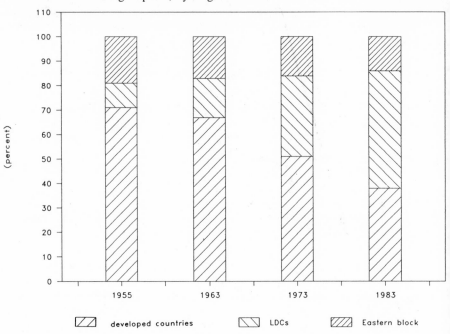

Source: GATT 1984.

As a result, in many developed countries, including the United States and the European Community (EC), imports of clothing from low-cost developing countries have become one of the most important political issues. In order to cope with the problem, many developed countries tried to establish a multilateral framework of restrictions on clothing trade, culminating in the Multifibre Arrangement (MFA) in 1974, which has become more and more restrictive over time.

Before examining the MFA, it is useful to consider the multilateral textile negotiations prior to the MFA, such as the STA. The United States played a decisive role in establishing the Short-Term Arrangement Regarding International Trade in Cotton Textiles (STA), which started in 1961 as the first multilateral restriction on textile products. By the 1950s, the U.S. textile industry succeeded in obtaining some domestic support for special protection against imports of cotton textiles. Keesing and Wolf (1980) noted that "two important ideas [were] especially strongly held in the United States, namely (i) that textiles were somehow special and fully deserving of exemption from general liberalization and (ii), a closely related idea, that without protection the industry could hardly survive."

They pointed out that there are both economic and political reasons for such special treatment of the U.S. textile industry. First, output and employment in the industry were stagnant and even declining in the 1950s. Although the stagnation could be attributed partly to international competition caused by a shift in comparative advantage toward low-wage countries, the main reason was a stagnant demand for textile products. The share of textile products in personal consumption expenditures in the United States fell from 14 percent in 1919 to less than 9 percent in 1959. Second, the industry was fairly large—employing 17 percent of the total manufacturing work force in industrial countries—and well organized as a political pressure group. Third, the only countries adversely affected by the protection were Japan and developing countries with little political clout.

Protectionism was reinforced when Japan applied for accession to the General Agreement on Tariffs and Trades (GATT) in 1955. Many countries worried about the potential of Japan, which was dramatically expanding cotton textile exports in those days. As Sampson (1986) argues, "restraining all suppliers would require restraint of more economically powerful countries and could prompt retaliatory action or request for compensation as provided for in Article XIX of GATT." Therefore, in 1957 the United States, a major importer of Japanese cotton products, negotiated an agreement on the Japanese five-year VER on the shipment of cotton textiles to the United States (examined in detail above). Although the United States succeeded in curbing Japanese cotton products, other Asian countries—especially Hong Kong—dramatically increased shipments to fill the gap (see table 2.1 above).

A diversion of import sources is common for textile and clothing products, because the production setup costs are relatively small. Faced with such a diversion, the United States began negotiations with Hong Kong on the VER (in vain) and brought the issue to GATT in an attempt to obtain a multinational framework for a restriction on textile and clothing products. Meanwhile, the United Kingdom formed bilateral agreements on the VER with Hong Kong, India, and Pakistan.

VERs are a derogation of GATT principles because they are discriminatory and quantitative restrictions. Therefore, the restricting countries—especially the United States—wanted to obtain international sanction for them. Exporting countries also wanted an international arrangement because, as Keesing and Wolf (1980) argue, "It was feared that uncontrolled restrictions, even if agreed on a 'voluntary' basis, would fundamentally impair the long-term opportunities of developing countries." In contrast to the MFA (as well as the STA and the LTA) which provides that new quota levels should not be lower than the actual shipments before the quota, the levels of VERs before 1960 were often substantially below the actual shipments of the previous year.

Thus, the interests of importing and exporting countries partly co-incided, and the international agreement on restrictions on textile and clothing trade (STA) came into effect in 1961. Man-made fiber and wool became important by the early 1970s and were included in the MFA when it was initiated in 1974. The MFA has been renewed three times; the current agreement, MFA IV, extends through July 1991.

As the GATT (1984) pointed out, the period under MFA I (January 1974–December 1977) was characterized by a period of "relative liberalization" of trade in textiles and clothing. During this time, many previous restrictions were abolished, consistent with MFA Article 2 (on the phasing out of pre-MFA restrictions). Not only had cotton textiles been subject to restrictions under the STA and LTA since 1961, but there were also trade restraints on wool and man-made fiber products that were outside of the STA and the LTA. Therefore, the period under MFA I "witnessed enhanced discipline in the regulatory measures compared to the autonomous and arbitrary methods of the past," as the GATT pointed out. The restrictions imposed during MFA I were more or less consistent with the spirit of the MFA text, which states in Article 1 that the aim of the MFA is "to achieve the expansion of trade, the reduction of barriers to such trade and the progressive liberalization of world trade in textile products, while at the same time ensuring the orderly and equitable development of this trade and avoidance of disruptive effect." Most importing countries preferred selective coverage of items (consistent with annex A of the MFA) rather than comprehensive restrictions; only the United States took comprehensive measures. Provisions of annex B (on the base level, minimum growth rate, and flexibility of quotas) were well observed by many importing countries.

MFA II (January 1978 to December 1981) proved more restrictive, primarily because of European Community (EC) initiatives. During the period under MFA I, the EC's textile and clothing imports increased dramatically, possibly because exports from developing countries shifted to the EC from the United States, where a comprehensive system of bilateral restriction had been set up in 1971. This increase occurred during a time of economic recession and high unemployment after the first oil crisis. Thus, although most of the MFA participants favored a simple extension of the MFA, the EC took a hard line.

The EC was responsible for a new provision included in the Protocol of Extension of the MFA—the possibility of "jointly agreed reasonable departures" from particular elements of the MFA provisions in certain cases. Although reasonable departures were intended to be only temporary, they have, in fact, been used for long periods. The departures consisted of reductions in quotas from their previous levels (or actual trade), reductions in flexibility, and annual growth rates of quota level below 6 percent as stipulated in the annex of the MFA text. During this period, the EC formed a system of comprehensive restrictions, dividing MFA products into 114 categories and 5 groups. In addition, it adopted a "basket extractor" mechanism whereby any exporter whose exports exceeded a threshold share of total EC imports would be subject to new controls.

Faced with the growing objections of exporting countries to the frequent use of departures under MFA II, the Protocol for MFA III (January 1982 to July 1986) excluded the reasonable departures clause. Instead, more specific provisions were introduced. One of the most important was an "antisurge" provision concerning underutilized quotas. Oddly, most of the MFA quotas are unfilled except for those imposed on a few superstars of textile and clothing exports. The utilization rate of other countries is sometimes as low as 10–20 percent. Importing countries thus added antisurge provisions to avoid sudden influxes of imports under unfilled quotas. To facilitate adjustment in importing countries, a permanent subcommittee of the Textiles Committee of the GATT was established to monitor adjustment policies. In spite of these changes, MFA III led to a further tightening of restrictions, as the Textile Surveillance Body of the GATT reported in December 1983.

Faced with dramatic import increases in the 1980s, the United States became even more restrictive. The most important change in the U.S. policy was a "call" system, announced in December 1983. Under this system, consideration of a possible case of market disruption can be initiated when imports have (*a*) reached 20 percent of domestic production; or (*b*) risen by 30 percent in the previous year, with imports from an individual supplier reaching 1 percent of the domestic production. The United States invited more than a hundred consultation calls in 1984–85, and in almost all cases new restrictions were imposed on textile and clothing exports from developing countries.

During MFA IV (August 1986 to July 1991), provisions for even broader coverage and tighter restrictions were introduced. The "reasonable departures" clause was restored, the product coverage was extended to include vegetable fibers and silk blends, and other small changes further restricted textile and clothing exports. The MFA has now been in effect for many years, and there is little prospect of its being abolished when MFA IV ends, although the future of the MFA is being negotiated actively under the Uruguay round.

It is noteworthy that, during the long period of MFA restriction, the

FIGURE 2.4 Clothing Trade of Japan

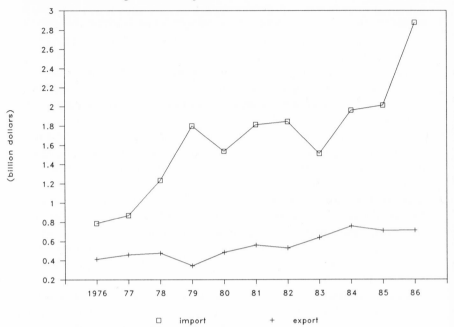

Source: United Nations, *Statistical Yearbook*.

role of Japan in the world textile and clothing trade has been rapidly changing from an exporter to an importer. This change is remarkable especially for the international clothing trade, which is more labor-intensive than textiles (in the narrower sense). Figure 2.4 shows the exports and imports of clothing by Japan since the middle 1970s. While the value of exports did not change very much, the value of imports increased from $0.8 billion in 1976 to $2.9 billion in 1986, an increase at an average annual rate of 14 percent. As a result, in 1986 the value of Japanese clothing imports has become four times higher than that of its exports. Although Japan (as well as Switzerland) has not taken an MFA restriction against its imports of clothing, it is uncertain whether Japan will continue a nonrestrictive policy, because it is expected that the imports of clothing from developing countries will further increase in the future for many reasons, including a shift in comparative advantage and a further appreciation of the Japanese yen.

ORDERLY MARKET AGREEMENT ON COLOR
TELEVISION SETS

Japanese Exports of Television Sets

The television set, especially the color television set, was one of the most important items involved in the U.S.-Japan trade conflict after the textile products conflicts subsided. While the U.S.-Japan textile negotiations occurred mainly in the 1950s and 1960s, the television set trade conflict became an important issue in the 1970s. In the 1970s business and labor in the American consumer electronics industry submitted many petitions to the Congress and the U.S. International Trade Commission in an attempt to expel Japanese television sets from the U.S. market. The trade conflict ended with the conclusion of the Orderly Market Agreement (OMA), in which the two countries agreed in 1977 to limit Japanese export of color television sets to the U.S. market. As examined in detail below, U.S. labor unions played a much more important role than before in erecting import restrictions on the Japanese product.

Before examining the U.S.-Japan television set trade conflict, it is useful to briefly consider the situations that the television industries in the two countries were facing in those years. As has happened with many manufactured goods, the United States took the lead in producing and marketing the television set, and Japan began production under licensing agreements with the United States. Such licensing agreements were concluded in 1953 for black-and-white television sets and in 1962 for color television sets. In the early years of the licensing agreements, Japanese television production was much smaller than that of the United States, and very few expected that Japanese television sets could ever be exported to the United States on a large scale. Later on, the Japanese television set manufacturing industry succeeded in marketing low-priced television sets produced by workers with lower wages than U.S. workers and succeeded in shifting from old-fashioned vacuum tube models to solid-state models more quickly than their U.S. counterparts.

Figure 2.5 shows the change in Japanese export of television sets to the United States and to the world since the early 1960s. Because of data limitations, exports of the black-and-white and color television sets are combined. The major export in the 1960s was black-and-white, and after the middle 1970s, the color television set. While the number of Japanese TV sets exported to the United States remained a mere 2 thousand and 5.6 thousand in 1962 and in 1963, respectively, it increased to 700 thousand in 1964, and by 1971 it reached 4 million. The dramatic

FIGURE 2.5 Japanese TV Exports

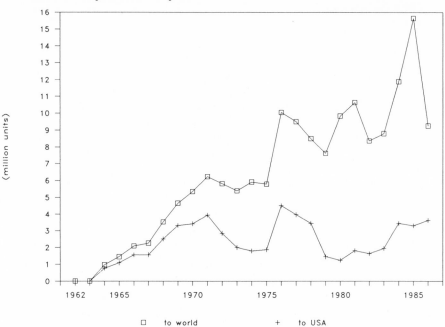

Source: United Nations, *Statistical Yearbook*.

increase in the latter half of the 1960s was then temporarily interrupted. Japanese TV exports to the United States declined for a few years, because the international competitiveness of Japanese television sets weakened due to the appreciation of the Japanese yen and increased competition from the NICs and because the U.S. demand for consumer durable goods as a whole declined due to the economic recession.

In spite of the temporary setback, as U.S. consumer demand shifted from vacuum tube models to solid-state models, the Japanese television sets gradually earned a reputation for better quality. American consumers thought that the Japanese sets had better picture quality and reliability than the U.S. sets. A Japanese producer, Hitachi, had been first to successfully market a solid-state television set. In the 1970s, American consumers bought the Japanese models not for price but for quality.

As the U.S. economy recovered from the first oil recession, Japanese export of television sets to the United States increased sharply in 1976 to 4.5 million units, double that of the previous year. Faced with the sharp increase in Japanese exports, the United States strengthened its protectionist attitude and demanded that Japan make concessions as

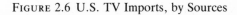

FIGURE 2.6 U.S. TV Imports, by Sources

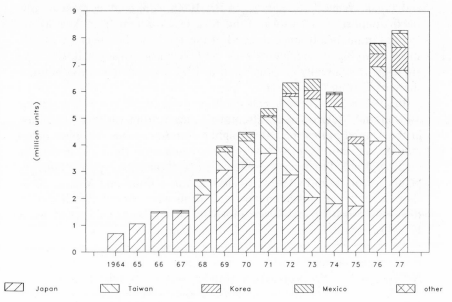

Source: United Nations, *Statistical Yearbook*.

had happened before with textile products. Due to U.S. pressure, Japan was obliged to accept the Orderly Market Agreement (OMA) on color television exports in 1977, and exports to the United States have declined sharply since then.

Fortunately, Japan succeeded in diversifying its export markets. As Figure 2.5 shows, in spite of the decline in exports to the United States after initiation of the OMA, Japanese exports to the world as a whole did not decline. While the share of exports to the United States in the total export of Japanese television sets had been as high as 70–80 percent in the 1960s, it gradually declined to 10–30 percent in the 1980s.

International Trade and Offshore Assembly

Although the U.S. protectionists chose the Japanese television set as a target for restriction and the Orderly Market Agreement was concluded with Japan in 1977, imports of television sets from newly industrialized countries, including Korea and Taiwan, increased dramatically in the 1970s. Television sets from these NICs often carried American brand names. Offshore assembly arrangements played an important role in rapidly increasing U.S. import of television sets. Figure 2.6 shows the U.S. imports of television sets by exporting sources from the middle

1960s to 1977 when the OMA was concluded between the United States and Japan. While U.S. imports in the 1960s were coming mostly from Japan, imports from Taiwan (and to a lesser extent from Korea) increased dramatically since the end of the 1960s, mainly because of off-shore assembly arrangements with the U.S. firms. As a result, the Japanese share gradually declined, and in 1977 it was below the combined share of Taiwan and Korea.

In 1967 a U.S. firm began offshore assembly of television sets in Taiwan and Mexico. In an attempt to escape from various difficulties in the United States, including higher domestic wages, stronger labor unions, and more severe government regulations, the U.S. television industry decided to move the assembly plants (and some part-producing plants) of black-and-white television sets to Taiwan and Mexico. Off-shore assembly arrangements by U.S. firms were extended to Korea in the 1970s. Since the mid-1970s, more than half of U.S. TV imports were U.S.-brand television sets assembled abroad.

Dramatic expansion of the offshore assembly arrangement resulted from encouragement by the governments of the United States and the NICs, as well as the economic incentives to the U.S. television industry mentioned above. The governments of host countries (i.e., NICs where the American firms built their overseas plants) provided various incentives for the U.S. firms to move production sites into their countries, because they thought that the production of relatively sophisticated and labor-intensive products like television sets would contribute a great deal to the economic development of their countries. A typical example of such an incentive is the establishment of free trade zones (FTZ). The free trade zone is a special production site, designated by the government of the host country, with preferential treatment given to the foreign firms operating there.

Even now, numerous free trade zones exist in many developing countries, and a wide variety of preferential treatments are given to assembly plants operated by the foreign firms. Normally, imports of capital goods and materials necessary for production in the FTZ are exempted from import tariffs and import quotas. Goods produced in the FTZ can be exported freely, without export duties or export restrictions. The profit of the foreign firms operating in the FTZ can be expatriated without regard to foreign exchange controls. In many cases, a long-term tax holiday is granted: the foreign firms operating in the FTZ are exempted from income taxes by the host country for a certain period (often more than 10 years). Further, often basic facilities, including electricity and water supply, are provided by the host country. In some cases, firms in the FTZ are not subject to the host country's labor laws, allowing them to operate more freely and at lower cost. Encouraged by preferential treatments in the FTZ, the television industry of the United States moved production facilities to NICs such as Taiwan, Korea, and Mexico.

In addition to encouragement by the host country governments, U.S. government policies contributed a great deal to the U.S. firms' decisions to move their production facilities to developing countries. For example, the U.S. government gives preferential tariff treatment to imports made with U.S. components. Since the revision of U.S. tariff law in 1963, when a country exports products made of, at least in part, certain U.S. components, the value of the U.S. components is exempted from the U.S. custom duties under the U.S. Tariff Schedule: lines 806.30 and 807.00.

Consider the case of a U.S. firm that shipped components, such as picture tubes, transistors, and switches, from its domestic part plant to its assembly plant in the FTZ of a developing country and shipped back assembled television sets for sale to U.S. consumers. In this case, the value of the parts shipped from the United States is exempted from U.S. custom duties, which are imposed only on the value added abroad.

This provision of the U.S. tariff arrangement is known as the "806–807 arrangement" from the line numbers in the U.S. Tariff Schedule (806.30 and 807.00). The 806–807 arrangement has greatly helped the foreign activities of U.S. multinational corporations. Because of lower wages and preferential treatment in the free trade zones of developing countries, the value added there is normally much less than the value of the U.S. component. Therefore, the U.S. multinational corporations must pay only a small tariff in order to exploit the lower production costs abroad.

As shown in figure 2.6, U.S. imports of television sets from Korea, Mexico, and Taiwan have rapidly and consistently increased, due to such economic reasons as lower wages and the policies of the governments in both host and home countries. While U.S. TV imports from Japan declined due to, among other factors, a sharp appreciation of the Japanese yen in the 1970s, imports from newly industrialized countries increased consistently due to offshore assembly arrangements by U.S. firms. Expansion of the offshore assembly arrangement produced a difference in views on import restrictions between U.S. business and labor, as will be examined in detail below.

Impact of the Orderly Market Agreement

As U.S. imports of television sets rapidly increased since the 1960s, the voice of the labor unions, as well as of the firms, calling for import restrictions became increasingly stronger. As shown in figure 2.6, while the number of television sets imported had been around 1.5 million units in 1967, it increased consistently every year to reach 6.5 million units in 1972. In other words, imports quadrupled in just five years. In contrast to the dramatic increase in imports, domestic production remained stagnant, largely because of the economic recession in the early 1970s. The stagnant domestic production resulted in frequent layoffs in the U.S. television industry. Faced with severe labor market conditions that coincided with the dramatic increase in TV imports, the labor unions repeatedly petitioned for import relief from the U.S. government.

In spite of their frequent petitions, the labor unions did not succeed in obtaining import relief in the early 1970s. In 1971, a petition for relief from foreign competition was submitted to the U.S. Tariff Commission by the three leading labor unions in the industry: the International Union of Electrical, Radio, and Machine Workers; the International Brotherhood of Electrical Workers; and the International Association of Machinists and Aerospace Workers. The petition asserted that the U.S. television industry was suffering serious injury caused primarily by the dramatic increase in imports after the Kennedy-round tariff reductions, and therefore, the tariff rate imposed on foreign television sets should be raised to 35 percent, or the tariff rate in the 1930s. The U.S. Tariff Commission rejected the petition, saying that during the Kennedy-round the tariff rate on television sets was decreased from 10 percent to 6 percent, which was too small a decline to cause a serious injury to the domestic industry. In 1970–77, the labor unions in the television set industry submitted a total of eleven petitions to the U.S. Tariff Commission, but all of them were rejected.

One of the reasons for these consistent rejections was that the labor unions' petitions were made under section 301 of the Trade Expansion Act of 1962. According to section 301 of the 1962 act, three conditions had to be met before import relief was granted: (a) the industry concerned must suffer a serious injury; (b) the injury must be primarily caused by the increase in imports; and (c) the increase in imports must result in major part from concessions granted under trade agreements. The Trade Reform Act of 1974 does not contain condition (c). Thus, import relief under section 301 of the 1962 Act was of limited applicability. Under the 1962 Act, even when the domestic industry suffered from serious injury primarily caused by the increase on imports, import relief was not granted unless condition (c) was satisfied.

There is another important reason for the lack of success in attempts by the labor unions to obtain import relief in the early 1970s. Manufacturers in the U.S. television industry did not join the initiative by the labor unions to obtain import relief from the U.S. Tariff Commission, because their interests had diverged. As discussed above, encouraged by lower wages and preferential treatment, more and more U.S. firms moved their assembly plants to developing countries and shipped back television sets assembled in free trade zones. An increasing part of the U.S. imports of television sets consisted of U.S.-brand products made in foreign countries under the offshore assembly arrangement, and the importance of imports from Japan was decreasing.

Under these circumstances, the labor unions' demand for higher tariffs on imported television sets in general was against the interest of the American multinational corporations. To the American multinationals, a restriction on TV imports in general was a restriction on sales of their own products produced abroad. Therefore, U.S. producers did not buy the idea that all imports of television sets should be restricted in order to protect domestic jobs. Unlike the labor unions, the producers wanted to restrict Japanese imports, leaving imports of products under offshore assembly arrangements intact. Instead of petitions for relief from import competition in general, the U.S. producers petitioned for relief from the Japanese competition alone, citing dumping and other unfair trade practices. A decision on the petition was not made until 1976.

Various petitions made by the producers and the labor unions in the U.S. television manufacturing industry in the early 1970s were unsuccessful, but, in the mid-1970s, the situation began to change, as the Trade Reform Act of 1974 was enacted and production of domestically made television sets decreased by 30 percent in the recessionary year 1975. As discussed above, conditions for import relief under the 1974 act were easier to meet than those under the 1962 act. This relaxation in the requirements coincided with a dramatic decline in domestic production. Producers and labor unions in the U.S. television manufacturing industry, who had independently submitted petitions, now felt that cooperative action was necessary to achieve effective protection.

After intensive talks between business and labor, a management-labor coalition, the Committee to Preserve American Color Television (COMPACT), was formed in 1976. In September 1976 COMPACT submitted a joint petition for import relief to the U.S. International Trade Commission (ITC), a successor to the U.S. Tariff Commission. Because imports of Japanese color television sets were dramatically increasing in 1976–77 and because the conditions for granting import relief were easier to meet than those under the 1962 act, the International Trade Commission quickly admitted the petition in March 1977 and sent a recommendation to the president that the tariff rate on imported color television sets be raised from the current 5 percent to 25 percent.

In April 1977 the U.S. Customs Court in New York made an important ruling. When the U.S. Treasury Department rejected a petition for countervailing duties on Japanese television sets, submitted by Zenith, Magnavox, and Sylvania, the three producers appealed the decision to the Customs Court. The court rejected the decision by the U.S. Treasury, and it ordered the treasury secretary to impose countervailing duties on Japanese imports.

While the Customs Court decided in favor of the petition by the U.S. producers, the Carter administration wanted to negotiate with Japan on "voluntary" export restraint. The U.S. administration preferred voluntary export restraint on the part of Japan to the explicit restrictive action by the United States, because multilateral trade negotiations for lowering tariffs were going on. Faced with intensified U.S. pressure, negotiation between the United States and Japan was quickly completed. In July 1977 they reached the Orderly Market Agreement (OMA) on the shipments of Japanese color television sets to the United States.

According to the OMA, which was to be in effect for three years, Japanese exports of color television sets to the United States were to be below 1.75 million units (1.56 million for completed products plus 0.19 million for semicompleted products). In addition to setting a ceiling on Japanese exports, the OMA provided that measures should be taken to encourage Japanese producers to build their production facilities in the United States. Since then, Japanese manufacturers have rushed to establish production bases in the United States in an attempt to avoid further trade conflict in the future. As a result, Japanese exports were curbed by the OMA, while the production of Japanese color television sets in the United States jumped (see chapter 7 for details).

Although Japanese exports were decreased by the OMA, the difficulties faced by the U.S. television manufacturing industry did not end. As happened in the textile industry before, the total imports of television sets did not decline, because the imports from newly industrialized countries such as Korea, Mexico, and Taiwan increased dramatically to fill the gap created by the OMA with Japan. In figure 2.7, the Japanese share of U.S. imports of television sets is compared with the joint share of Korea and Taiwan. As the figure shows, the share of Korea and Taiwan was rapidly increasing, while the Japanese share declined after the Orderly Market Agreement went into effect in 1977.

Such a trade diversion after restrictions is not limited to color television sets. When an increase in imports results from the weaker international competition of domestic industries, trade restrictions are often unsuccessful, because the fundamental reasons for the weak international competition (e.g., imperfections in the product and labor markets in the domestic industry) are strengthened, rather than rectified, by the trade restrictions. A similar phenomenon is observed in the automobile industry, as discussed below.

FIGURE 2.7 U.S. TV Imports, by Sources

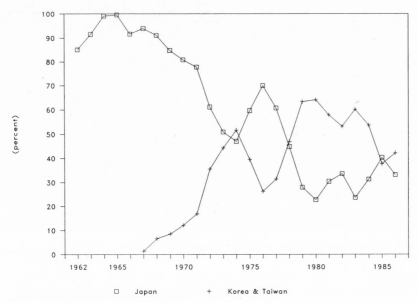

Source: United Nations, *Statistical Yearbook*.

VOLUNTARY EXPORT RESTRAINT ON JAPANESE AUTOMOBILES

Recent Developments in U.S.-Japan Automobile Trade

Product categories involved in the Japan-U.S. trade conflict have changed over time from labor-intensive products to more capital-intensive products. As discussed above, textile and clothing products were the most important items in the Japan-U.S. trade negotiations in the 1960s; in the 1970s color television sets became a hot issue. But, when Japan dramatically increased the export of automobiles to the United States, especially after the second oil crisis in 1979, the emphasis of trade restrictions shifted toward automobiles in the 1980s.

In spite of various restrictions, automobiles are the largest export items of Japan in the 1980s. In view of this, the theoretical and empirical analyses in this book will emphasize the Japan-U.S. automobile trade and its restrictions. Before examining the effects of restrictions on automobile trade (which will be carried out in later chapters of the book) the history of the Japan-U.S. automobile trade since the 1970s will be outlined.

The United States and Japan are the two largest auto-producing

FIGURE 2.8 Auto Production and Export (Japan)

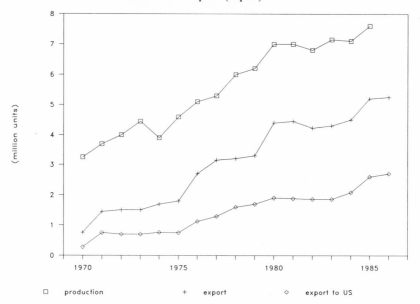

Source: Prime Minister's Office of Japan, Statistical Yearbook of Japan; United Nations, Statistical Yearbook.

countries in the world. For example, in 1983 the production of passenger cars in the United States and Japan was 6.8 million and 7.2 million units, respectively. In 1984, the United States was the largest producer in the world: production in the United States and Japan was 7.7 million and 7.1 million, respectively. The combined share of the two countries in world automobiles production is as much as 50 percent. Therefore, it is predictable that developments in the two countries have a great impact on the world automotive market. Although the size of the automobile industries in the two countries has been very similar in recent years, there are striking differences between the two.

First, the Japanese automotive industry has grown dramatically in the 1970s, while there has been no comparable growth in the U.S. counterpart. As shown in figure 2.8, Japanese passenger car production in 1970 was 3.2 million units (just one-third of the U.S. production in the same year). But, with the exception of the minor setback in 1974, Japanese production has continued to grow at a very high rate, and it has equaled the U.S. level since the late 1970s. Japanese production at the end of the 1970s was twice the 1970 level. On the other hand, U.S. production did not show any increase comparable to the Japanese counterpart. While U.S. production of passenger cars in 1970 was more than

TABLE 2.2.
Japan's Imports of Passenger Cars (in Thousands)

Year	Total	American	Year	Total	American
1970	19.1	5.3	1979	64.8	20.7
1971	18.6	4.6	1980	46.3	10.4
1972	24.8	5.5	1981	31.9	4.2
1973	36.9	12.0	1982	36.5	4.2
1974	42.2	14.9	1983	37.3	2.7
1975	45.5	16.6	1984	44.1	2.3
1976	40.4	13.8	1985	52.2	1.5
1977	41.4	14.4	1986	73.5	3.3
1978	54.5	13.3	1987	108.3	5.8

Source: United Nations, *Statistical Yearbook*.

8 million units, production fluctuated according to general economic conditions. In the early 1980s, auto production in the United States was substantially below that of 1970 due to the recession and foreign competition.

Second, a quick inspection of figure 2.8 reveals another interesting fact, namely, that the Japanese automotive industry is heavily dependent on overseas markets, mostly on the U.S. market. Throughout the 1970s, most of the growth in Japanese automobile production was supported by the expansion of export markets. While the share of exports in total Japanese automobile production was 24 percent in 1974, it increased to more than 50 percent in the 1980s.

On the other hand, imported cars are almost insignificant in the Japanese market. Although Japan abolished import tariffs on automobiles in the late 1970s, the import share was around 1 percent of total domestic sales in Japan. Further, of all the imported cars in Japan, American cars are disastrously unsuccessful. As shown in table 2.2, Japanese imports of American cars in the 1980s remained far below ten thousand units, while Japan exported about two million cars to the United States. The strong performance of Japanese automobiles in the world market (especially in the U.S. market) and its dramatic growth in the 1970s have captured world attention, and many importing countries have imposed restrictions on Japanese imports in recent years.

In contrast, imported cars play an important role in the U.S. domestic market, while automobile exports are not very important to the United States. For example, the share of exports in the U.S. total production of passenger cars is less than 8 percent, most of which are exported to its neighbor, Canada. On the other hand, imports of foreign-made (mostly Japanese-made) cars are increasingly important in the U.S. market.

FIGURE 2.9 U.S. Car Market

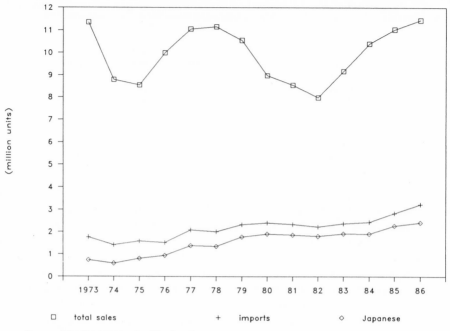

□   total sales   +   imports   ◇   Japanese

Source: *Ward's Automotive Yearbook.*

Figure 2.9 shows the trend in sales of passenger cars, including imported cars, in the United States since 1970. It should be noted that sales of imported automobiles in the United States have increased almost consistently through the 1970s. As the price of gasoline rose after the first oil crisis, the share of the Japanese imports increased greatly.

On the other hand, sales of domestic cars have fluctuated widely according to general economic conditions, with no trend toward growth. The share of imported cars in the U.S. market exceeded 20 percent in 1979 after the second oil crisis. In spite of the Japanese voluntary export restraint, the share of imports in the U.S. market has been around 30 percent in the 1980s. The share of Japanese-made cars is 20–25 percent, while the share of American cars in the Japanese market is far below 1 percent.

Recession in the U.S. Auto Industry and the VER

The second oil crisis and the succeeding economic recession gave a serious blow to the American automotive industry. When the price of gasoline exceeded a dollar per gallon and long lines formed at many gas

FIGURE 2.10 American Autoworkers

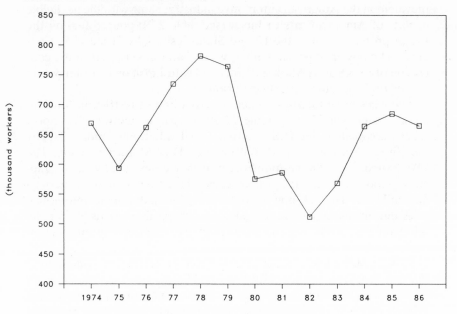

Source: U.S. Department of Labor, *Employment and Earnings*.

stations, American car buyers moved away from domestic "gas-guzzlers" to fuel-efficient Japanese imports. Consequently, domestic car production in 1980 plunged to the lowest level since 1962. The drop in domestic auto production continued, and in 1982 it plunged to a mere 5.8 million units, while the average production in the 1970s was more than 8 million units. One of the "Big Three," Chrysler, was faced with possible bankruptcy, and the federal government bailed out the third-largest carmaker in the United States.

Predictably, the dramatic decline in domestic automobile production had a serious effect on American autoworkers. Figure 2.10 shows the number of production workers in the U.S. auto industry. Immediately after the second oil crisis, the number of American autoworkers declined from 764,000 in 1979 to 575,000 in 1980, a 25 percent decline. In other words, one in every four workers was laid off within a year. The decline in auto employment continued until 1982.

While sales of American cars plunged to the lowest level since the early 1960s, Japanese imports continued to increase, as shown in figure 2.9. From 1979 to 1980 Japanese imports increased by 9.1 percent to 1.9 million cars, while sales of domestic cars declined by 20.1 percent in the same period. This strong performance in sales of Japanese cars in a period threatening the bankruptcy of Chrysler and huge unemployment in the American automotive industry, along with the negligible exports of American cars to Japan (see table 2.2), poured fuel on the fire of protectionism in the United States, especially in the U.S. Congress. The power of protectionists, which had weakened since the conclusion of the Orderly Market Agreement with Japan on color television sets in 1977, became very strong again.

Many concerned parties argued for strict import restrictions on Japanese automobiles. For example, in 1980 separate petitions for import relief were made to the U.S. International Trade Commission (ITC) by the United Auto Workers (UAW) and by Ford Motor Company. The ITC turned down the petitions because they determined that the Japanese imports were not the primary cause of the troubles in the American auto industry. The ITC pointed out that a general decline in automobile sales due to the economic recession was primarily responsible for the misfortune of producers and workers in the American automobile industry.

In spite of the unfavorable ITC decision, protectionism continued in the U.S. Congress. Several bills that would have restricted Japanese car imports were submitted, the most famous (or notorious) being the bill introduced by Senators Danforth and Bentsen in 1981. Their proposed bill provided ceiling on the Japanese imports was far below the actual imports in 1980.

As happened before, during the negotiations on textiles and color television sets, Japan gave in to the U.S. pressures. In May 1981 the Japanese government announced that Japanese exports of passenger cars to the United States would be limited to 1.68 million vehicles in 1981 (when utility vehicles and exports to Puerto Rico are included, the ceiling becomes 1.83 million) and that the ceiling would be increased by 16.5 percent of growth in the U.S. market in 1982 and 1983. The initial "voluntary" export restraint on Japanese automobiles was extended to March 1985. Although the U.S. government insisted that the VER requested by the United States was officially lifted in March 1985, the Japanese VER did not end then. When the Japanese government announced in April 1985 that Japan would increase its automotive exports to the United States by 25 percent, an amount that was well below what would have been realized under free trade, frantic protectionism against Japan arose in the U.S. Congress. The Japanese government again gave in. The voluntary export restraint continued, and there is little hope for its imminent termination.

The Japanese VER on automobiles invited an increase in imports from other sources, as happened earlier when Japan agreed to limit its shipments of textiles and color television sets. For example, sales of the

Korean-made Hyundai Excel increased dramatically after imposition of the Japanese VER. As discussed in detail in later chapters, the weak international competitiveness of the American automobile industry seems to result from higher production costs, which, in turn, are due to imperfect competition in the labor market. Therefore, when the United States imposes import restrictions without correcting such market imperfections, consumer costs become very large through the price markup. Restrictions present more problems, rather than solutions, to the industries facing foreign competition.

JAPANESE IMPORT OF AGRICULTURAL PRODUCTS

In the previous sections, we have examined the U.S.-Japan trade conflicts on the three commodities for which Japan has (or used to have) a comparative advantage over the United States: textiles and clothing, color television sets, and automobiles. For these commodities, trade conflicts ended with Japanese voluntary export restraints after intensive negotiations between the two countries. To conclude our discussion of U.S.-Japan trade conflicts, we will examine conflicts on agricultural products, in which the United States has a substantial competitive edge over Japan.

A Change in U.S. Trade Policy—From Defense to Offense

In the 1980s, an important change in the pattern of U.S.-Japan trade conflicts has emerged. Until the early 1980s, the main issue in the U.S.-Japan trade conflict was how to cope with a sharp increase in Japanese exports to the United States. Faced with growing Japanese exports, the United States requested (or sometimes coerced) Japanese voluntary export restraints on the commodities concerned. In other words, the United States was following defensive trade policies. Since the beginning of the 1980s, U.S. trade policies have changed from defense-oriented to offense-oriented ones. The United States began to aggressively demand the opening up of the Japanese market to American exports.

Probably, the change in U.S. trade policy resulted from U.S. frustration about the huge trade deficit with Japan. As shown in figure 1.1, the U.S. deficit with Japan has widened considerably since the end of the 1970s. Although the overall U.S. deficit widened in the 1980s partly because of the overvaluation of the U.S. dollar, the increase in imports from Japan was much more dramatic than those from other countries. Figure 2.11 shows Japan's share in the exports and imports of the United States. As this figure shows, while the share of the Japanese imports in

FIGURE 2.11 Japanese Share in U.S. Trade

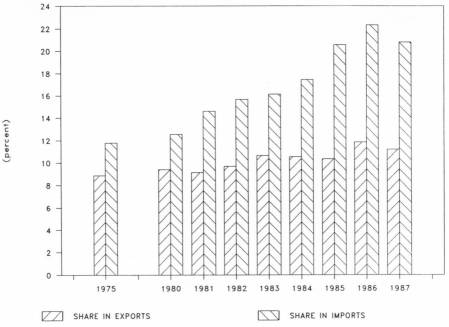

☑ SHARE IN EXPORTS   ◩ SHARE IN IMPORTS

Source: United Nations, *Statistical Yearbook*.

the total imports of the United States was 11.8 percent in 1975, it increased consistently and sharply to become as high as 20.5 percent in 1985. In contrast to this sharp increase, the Japanese share in U.S. exports grew very little: it increased from 8.9 percent to 10.3 percent in the same period.

Faced with the slow growth of U.S. exports to Japan, the United States decided to take a very hard line, and the emphasis in U.S.-Japan trade negotiations has shifted from how to contain the Japanese exports to how to increase U.S. exports to Japan. The "opening up of the Japanese market" became a key phrase among U.S. trade negotiators in the 1980s. In addition to the long-standing concern with agricultural products, many other issues have been put on the negotiation table, from semiconductors to construction projects. While some of these issues were settled after intensive negotiation, many issues remain.

Pressure to opening up the Japanese markets became more severe when the U.S. Congress enacted the Omnibus Trade Bill in the summer of 1988. The bill was intended, among other things, to strengthen the power of the United States Trade Representative (USTR). The strengthened USTR issued a report titled *Foreign Trade Barriers* in April 1989.

This report listed more than thirty categories as Japanese trade barriers, which varied from supercomputers to the Japanese law on large retail stores.

U.S. pressure to open up the Japanese market culminated when, based on the super 301 under the Omnibus Trade Bill of 1988, the USTR named Japan, Brazil, and India in May 1989 as priority countries for negotiation to correct their unfair trade practices. Although, as examined in detail below, the trade conflict on agricultural products was settled (except for rice) in 1988, many areas remain to be negotiated between the two countries.

Weakness of Japanese Agriculture in International Competition

Just as the internationally weak American automobile industry has won protection from Japanese competition, the weak Japanese agriculture has been protected from foreign (mostly American) competition by various trade restrictions, from high tariffs to quotas. For many years, the Japanese farmers have been organized as Nokyo, and its political wing Zenchu has exercised strong influence on Japanese trade policies. Just as the well-organized American autoworkers achieved protection from foreign competition, the politically strong Japanese farmers won strict import restrictions. With its strong political power, Japanese agriculture has been mostly insulated from foreign competition.

In spite of severe import restrictions, the international competitiveness of Japanese agriculture is so weak that the value of Japanese imports of agricultural products is about thirty times larger than that of exports. In other words, while Japan is importing large amounts of agricultural products from abroad, she is unsuccessful in competing in the international market.

Many indicators demonstrate the high degree of protection of Japanese agricultural products. Although Japan's average tariff rates on industrial products are among the world's lowest (at about 2 percent), the average tariff rates on agricultural products are much higher. For example, tariff rates on fresh and preserved fruits are 26 percent and 24.7 percent, respectively. The corresponding figures in the United States are 1.5 percent and 11.6 percent (Balassa and Noland [1988]). In addition to the higher tariffs, Japanese agriculture is protected by various nontariff barriers, primarily strict quotas. For example, according to Balassa and Noland (1988), Japan has twenty-two quotas on agricultural and fishery products while the United States has only one.

As a result of this high protection, domestic prices of agricultural products in Japan are much higher than world prices. The high domestic prices in Japan are evident in table 2.3, which summarizes ratios of

TABLE 2.3.
Ratios of Domestic Producer Price to World Market Price
(1980–1982)

	Japan	European Community	United States
Wheat	3.80	1.25	1.15
Coarse grains	4.30	1.40	1.00
Rice	3.30	1.40	1.30
Beef & lamb	4.00	1.90	1.00
Pork & poultry	1.50	1.25	1.00
Dairy product	2.90	1.75	2.00
Sugar	3.00	1.50	1.40
Weighted average	2.44	1.54	1.16

Source: The World Bank, *World Development Report*.

domestic producer prices to world market prices for selected agricultural products. While the domestic prices are more or less similar to the world prices in the United States, large markups exist in Japan. For example, the domestic price of beef and lamb (85 percent of this category consists of beef) is four times the world market price, which is very different from the situation in the United States where there is no markup.

In the middle 1980s, the OECD published an interesting indicator showing the magnitude of agricultural protection in various countries, which is called the "producer subsidy equivalent (PSE)." The PSE is an aggregate measure of government assistance to agriculture, which includes both import restrictions and domestic subsidy. According to the OECD report, the PSE in Japan was consistently higher than in most countries. For example, in 1986 Japan's PSE was as high as 78.5. In other words, 78.5 percent of farmer's income was generated by government interventions in Japan.

Since agricultural products are among the hottest export items for the United States, pressure to open up the Japanese agricultural market was one of the most important issues in U.S.-Japan trade negotiations in the 1980s. The details of U.S.-Japan agricultural negotiations are discussed below.

Opening Up the Japanese Market

In the 1980s, U.S. agriculture was in a difficult situation due to a decline in exports of agricultural products. Figure 2.12 shows the value of U.S. agricultural exports to the world and to Japan in the 1980s. As this figure shows, agricultural exports decreased by 40 percent from $43.8 billion in 1981 to $26.6 billion in 1986. Due to this decline, pressure

FIGURE 2.12 U.S. Agricultural Exports

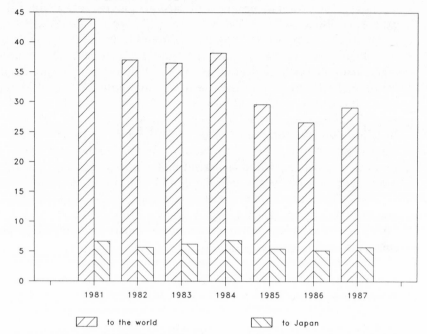

Source: United Nations, *Statistical Yearbook*.

for the opening up of the Japanese market became more intensified. Indeed, Japan is one of the most important markets for the American agricultural products. For example, in 1981 agricultural products amounted to 30 percent of the total value of U.S. exports to Japan, and more than 15 percent of the U.S. agricultural exports were directed to Japan.

Since severe restrictions were imposed on agricultural products for many years, there had been a series of external pressures for the opening up of the Japanese agricultural market even in the 1970s. The U.S. pressure became very strong as the trade imbalance between the United States and Japan widened sharply in the 1980s. In fact, since the middle 1980s agricultural products, especially beef and citrus, symbolized the closed nature of the Japanese market. Until it was settled in the summer of 1988, the negotiation on beef and oranges was one of the toughest trade conflicts between the United States and Japan.

The U.S.-Japan trade negotiations on beef and citrus have continued for many years. In 1978 and 1984, packages of agreements on these products were signed after intensified negotiations between the United States and Japan. In these negotiations, Japan agreed to expand quotas.

Although in the beginning the United States demanded the liberalization of imports (i.e., total abolishment of existing quotas), it settled for the expansion of quotas.

The negotiation in 1988, however, differed from the previous ones: the United States took a very hard line, partly supported by the General Agreement on Tariffs and Trade (GATT). Although a 1984 agreement was in effect for beef and citrus for four years (until the end of March 1988), the United States had brought to the GATT in 1986–87 twelve other Japanese agricultural quotas, including dairy products and starch. In February 1988, the report of the GATT panel on the twelve agricultural products (GATT 12) was adopted in the meeting of the GATT Council. The panel report concluded that ten of the twelve quotas were fundamentally inconsistent with the GATT obligations of Japan.

The timing of this GATT report was excellent for the American trade negotiators because the U.S.-Japan agreement on beef and citrus was about to expire at the end of March 1988. Partly encouraged by the report, the United States took a very hard line, demanding immediate abolishment of existing Japanese quotas on beef and citrus. Japan resisted the U.S. pressure because the producers of beef and citrus were politically very important to the incumbent Liberal Democratic Party.

As a result, the negotiation between the two countries turned out to be very tough. Trade negotiators of the two countries, including U.S. Trade Representative Yeutter and Japanese Minister of Agriculture Sato, flew back and forth between Washington and Tokyo for heated talks. However, negotiations broke down in April and the United States brought the case to the GATT.

In spite of Japanese resistance, in May 1988 the GATT decided to establish a dispute settlement panel on Japanese imports of beef and citrus. Faced with these pressures, Japan gave in. At the Toronto Economic Summit, agreement was reached between President Reagan and Prime Minister Takeshita on the gradual liberalization of Japanese quotas on beef and citrus. The final text of the U.S.-Japan agreement was signed on 5 July 1988, and the United States withdrew its complaints to the GATT on beef and citrus: the beef quota will end in three years, the fresh orange quota in three years, and the orange juice quota in four years.

The essence of the agreement was that Japan would replace quotas on these products with higher tariffs, which are more transparent restrictions. For example, after three years, or after 1 April 1991, Japan will raise its tariff on beef from the current 25 percent to 70 percent in fiscal year 1991. It will be lowered to 60 percent for fiscal year 1992 and further lowered to 50 percent thereafter. In addition, during the three years after the 50 percent tariff is realized, an emergency safeguard system will be provided.

Soon after settlement of the beef and citrus issues, Japan signed an agreement with the United States on other agricultural products. The agreement was based on the GATT recommendation in February 1988 mentioned above. As a result, most of the problems in U.S.-Japan agricultural negotiations were settled, with one big exception, import restrictions on rice. However, many issues remain on the opening up of the Japanese market, even after the disputes on agricultural products are more or less settled.

CHAPTER THREE

Labor Problems Underlying
Trade Conflict

THE PREVIOUS chapter examined some trade conflicts that occurred between the United States and Japan. After the U.S.-Japan textile negotiation was detailed as a historical example, more recent trade conflicts on color television sets and automobiles were discussed. These discussions showed that international trade problems are closely related to domestic labor problems in the importing country. Trade conflicts often coincided with serious unemployment problems in the importing country; when trade restriction became a big political issue, the labor unions played an important role in the importing country. In view of this interrelation between international trade problems and domestic labor problems, the labor market situation in the United States is carefully examined below and compared with the Japanese situation.

The following discussion, first of all, briefly examines recent employment, wages, and labor-management relations in the United States. Emphasis is placed on industries that were involved in serious trade conflicts with Japan, such as the automobile and steel industries. The examination shows that in these industries the power of labor unions is much stronger than in other industries, and the wage rate is much higher than average. Later discussions suggest that imperfect competition in the labor market contributes to the weaker international competitiveness of certain industries in the United States.

Second, by using an econometric method, wage level and flexibility in the American automobile industry is examined. It is shown that the higher and less flexible wage rate, which the stronger labor unions greatly influence, is responsible — at least to some extent — for the huge unemployment in the American automobile industry during economic recessions.

Third, a new trend in labor-management relations in the United States is discussed. As examined in detail below, cooperation of labor and management has become more common since the second oil crisis in those industries that experienced serious trade conflicts with Japan. In

FIGURE 3.1 Unemployment in the United States

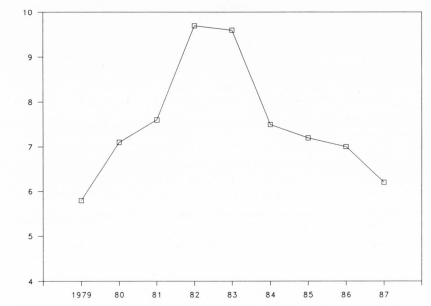

Source: U.S. Department of Labor, *Employment and Earnings*.

an attempt to strengthen their international competitiveness, labor and management in these industries began to take more cooperative measures for higher productivity. In the 1980s, labor contracts in these industries sometimes contained Japanese-like provisions, such as emphasizing job security over higher wages. At the end of this chapter, the salient features of the Japanese labor market are briefly examined. The examination reveals that the flexibility of the labor market is one of the most important reasons for the strong international competitiveness of the Japanese industries.

RECENT SITUATIONS IN THE U.S. LABOR MARKET

Massive Unemployment after the Second Oil Crisis

First of all, let us examine employment (and unemployment) in the U.S. economy as a whole. Figure 3.1 shows the unemployment rate in the United States since the second oil crisis in 1979. It is clear from the figure that the unemployment rate increased dramatically. Due to a time lag between the decline in production and the reduction in employment, the unemployment rate in 1979 was fairly low (5.8 percent). In 1980 it

FIGURE 3.2 Number of Workers by Industries (U.S.)

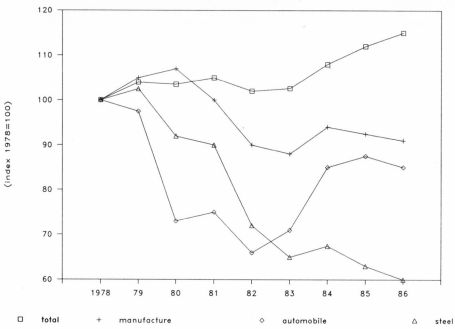

Source: U.S. Department of Labor, *Employment and Earnings*.

jumped to 7.0 percent, partly because of massive layoffs in the automobile industry. The unemployment rate increased to 9.5 percent in
1982 and 1983, the highest level since the end of World War II. In other
words, one in every ten American was unemployed in those years. Since
then, as the U.S. economy began to recover from the second oil recession, the unemployment rate declined. But, the trauma of the high
unemployment rate in the few years after the oil crisis persisted in
people's minds. Since the high unemployment rate coincided with an
increase in imports (especially imports from Japan), many people felt
that some restrictive measures against imports were necessary to save
American workers.

However, all American industries did not suffer from severe unemployment. The decline in employment varied widely from industry to
industry. While the employment level in the service sector did not decline, the decrease in employment in the manufacturing sector was large.
The decline in the automobile and steel industries was strikingly large.
Figure 3.2 shows the disparity in the labor market situations of selected
industries in the United States. The figure shows the total employment
change and those of selected industries, manufacturing, automobile, and

steel. The total employment in the economy since the second oil crisis
may seem puzzling. Although the unemployment rate jumped from 7.5
percent to 9.5 percent in 1981–82, the number of production workers
in whole industry did not decline very much in the same period: it
declined by a mere 2.4 percent from 60.9 million in 1981 to 59.5 million
in 1982. Immediately after the oil crisis, it actually increased from 60.3
million to 60.9 million during 1980–81, but, in spite of the increase in
employment, the unemployment rate increased from 7.0 percent to 7.5
percent.

Since the early 1970s, the labor supply in the United States has increased consistently due to the inflow of women and immigrants into
the labor market. In the 1970s, this increase in labor supply was absorbed
by the rapid increase in labor demand. But, in the early 1980s, the labor
demand slowed and even declined a little, which resulted in huge unemployment (as shown in figure 3.1). In other words, as far as the U.S.
economy as a whole is concerned, the decline in employment was not
so serious. Rather, the record high unemployment rate was brought
about by the strong pressure of increased labor supply.

In the manufacturing sector, the decline in employment was a very
serious problem. During 1979–83, the number of employed workers in
the U.S. manufacturing sector declined by 2.2 million to 12.5 million,
a 15 percent decline in four years. In spite of economic recovery after
that, manufacturing employment did not increase very much. The decline in employment in the automobile and steel industries was especially
remarkable. The number of production workers in the American automobile industry decreased by 25 percent within the year immediately
after the second oil crisis. The number of American autoworkers in 1980
was 35 percent below the precrisis level in 1978. In other words, during
the second oil crisis, one in every three American autoworkers was out
of work. Similarly, in the steel industry, the number of workers declined
by as much as 37 percent in 1979–83.

While employment declined drastically in both the automobile and
the steel industries (a decline of more than 30 percent), the developments during the years of economic recovery are very different. The
number of workers in the steel industry continued to decline even after
1983, but employment in the automobile industry increased again, because U.S. automobile sales (both domestic and imports) recovered,
and many U.S. consumers had to buy (less satisfactory) domestic models
due to the scarcity of Japanese models created by the Japanese VER.

Thus, while the decline in employment in the U.S. economy as a
whole was not so large after the second oil crisis, the decline in manufacturing industries, especially the automobile and steel industries, was
remarkable. As is discussed in detail below, one of the reasons for the

dramatic decline in employment in these industries was their imperfectly competitive labor markets. Wages in these industries are much higher and less flexible than average, and the labor unions seem to be responsible for the imperfectly competitive wage determination, at least to some extent. Imperfect competition in the labor market causes a rigid wage rate in recessionary years, so the necessary adjustment is made through a change in employment. Some statistical evidence on the relationship between imperfect labor market and employment fluctuation in the United States will be presented below.

Industrial Wage Differentials

A comparison of wage rates in different industries reveals an interesting fact: in some of the U.S. industries that were often involved in trade conflicts with Japan, such as the automobile and steel industries, the wage rate is substantially higher than in other industries; and a sizable wage hike was realized in the inflationary years of the early 1980s in spite of the dramatic decline in production and employment in these industries.

Table 3.1 shows the wage rates of production workers by industries. While the hourly wage rate of U.S. industry as a whole in 1986 was $8.76, the rate varies from industry to industry. The wage rate of the highest paid industry, petroleum, ($14.18) was 2.5 times that of the lowest paid industry, clothing, ($5.84). Leather ($5.92), retail sales ($6.03), and textiles ($6.93) are among the industries with the lowest wage rates. On the other hand, along with petroleum, steel ($13.73), automobile ($13.45), and tobacco ($12.85) are among the industries with the highest wage rates.

The pattern of industrial wage differentials is not necessarily universal across countries. Then, what creates such huge wage differentials in U.S. industries? Generally speaking, economic theory predicts that, the wage rate is an increasing function of the capital-labor ratio (K/L) in the industry. The wage rate (the price of the labor supply) is determined by the marginal productivity of labor. The higher the marginal productivity, the higher the capital-labor ratio. Therefore, there should be a positive correlation between wage rate and capital-labor ratio in the industry.

A quick inspection of table 3.1 suggests that this proposition generally holds. The production of clothing and leather products is fairly labor-intensive, and the capital-labor ratio in these industries is relatively low. Due to the lower marginal productivity that results from a lower capital-labor ratio, the wage rates in these industries are lower than average. On the other hand, the petroleum industry requires a huge amount of

TABLE 3.1.
Hourly (U.S.) Wage Rate by Industry (in Dollars)

	1985	*1986*
Total	8.57	8.76
Mining	11.98	12.44
Construction	12.32	12.47
Manufacturing	9.54	9.73
Lumber and wood products	8.22	8.33
Furniture and fixtures	7.17	7.46
Stone, clay, and glass products	9.84	10.05
Primary metal	11.67	11.86
Iron and steel	13.33	13.73
Fabricated metal products	9.70	9.89
Machinery, except electrical	10.29	10.59
Electric and electronic equipment	9.46	9.65
Transportation equipment	12.71	12.81
Motor vehicles	13.39	13.45
Instruments and related products	9.17	9.47
Food products	8.57	8.74
Tobacco	11.96	12.85
Textile mill products	6.70	6.93
Apparel	5.73	5.84
Paper and allied products	10.83	11.18
Printing and publishing	9.71	9.98
Chemicals	11.56	11.98
Petroleum and coal products	14.06	14.18
Rubber and plastics	8.54	8.73
Leather and leather products	5.83	5.92
Transportation and utilities	11.40	11.70
Wholesale trade	9.16	9.35
Retail trade	5.94	6.03
Finance, insurance, real estate	7.94	8.35
Services	7.90	8.10

Source: U.S. Department of Labor, *Monthly Labor Review*.

capital and employs few workers. Because of the high capital-labor ratio, the wage rate is higher in the petroleum industry. Similarly, other high-wage industries, such as automobile and steel, are relatively capital intensive, where labor productivity is expected to be higher than average. Thus, the prediction of orthodox economic theory seems to be correct in many cases.

As becomes clearer in the next section, however, while the wage rate in the American automobile industry, where the labor union is very strong, is 50 percent higher than the U.S. average, such a huge wage markup in the automobile industry is not universal. In Japan, for ex-

TABLE 3.2.
Annual Growth Rate of Wage and Employment in the United States (%)

	1980	1981	1982	1983	1984	1985	1986
Total							
Employment	−0.1	1.0	−2.4	1.0	5.6	3.4	2.2
Wage	8.2	8.9	5.9	4.4	3.7	3.0	2.2
Manufacturing							
Employment	2.3	−5.7	−10.4	−1.7	6.0	−1.4	−1.5
Wage	8.5	9.9	6.3	4.0	4.1	3.8	2.0
Motor vehicles							
Employment	−24.7	1.8	−12.7	9.2	18.9	3.1	−2.9
Wage	8.5	12.1	5.4	4.6	4.9	5.2	0.7
Primary metal							
Employment	−11.0	−1.8	−20.7	−9.3	5.1	−6.1	−7.4
Wage	8.8	10.6	4.8	0.2	1.1	1.7	1.6
Consumer price index	13.5	10.4	6.1	3.2	4.3	3.6	1.9

Source: U.S. Department of Labor, *Employment and Earnings* and *Monthly Labor Review*.

ample, the wage rate of autoworkers is not very different from that of an average Japanese worker. Further, while in the United States, the wage rate in the manufacturing sector ($9.73) is higher than the industry average ($8.76), the industrial wage differential in Japan is opposite to that of the United States. In Japan, due to the high wage in the banking and insurance industries, which have been relatively well protected from foreign competition, the wage rate in the tertiary sector is higher than that in manufacturing sector.

An annual increase in wage rate varies widely from industry to industry in the United States. As shown in table 3.1, the wage level in the automobile and steel industries is much higher than average. In addition, the labor unions in these industries could achieve much higher wage increases during the years of high inflation and high unemployment after the second oil crisis. Table 3.2 shows the annual percentage changes in total wage rates and employment and those of selected industries, manufacturing, automobiles, and metal (mostly steel), along with the annual rate of increase in the consumer price index.

As shown in the table, the inflation rate immediately after the second oil crisis was very high: 13.5 percent and 10.4 percent in 1980 and 1981, respectively. Under the high inflation, the labor unions demanded large wage increases in order to maintain the workers' real wage. Although the rate of wage increase in those years was lower than the inflation rate, the workers could achieve notable wage increases during the recession: in industry as a whole, the rate of wage increase was 8.2 percent and 8.9 percent in 1980 and 1981, respectively. The wage increases in the automobile and metal industries were greater than in industry as a whole. In the automobile industry, the wage rate was raised by 8.5 percent in 1980, and in 1981 it was further increased by 12.1 percent, which was much higher than the 8.9 percent increase in the total economy. In the metal industry (mostly steel), a similar phenomenon was observed, where the rates of wage hikes in 1980 and in 1981 were 8.8 percent and 10.6 percent, respectively.

The labor unions in the automobile and metal industries achieved higher wage increases than average in spite of more severe unemployment situations than average. The higher wage increase under more severe unemployment is contrary to the prediction of orthodox economic theory. Orthodox economic theory predicts a negative correlation between wage increase and unemployment: during recessionary years when the unemployment rate is high, the rate of wage increase tends to decrease; in the boom years when the unemployment rate is low, the workers can obtain a higher wage increase. The negative correlation between wage hike and unemployment is known as the "Phillips curve," whose validity has been proved in many cases.

However, the developments in wage hikes and unemployment in the automobile and steel industries in the United States immediately after the oil crisis seem to contradict what the Phillips curve predicts. As examined in detail above, employment in these industries during the recession declined dramatically, a much larger decline than the industry average in the United States. While the number of workers in the U.S. economy remained almost constant (or increased a little) in 1980–81, employment in the automobile and metal industries decreased dramatically (as shown in table 3.2). Consequently, workers in these industries deplored the critical situation in the labor market, and they insisted that foreign (mostly Japanese) competition was responsible for their misfortune. It should be noted that wage increases well above average in these industries were achieved during a critical employment situation.

The development in the labor markets of the U.S. automobile and steel industries (a higher wage increase under higher unemployment) presented an apparent contradiction to the prediction of orthodox economic theory which is based on the Phillips curve. This phenomenon can be explained by a new economic theory based on imperfect competition in the labor market (discussed in detail in the next chapter). The power of labor unions in these industries is much stronger than average. It seems likely that, because of the strong bargaining power of their labor unions, workers in these industries could achieve a higher wage increase in an attempt to maintain their real wage, in spite of severe labor market conditions. A more rigorous econometric analysis is made below on the impact of labor unions on the level and flexibility

TABLE 3.3.
Percentage Unionized in the United States

Year	Percentage Unionized	Year	Percentage Unionized
1970	27.3	1980	23.0
1972	26.4	1983	20.1
1974	25.8	1984	18.8
1976	24.5	1985	18.0
1978	23.6	1986	17.6

Source: U.S. Department of Labor, Employment and Earnings.

of wages in various U.S. industries, with an emphasis on the American automobile industry.

It should be also noted in table 3.2 that the pattern of wage increases for U.S. metalworkers differed from that of autoworkers since the middle 1980s. While the metalworkers could achieve wage increases higher than average in 1980 and 1981, the annual rate of increase in their wages has been as low as 1 percent since 1983, when it was far below the average. Faced with extremely severe unemployment, some of the strongest labor unions, including the United Steel Workers, began to think that a lower wage increase is, at least in some cases, necessary to avoid unemployment.

In the 1980s the unemployment problem in the U.S. metal industry was extremely severe: employment declined by 40 percent in 1980–86. This severe unemployment situation, which coincided with an increase in foreign competition, has created a new trend in the labor-management relationship in U.S. industry: labor and management have begun to cooperate with, rather than confront, each other in an attempt to survive the competition from abroad. The new cooperative trend between labor and management in the U.S. automobile and steel industries is discussed in more detail in later sections of this chapter.

Power of Labor Unions

As became clear when we examined some examples of U.S.-Japan trade conflicts, international trade conflicts were often initiated by the demands of the labor unions in the importing country. The influence of labor unions seems to become stronger over time. However, in the United States, the percentage of labor that is unionized has declined for a long period of time. Table 3.3 shows the percentage of U.S. workers that are unionized, or the proportion of unionized workers in the total employees. As this table shows, the percentage unionized has declined

TABLE 3.4.
Percentage Unionized by Industries (United States, 1985)

	Employees (×1,000)	Union Members (×1,000)	Percentage Unionized (%)
Total	94,521	16,996	18.0
Transport equipment (excluding shipbuilding)	1,519	974	64.1
Iron and steel	808	712	88.1

Source: U.S. Department of Labor, *Employment and Earnings.*

consistently since 1970. In 1970, for example, the percentage unionized was 27.3 percent, or one in every 3–4 workers was in a labor union. But, in the 1980s the percentage unionized has declined rapidly. The percentage unionized in 1986 was a mere 17.6 percent. In other words, more than 80 percent of American workers were nonunion.

While the percentage of American workers unionized in the whole economy is very low (American workers are much less organized than the Japanese workers), the percentages in the automobile and steel industries are fairly high. Table 3.4 shows the percentage unionized among American workers by industries in 1985. As the table shows, the percentage unionized in industries involved in the trade conflict with Japan is much higher than the industry average. While the percentage unionized in the whole industry in 1985 was only 18 percent, the corresponding figure in the steel industry was 88.1 percent.

In the transport equipment manufacturing industry, the percentage unionized was four times higher than average. Since the percentage unionized in the automobile industry was not available, table 3.4 shows the figure for the transport equipment manufacturing industry, which includes the manufacture of airplanes. But, if the automobile industry could be singled out, the figure is probably much higher than 64.1 percent. In fact, almost all of the production workers in the U.S. automobile industry were organized in one strong labor union, the United Auto Workers (UAW).

Thus, in the automobile and steel industries, various aspects of the labor market, including employment levels, wages, and the percentage unionized, are very different from those of the average industry in the United States. At the risk of oversimplification, the following can be said about the labor markets in the two industries that were involved in serious trade conflicts with Japan:

1. The power of labor unions is very strong (percentage unionized is well above average).
2. Employment declined drastically and unemployment was very serious after the second oil crisis.
3. The wage level is much higher than the industry average, and during the years of high inflation after the second oil crisis the rate of wage increase remained higher in spite of more severe unemployment.

The above stylized facts suggest that the weak international competitiveness of the automobile and steel industries in the United States resulted, at least to some extent, from imperfect competition in these industries. In an attempt to make a more rigorous analysis, an econometric study of the impact of labor unions on the level and flexibility of wages is given in the next section.

LABOR UNIONS AND WAGES

In the previous section, we have examined recent developments in the U.S. labor market. Unemployment, wages, and labor unions in the industries involved in trade conflicts with Japan (such as the automobile and steel industries) have been compared with the industry averages in the United States. Our conclusion could be summarized as follows: In many industries involved in serious trade conflicts, the labor market is far less perfectly competitive than orthodox trade theory usually assumes. Strong labor unions have achieved a huge wage markup, and the higher labor cost often causes weaker international competitiveness in these industries. The weak competitiveness due to labor market imperfections often invites an increase in imports, which in turn brings about high unemployment in a recession.

But, many factors are responsible for the industrial differential in wage rates and unemployment. The data on wages and unemployment by industries only *suggest* that in certain industries, imperfect competition in the labor market is partly responsible for a higher wage rate and a wider fluctuation in employment than in an average industry. It is not possible to conclude a causal relationship from the data. In view of this, the impact of labor unions on the level and flexibility of wages in the U.S. automobile industry is more rigorously examined below.

TABLE 3.5.
Relative Wage of Autoworkers

Manufacturing = 100.0

	1970[a]	1975	1980	1984	1985	1986
Japan	107.8	108.3	113.8	113.8	114.6	n.a.
U.S.	126.3	134.0	135.2	138.2	140.4	138.2

All Industries = 100.0

	1970[a]	1975	1980	1984	1985	1986
Japan	101.0	100.0	105.7	107.1	108.2	n.a.
U.S.	131.0	142.8	147.7	152.2	156.2	153.5

Sources: Japanese Ministry of Labor, *Yearbook of Labor Statistics*; U.S. Department of Labor, *Employment and Earnings*.
[a]For Japan, data for 1971.

Wage Markup in the United States and Japan

First of all, let us examine the relative wages of autoworkers in the United States and Japan (i.e., the wage rate of autoworkers in each country relative to that of the average workers in the same country). Table 3.5 lists the relative wages of autoworkers in the two countries since 1970. The table shows that American autoworkers are paid much better than average American workers, while in Japan the difference is relatively small.

For example, in 1985, the wage rate of American autoworkers was 40.4 percent higher than that of average American workers in the manufacturing sector as a whole (56.2 percent higher than the economy-wide average). This difference increases when we include other fringe benefits. For example, according to Crandall's estimate (1984), the total hourly compensation in the motor vehicle industry in the United States is 54.5 percent higher than in the manufacturing sector as a whole (almost double the economy-wide average). On the other hand, in Japan, a big wage markup in the auto industry is not observed. As table 3.5 shows, the wage rate of the Japanese autoworkers in 1985 was only 14.6 percent higher than that of the average manufacturing workers (merely 8.2 percent higher than that of the average workers in all industries). Further, this small difference may result from differences in labor productivity among industries rather than from a markup by the imperfect labor market structure.

Table 3.6 shows the relative wage of Japanese autoworkers by the

TABLE 3.6.
Relative Wage Rate of Transport Equipment Industry by Size of
Establishment (Japan)

No. of Employees	Relative Wage I (Manufacturing = 100)	Relative Wage II (All Industries = 100)
5–29	110.8	98.6
30–99	103.5	84.6
100–499	104.1	94.4
500 and over	89.7	86.4

Source: Compiled from data in Yearbook of Labor Statistics.
Note: Data are for 1985.

size of establishments. Table 3.6 uses data on the wage rate of the transport equipment manufacturing industry, because data on the auto wage rate by size of establishment were not available. Although the wage rate in the transport equipment industry as a whole is 15.2 percent higher than in the manufacturing sector (8.8 percent higher than in all industries), when we compare the wage rate by size of the establishment, the difference in wage rate between the transport equipment manufacturing industry and the manufacturing sector as a whole almost disappears, except for the case of very small-size establishments. Moreover, in the large-size establishments (more than 500 workers), the wage rate of autoworkers is 10 percent less than that of manufacturing industry as a whole. In other words, although the workers in the transport equipment industry are paid a slightly higher wage than the average manufacturing workers, the difference seems to result from the fact that the average establishment size in the transport equipment manufacturing industry is bigger than most industries.

As table 3.7 shows, the wage rate in Japan varies widely according to the size of the establishment, and the gradient of the size difference

TABLE 3.7.
Wage Rate by Size of Establishment (Japan)

No. of Employees	Transport Equipment	Manufacturing	All Industries
5–29	67.8	54.9	59.4
30–99	72.6	62.9	74.1
100–499	89.4	77.1	81.8
500 and over	100.0	100.0	100.0

Source: Compiled from data in Yearbook of Labor Statistics.
Notes: Wage rate of establishments of 500 and over = 100. Data are for 1985.

is very similar in various industries. For example, the wage rate in the very small establishments (where the number of employees is less than 30 persons) is about 60 percent of that in the big establishments (with more than 500 employees) where probably the labor productivity is higher than in the small establishments due to higher capital intensity. Thus, it seems that the wage rate in the Japanese auto industry is a little higher than average not because there is a wage markup due to labor market imperfection but because the size of automobile plants is above average. Therefore, the wage rate in the Japanese auto industry seems to be determined fairly competitively, which is very different from the situation in the U.S. automobile industry.

An interesting phenomena is observed in table 3.5: while the relative wage of American autoworkers had increased consistently until 1985, it declined in 1986. As shown in the table, in 1970 the wage rate of American autoworkers was 31 percent higher than that of average workers. The wage gap increased consistently since then, and in 1985 the wage rate of the auto industry was almost 60 percent higher than average. But, for the first time since 1970, the wage gap narrowed a little in 1986 when the auto wage was 53.5 percent higher than in industry as a whole.

A similar decline in the relative wage rate is observed in the U.S. steel industry. As discussed in detail below, faced with a severe unemployment problem after the second oil crisis, workers and management in the industries involved in trade conflicts began to emphasize job security over higher wages.

Higher Wages and Labor Unions

Above, we have examined various data that suggest that the wage rate of U.S. autoworkers is much higher than that for average American workers, while there is no significant difference in Japan between wages in the automobile industry and in industry as a whole. We now examine the relationship between the higher wage and unions, because most of the American autoworkers are organized as the UAW and it is suspected that this strong union is responsible for the huge wage markup in the American auto industry.

Many studies have suggested a positive correlation between the union and the higher wage rate in the United States. For example, Lewis's classical study (1963) found that the union causes wage rates to be 15 percent higher than they would be otherwise. Since then, many studies have been made on the impact of labor unions on wage rates. Unfortunately, most of these later studies have been concerned with unionism in broad sectors, although the impact of the union on wages may differ from industry to industry. But, recently, Weiss (1985) estimated the

TABLE 3.8.
Union-Wage Effect by Industry (United States)

Log($WAGE$) = 0.385 + 0.118 Log($UNION$) + 0.321 Log(LPP)
          (1.69)   (3.38)   (5.46)

        R^2 = 0.7044, # of observations = 25
        t is shown in ( )

where $WAGE$ = Hourly compensation for worker (dollars)
                $UNION$ = Unionization rate (%) (proxy for the power of the union)
                LPP = Labor productivity (value of shipment per worker,
                                   thousand dollars)

Source: Author's estimate. See text for details.

union-wage effect by industries, and found that in the automotive industry the union causes the wage rate to be 26.5 percent higher for males and 44.0 percent higher for females than it would be otherwise. He also estimated that in the whole industry the union caused the wage rate to be 21.8 percent higher for males and 15.0 percent higher for females. Further, he found that this union-wage effect was much smaller in the industries with lower unionization rates.

In order to examine the relationship between union strength and the wage rate by industries, we have run a cross-section regression. The findings are summarized in table 3.8. Data on union members by detailed industries were not available after 1978. Therefore, using data from 1978, we estimated the elasticity of the wage rate with respect to the power of the union, which was represented by the percentage unionized in each industry. As the table shows, we found that the greater the union power in the industry, the higher the wage rate. Of course, strictly speaking, there are various shortcomings in the regression. For example, if the percentage unionized in the industry is an increasing function of the wage rate, the estimate of the coefficient for the variable $UNION$ in table 3.8 may be an overestimate because of simultaneity. Therefore, the regression only serves to suggest a positive relationship between union power and the wage rate in the automobile industry. For an accurate estimate of the union wage effect in the U.S. automobile industry, further studies would be needed. But, the regression result in table 3.8, along with the study by Weiss, suggests that the strong union would be heavily responsible for the higher wage in the American automobile industry.

TABLE 3.9.
Elasticity of Wage Bill by Industries (United States)

	High Unionization		Low Unionization		
	Transport Equipment	Primary Metal	Textile	Chemical	Instrument
Unionization rate (%)	56.7	64.2	17.1	20.1	8.9
Elasticity					
wage (w)	0.0174	0.1217	0.2805	0.2625	0.2057
employment (e)	0.5561	0.3266	0.4151	0.2101	0.2267
hour (h)	0.1394	−0.0123	0.2392	0.0280	0.0408
w + e + h	0.7129	0.4360	0.9349	0.5004	0.4731

Source: Author's estimates. For methodology, see the discussion in the text.

Wage Flexibility and Labor Unions

In the previous subsection, we examined the relationship between the wage markup and labor unions. We found a substantial wage markup in the U.S. automobile industry and showed that the union is, at least to some extent, responsible for the wage markup. When we look at the short-run fluctuation in employment, the flexibility of the wage rate is important (as well as the wage level itself) because if the wage rate is less flexible, it is more likely that the larger part of the adjustment for a sales decline would be made through a reduction in employment. In industries where the wage adjustment is less flexible, the unemployment problem becomes more serious during a recession than it would be otherwise.

Gordon (1982) presented a study of wage flexibility. He compared the elasticity of the wage rate with respect to the output change in the manufacturing industry as a whole in the United States, the United Kingdom, and Japan. He found that the wage rate of the U.S. manufacturing sector is much less flexible than its Japanese counterpart. While Gordon's study concerned the elasticity of wage rate in the manufacturing sector as a whole, we have made a similar estimate by industries in order to examine the relationship between wage flexibility and the labor unions. Table 3.9 summarizes our findings. As discussed in detail below, we found some evidence to suggest that the wage rate in the American automobile industry is less flexible than in most industries and that the union is likely to be responsible for this.

Our estimation method is similar to Gordon's. First, wage rate, employment, and weekly working hours in each industry were each regressed to a constant and time trend in order to get the de-trended and de-meaned variables (normalized variables). Second, the logarithm of each normalized variable was regressed to a constant term, time trend, and the logarithm of a normalized production variable (and its lagged variables up to four quarters). Third, the estimated coefficients of five regressors (current production and lagged production up to the fourth quarter) were added to get the elasticity. Table 3.9 summarizes the estimated elasticities of various industries.

First of all, it should be noted that in the transport equipment manufacturing sector (proxy for the automobile industry) the elasticity of the wage rate with respect to output change is very low while the elasticity of employment is high. In other words, in the American automobile industry, the adjustment to a change in production is made through a change in employment level rather than a wage change. Therefore, in a recession, the unemployment problem in the industry tends to be more serious than in other industries, which conforms with the actual situation in the labor market of the American automobile industry after the second oil crisis.

Secondly, the wage rate elasticity in highly unionized industries (e.g., transport equipment and primary metals) is clearly below that of low unionized industries (e.g., textile mill products, chemicals, and instruments). For example, in the textile mill industry, where the percentage unionized is 17.1 percent, the elasticity of wages is 0.28, while in the transport equipment manufacturing industry, where the percentage unionized is 56.7 percent, the elasticity of wage is only 0.017.

From the estimate in table 3.9, it seems that in highly unionized industries, such as the American automobile industry, the wage rate is not only higher but also less flexible than in other industries. In these industries, international competitiveness tends to be weaker due to the higher labor cost, and the adjustment to a decline in production is made through large-scale layoffs during a recession.

Flexible Wage Determination in Japan

Some evidence has been presented above to show that in Japan the wage rate of autoworkers is not very different from that in other industries, while in the United States the auto wage is much higher and less flexible than that in the average American industry, for which the labor unions seem to be responsible at least to some extent. The theoretical analysis in chapters 4 and 5 rigorously demonstrates that the higher wage rate brought about by the imperfectly competitive labor market (i.e., the big union wage markup) constitutes a comparative disadvantage in the American automobile industry. In the rest of this section, some institutional facts concerning the competitive wage determination in Japan will be briefly discussed. Three institutional reasons, among others, could explain why the wage rate in the Japanese automobile industry is determined more competitively than its American counterpart.

First, in Japan, unions are organized by companies rather than by industries, while there are strong industrial unions, such as the UAW, in the United States. Further, Japanese "enterprise unions" consist of both blue-collar and white-collar workers. (Note that, in Japan, the union by companies is called an "enterprise union" rather than a "company union" in order to avoid the bad connotations of the latter.) Naturally, an enterprise union is much more cooperative with management than are industrial unions. The number of labor disputes in Japan is well below that in the United States. For example, days lost in labor disputes in 1973–83 were 535,000 man-days annually in Japan and 17 million man-days in the United States. In the Japanese enterprise-union system, economic conditions are given more weight when the wage rate is negotiated between management and workers. This is considered to be the primary reason for setting the wage rate in each industry at a competitive level in Japan.

Second, in Japan, the annual bonus is a significant part of the annual wage of workers, and this bonus system plays an important role in the flexibility of wages, especially in a critical period. Normally, workers (especially those in big companies) receive bonus payments twice a year, whose amount is more than five months' pay, and the bonus is considered to be a part of the total wage. The amount of such bonus payments fluctuates widely according to the business conditions of the company. For example, if the company's business conditions are extremely bad, there may be no bonus. On the other hand, if the company's business goes very well, the bonus could be ten months' pay. Through this "bonus system," as well as the annual wage contract (discussed below), the wage rate of Japanese workers, including autoworkers, is very responsive to business conditions.

Third, there is an important difference in the duration of wage contracts in the United States and Japan. In the United States, most wage contracts are binding for three years. For example, the UAW makes three-year contracts with auto producers, while in Japan wage contracts are negotiated annually. In other words, in the United States the wage rate is inflexible for three years regardless of changes in business conditions, while in Japan the wage rate is negotiated annually and determined by taking into consideration various changes in business conditions during the previous year. Of course, in the United States, such three-year contracts are subject to renegotiation, but in Japan the annual negotiation is institutionalized. The longer duration of the wage contract in the American automobile industry seems to be responsible, to a great extent, for the inflexibility of the wage level, which, in turn, contributes to the wider fluctuation in employment levels in the industry.

UNION-MANAGEMENT ACCORD AND JOB SECURITY

Traditionally, in the U.S. industries involved in a serious trade conflict with Japan (e.g., the automobile and steel industries) the wage determination has been made in an imperfectly competitive labor market. Backed by strong labor unions, the workers in these industries could achieve higher wage increases, without regard to the economic condition. The higher production cost due to the higher wage rate caused the weaker competitiveness of these American industries in comparison with their Japanese counterparts. Further, since the wage rate in these industries in the United States is inflexible even in a recessionary period, the adjustment to a decline in production was made through a reduction in employment, and therefore, unemployment in these industries became much more serious than the industry average during the severe recession after the second oil crisis.

Recently, however, a new trend is emerging in the labor market in the United States. After the bitter experience of huge unemployment, the American workers in many industries, including the automobile and steel industries, began to realize that cooperation (rather than confrontation) between labor and management is important to protect their jobs. In other words, although imperfect competition in the labor market was one of the important reasons for the weakness of American industries for many years, there was a change in the American labor market after U.S. industries experienced strong foreign competition (mostly Japanese competition) in recent years. Below we shall examine some of these changes in the U.S. labor market, emphasizing the automobile and steel industries.

Job Security over Higher Wages

For many years, only the pecuniary aspects of labor conditions, such as wage rates and fringe benefits, had been emphasized in labor-management negotiations in the United States. Job security was not a big issue in the negotiations except for the seniority arrangement in the order of layoffs. This is probably because the mobility of workers in the

U.S. labor market is much greater than it is in Japan. Job security had not been a major labor union demand because unemployed workers in the United States could find another job more easily than their Japanese counterparts due to the greater mobility in the U.S. labor market. But, American workers in certain industries, such as the automobile and steel industries, experienced extremely severe unemployment after the second oil crisis, and the trauma of this unemployment brought about a change in the labor unions' demand: many workers in these industries began to consider job security more important than a higher wage. Some examples of labor-management accord to save domestic jobs are discussed below.

JOB OPPORTUNITY BANK

Job security was first introduced in a major labor-management contract, when the wage contracts were concluded in 1984 between General Motors and the UAW and between Ford Motor Company and the UAW. The production of automobiles in the United States declined dramatically after the second oil crisis, because the demand for consumer durable goods, including automobiles, declined due to the recession and because the consumer demand for automobiles shifted from big domestic models to fuel-efficient Japanese models. As a result of the decline in sales, many workers were laid off in the American automobile industry. One in every four autoworkers was laid off within the year immediately after the oil crisis, and employment in the American auto industry in the bottom year (1982) was one-third below the precrisis level (1978). After experiencing this severe unemployment situation, the labor union gave up the idea of a high wage increase to maintain the real wage in the labor-management negotiations in 1984. Rather, the negotiations emphasized such matters as the strengthening of international competitiveness of the American automobile industry and the job security of American autoworkers.

The 1984 wage negotiations between management and labor in the American automobile industry attempted to protect workers from layoffs. The contracts between the two largest auto producers and the UAW contained provisions for a "job opportunity bank." The job opportunity bank was funded entirely with the company's money. The fund was to be used to pay expenses for vocational training and other education when workers were obliged to change jobs inside or outside the company.

While the job opportunity bank is fairly innovative in the United States, it is very common in Japanese companies. As examined in detail below, a typical employment practice in a Japanese company (especially in the large Japanese corporations) is as follows: after hiring new graduates who lack skills and experience that are directly applicable to the production activities of the firm, the firms provide free, on-the-job training to them. The wage rate of workers depends less on their skills than on their number of years of service in the company under the so-called lifetime employment system. In Japan, it is considered proper for companies to bear the cost of training and educating their employees, and companies have full discretion to transfer their employees from one division to another within the company, even when the transfer involves a geographical relocation of workers.

The situation in the United States is very different from that in Japan. There are numerous job categories in the large U.S. corporations, and the wage rate is determined by the job. (In the Japanese counterpart the wage rate is determined very much according to the number of years of service in the corporation.) In the United States, therefore, workers often pay to acquire the skills necessary for a new, more favorable job. Accordingly, the American corporation cannot transfer its employees as readily as its Japanese counterpart can. When a labor surplus occurs for job category A at the same time as a labor shortage occurs for job category B within a company, the large U.S. corporation normally lays off some workers in job category A and hires new workers for openings in job category B from applicants both within and outside the company. When large Japanese corporations have a similar disparity of labor demand among different jobs, their typical practice is to transfer some employees from job category A to job category B after giving them the training necessary for the new category (at the company's expense, of course). This Japanese practice, training-transfer, is not common in American companies.

However, having experienced the record high unemployment after the second oil crisis, labor and management in the American automobile industry began to agree that the Japanese training-transfer practice should be introduced to their companies. They thought that in order to avoid the recurrence of massive unemployment the American auto producers had to increase international competitiveness, for which the adoption of the Japanese training-transfer practice was necessary. As a result, the job opportunity bank was institutionalized in union-management contracts in 1984. According to the provision, General Motors and Ford Motor Company agreed to bear the training costs of their employees when they were forced to change jobs. For example, in 1984, General Motors agreed with the UAW to contribute to its job opportunity bank a total of $1 billion in the following six years. Similar provision was made in the 1985 contract between Chrysler and the UAW. Thus, the job opportunity bank, which is largely based on a Japanese practice, was institutionalized in the American automobile industry after severe

TABLE 3.10.
Wage Increase in Major Union Contracts (United States)

| Year | Wage Increase[a] (%) | | Effective Wage Increase[b] (%) |
	First Year of Contract	Average in the Entire Term of Contracts	
1980	9.5	7.1	9.9
1981	9.8	7.9	9.5
1982	3.8	3.6	6.8
1983	2.6	2.8	4.0
1984	2.4	2.4	3.7
1985	2.3	2.7	3.3
1986	1.2	1.8	2.3

Source: U.S. Department of Labor, *Monthly Labor Review*.
[a]The major union contract covers more than a thousand workers.
[b]Including cost of living adjustment (COLA).

trade conflict with Japan. A similar idea spread to other industries, most notably to the U.S. steel industry, as discussed below.

WAGE CUT IN THE STEEL INDUSTRY

As shown in Table 3.2, employment in the American steel industry continued to decline in the 1980s, because of a world-wide decline in demand for steel products and because of foreign competition (mostly from Japan and Korea). Faced with severe unemployment, an unusual agreement was made between labor and management in the American steel industry during the wage negotiations in 1986: the nominal wage rate in the American steel industry was cut to a lower level than in the previous year in spite of a general price increase.

The wage cut in the steel industry was agreed under a moderating wage increase in the U.S. economy as a whole. As the U.S. economy began to recover from the high unemployment and high inflation due to the second oil crisis, the rate of wage increase became smaller and smaller. Table 3.10 shows the wage increases in major union contracts that cover more than a thousand workers. The first column gives the rate of wage increase in the first year of each union wage contract. Mostly due to the high inflation rate, the agreed rates of wage increase immediately after the oil crisis were very high: 9.5 percent and 9.8 percent in 1980 and 1981, respectively. But, the rate of wage increase declined rapidly after that. In 1983, it fell below 3 percent, and in 1986 it further declined to 1.2 percent, the lowest level since the U.S. Department of Labor had started collecting data in 1968.

The wage contracts of the U.S. steel industry in 1986 were negotiated during a decline in the rate of economy-wide wage hikes. After the often hostile negotiations, American steel workers were obliged to accept the unusual wage cut. As described in detail below, wage negotiations in the U.S. steel industry in 1986 were unusual from the very outset. Until 1986, the United Steel Workers (USW) had normally negotiated collectively with the five largest steel makers, and the other smaller steel makers followed the agreement between the USW and the big five. In 1986 the steel makers refused to negotiate collectively. Instead, they proposed separate wage negotiations in individual firms. The American steel makers insisted that since the business conditions of individual steel makers differed widely, due to the severe steel depression, the steel industry could not give a collective response to the union's demand for a wage hike. The USW had to give in to the hard line of management, and it accepted separate negotiations with individual firms.

The USW was obliged to first negotiate with the second largest steel maker, the LTV, where business conditions were very bad. After a relatively quick negotiation, a wage contract was agreed between the union and management, in which the USW accepted a 10 percent cut in the hourly wage rate, in view of the severe conditions the LTV was facing. Further, the union had to agree on the reduction of fringe benefits, such as the number of days granted as paid annual leave. In return for the workers' concessions, LTV management agreed to share the training and education costs of workers in case of job changes and to make payment to the "steel depression fund" that the union had institutionalized on its own. Further, management promised a profit-sharing: when business conditions improved in the future, the workers would receive a special bonus and share the company's profit.

A similar wage-cut provision was agreed on in the following negotiations with National Steel, the sixth-largest steel producer in the United States. A job security provision was included in the labor-management contract. In return for the wage concession by the labor union, the company promised that no workers would be laid off except for emergencies, such as plant closure, bankruptcy, or an extremely bad financial situation in the firm. While the company expected that a 25–30 percent reduction in the work force would be necessary in the following four years, the reduction would be made, as far as possible, through natural attrition, such as retirement and quitting, rather than layoffs. If the necessary reduction were not achieved by the autonomous measures, the company would resort to an early retirement system, and forced measures such as layoffs would be avoided if possible.

After these successive agreements on wage reduction, the USW started wage negotiations with the largest steel producer in the United States, USX Corporation. In an attempt to reverse the trend of wage cuts, the USW went on strike on 1 August 1986 when the old wage contract expired. While the USX insisted on a wage cut similar to those at the smaller companies, the USW tried to limit its concession to a wage freeze rather than a wage cut. The strike continued longer than expected. In the middle of January 1987, it finally ended after 170 days, which was the longest strike against a major steel company in the United States. In spite of the strike that continued almost for half a year, the wage contract at the USX turned out to be similar to those at the smaller companies. In order to protect their jobs the workers were obliged to accept a wage cut, while the firm, in return, agreed to share future profits with workers in the form of special bonuses if the business conditions of the company improved.

As was the case in the automobile industry, labor and management in the American steel industry agreed that strengthening their international competitiveness was necessary for survival and job protection in difficult years. The workers had to agree on a cut in wages and fringe benefits to lower labor costs, which was essential for winning the international competition.

Toward Union-Management Accord

As examined above, after experiencing a dramatic decline in employment, which, at least in part, resulted from weak international competitiveness, labor and management in the automobile and steel industries began to agree that job security is sometimes more important than higher wages. Recently, a new trend of labor-management cooperation has been emerging. In order to increase labor productivity, which is essential for stronger competitiveness in the international setting, unions and management in many industries began to cooperate with rather than to confront each other.

DECREASING LABOR DISPUTES

The emergence of union-management accord is not confined to the automobile and steel industries. The labor-management relationship has recently become more peaceful in the U.S. economy as a whole. Table 3.11 catalogs labor disputes since the middle 1970s in U.S. companies that employed more than a thousand workers. As the table shows, the seriousness of labor disputes remained almost constant throughout the 1970s. An average annual picture of labor disputes in the United States in those days was as follows: a little more than one million workers participated in about 200 major strikes, due to which 20 million mandays were lost. But, after the second oil crisis, labor disputes in the United States rapidly declined. For example, the number of major labor

TABLE 3.11.
Labor Disputes in the United States

Year	Number of Work Stoppages	Workers Involved (×1,000)	Days Idle (×1,000)
1975	235	965	17,563
1976	231	1,519	23,962
1977	298	1,212	21,258
1978	219	1,006	23,774
1979	235	1,021	20,409
1980	187	795	20,844
1981	145	729	16,908
1982	96	656	9,061
1983	81	909	17,461
1984	62	376	8,499
1985	54	324	7,079
1986	69	533	11,861
1987	46	174	4,468

Source: U.S. Department of Labor, Monthly Labor Review.
Note: Excludes work stoppages involving fewer than 1,000 workers and lasting less than 1 day.

disputes in 1985 was about one-fourth of that of any year in the 1970s. Although labor disputes increased a little in 1986, mostly due to the above-mentioned strike against USX and the strike against American Telephone and Telegraph (ATT), they resumed a declining trend in 1987. Thus, labor-management relations in the United States have become more peaceful in the 1980s, after the severe unemployment in the industries that faced tough competition from abroad.

In addition to the peaceful labor-management relationship, there is one more noticeable trend in the U.S. labor market: a continuous decline in union power. As shown in table 3.3, until the middle 1970s the percentage unionized (an indicator of union power) was stable at around 25–30 percent, but since then it declined consistently to reach 17.6 percent in 1986. In other words, only one in every six workers is unionized these days. Faced with this alarming decline in its membership, the AFL-CIO has been trying to prevent workers from leaving labor unions and trying to establish their union at newly constructed plants.

In spite of such union efforts, the decline seems to continue. For example, the UAW has been unsuccessful in forming unions in automobile factories run by the Japanese auto producers (as examined in detail in chapter 7). The American employees working at Japanese auto plants are often hostile toward labor unions, because they think the unions are often detrimental to higher productivity at the plants.

A NEW TYPE OF LABOR CONTRACT

In August 1985, a very cooperative union contract was agreed on between General Motors and the UAW. The contract covered future workers at the GM small-car plant that was under construction in Tennessee. The contract emphasized productivity increase through cooperation of labor and management. It contained various elements that were unusual in the United States, although such elements had a long history in the labor contracts of other countries, including Japan and West Germany. Some of them are briefly discussed below.

First of all, employee participation in management was institutionalized in the contract. The union contract emphasized the importance of employee participation in decision making in an attempt to strengthen the competitiveness of General Motors domestically and internationally. A new joint committee, called the Strategic Advisory Committee (SAC), was established by the contract. The members of the SAC would be selected from both management and workers, and it was given an advisory role in certain important decision making functions at the plant.

In addition to the SAC, various joint committees were introduced to ensure workers' participation in some details of management. While the employee participation had long been institutionalized in West Germany, it was fairly unusual in the United States, where running the company had been considered to be the sole responsibility of management (not of production workers or labor unions).

Second, the 1985 union contract provided that employees would not be laid off except for unpredictable events or extremely serious business conditions, which had some similarity to the Japanese "lifetime employment" system. This provision went a step further than the job opportunity bank in the previous union contracts. Instead of giving training to those laid off, the union contract tried to explicitly give the workers job security.

Third, the abolishment of detailed job classifications should be noted in the union contract. While numerous job categories had existed in the assembly plants in the United States, the union contract of the Tennessee plant of General Motors unified various job categories: only one category for unskilled workers and a few categories for skilled workers. Since Japanese production workers are not classified into numerous job categories, the Japanese firms could transfer workers from a position in division A to a position in division B when there was a labor surplus in division A and a labor shortage in division B of the same company. This ease of worker-transfer in Japanese firms contributed a great deal to their higher productivity and the stronger competitiveness of Japanese industry. GM's Tennessee contract intended to follow the Japanese practice in order to make the plant more productive.

Fourth, the idea of the equality of all workers in the plant was emphasized in various parts of the union contract. For example, all workers in the plant were equal and classified as "salaried work force." This was also a Japanese element, and it was unlike the U.S. tradition. In most factories in the United States, white-collar workers and blue-collar workers are considered to be salaried workers and hourly wage workers, respectively, and these two categories of workers are treated very differently. The GM contract in the Tennessee plant tried to abolish this tradition and ensure equal treatment of all employees there.

The idea of "union-management cooperation for job security" was maintained in the more recent contracts in the U.S. automobile industry (e.g., union contracts with General Motors and with Ford Motor Company in 1987). As far as the U.S. automobile industry is concerned, it has become a pattern in many union contracts in the 1980s. Thus, after severe unemployment under fierce foreign competition, the union-management relationship has been changing. Unions began to agree with management that in order to save jobs the competitiveness of the company should be strengthened, and they realized that in order to strengthen the competitiveness, in turn, a reduction in working conditions, including the wage rate, is sometimes necessary. International trade has thus affected union-management relations in the United States.

CHAPTER FOUR

A General Theory
of International Trade

NEED FOR A NEW FRAMEWORK

Trade-Off between Rigor and Practicality

The discussions of the previous chapters (chapters 1–3) are, in some sense, a prelude to the later chapters, where the interactions between international trade problems and domestic labor problems are analyzed more rigorously. In the previous discussions, a need for a new framework for integrated analysis of the two types of problems was pointed out. The new framework might be called labor-oriented international economics. In chapter 2, the important facts of trade conflicts were summarized, taking the U.S.-Japan trade relationship on four major industries as examples: textile and clothing, color television sets, automobiles, and agricultural products. In chapter 3, various aspects of the domestic labor market were discussed, with an emphasis on the U.S. automobile industry after the second oil crisis. Through these discussions in the previous chapters, it was suggested that developments in the trade conflicts were greatly influenced by the domestic labor market in the importing country and that the domestic labor market was often affected by external economic conditions. This book has two major purposes: (*a*) to develop a formal general equilibrium trade model based on new realistic assumptions and (*b*) to demonstrate that the rigorous model can be easily applied to actual situations, such as the U.S.-Japan automobile trade.

This chapter serves the first purpose (i.e., establishment of a rigorous theory). In this chapter, the interaction of international trade and domestic labor market is rigorously examined by using a general equilibrium framework based on realistic assumptions. In other words, the model developed in this chapter is intended to be both rigorous and practical: while it has firm microeconomic foundations, it incorporates various realities of actual trade relationships in recent years.

Generally speaking, orthodox trade theories have been based upon three basic assumptions: (a) perfect competition, (b) constant returns to scale, and (c) a homogeneous product. The assumptions are often unrealistic when applied to recent international trade in the real world. For the sake of rigor and simplicity in their models, orthodox trade theories did not incorporate either imperfect competition in the product market (such as monopoly and oligopoly) or labor-market imperfections (such as wage markup by labor unions and unemployment).

On the other hand, the usual discussions of actual trade conflicts often lacked a firm economic foundation. For example, when people discuss the impact of foreign competition on domestic unemployment or the impact of labor unions on the trade policies of a country, they often become emotional. In an attempt to fill the gap, the analysis of this chapter is intended to establish an economic model that is based upon realistic assumptions and at the same time has a firm microeconomic foundation.

Chapters 5 and 6 are intended to serve the second purpose of the book: to demonstrate that the rigorous general equilibrium model can be easily applied to an actual situation, such as the U.S.-Japan automobile trade. As most economic students would admit, the gap between pure economic theory and applied econometrics is often large. Students of pure economic theory (especially mathematical economics) deal with rather abstract subjects. In an attempt to achieve extreme rigor in their theories, they try to prove very abstract propositions by using more and more complicated mathematical tools, and little attempt seems to be made to apply the rigorous theory to phenomena in the real world. On the other hand, since the pure economic theorist does not provide them with readily applicable models, econometricians try to explain real world phenomena by running a regression, with explanatory variables on the right-hand side which were obtained rather intuitively. Such a regression often has no firm foundation in economic theory. In view of such a gap, this book tries to narrow it by applying a rigorous general equilibrium theory to an important case in the real world, the U.S.-Japan automobile trade conflict. After the theoretical analysis of the U.S.-Japan automobile trade in chapter 5, the rigorous model developed in this chapter is used in chapter 6 to estimate the cost of the Japanese automobile voluntary export restraint on the domestic economy of the United States.

Of course, it is beyond the capacity of this book to unify pure economic theory and practical econometrics, but we tried to make the analysis of this book a stepping-stone toward such an integration. Since mathematical expositions in this chapter (and chapter 5) may seem complicated, an intuitive interpretation is provided after the mathematical proofs in order to ensure easier understanding of the argument.

Three Characteristics of the Manufactured Goods Trade

When we look at the pattern of world trade since World War II, we notice a shift from a trade in primary products to the manufactured goods trade. "Intra-industry trade" of manufactured goods among developed countries has been rapidly expanding. Intra-industry trade means an exchange of goods from the same industries between different countries. For example, when Japan exports Toyotas to West Germany while importing Mercedes from West Germany, the two countries are engaging in intra-industry trade: both countries export some types (or models) of automobiles while importing other types of automobiles. The intra-industry trade of manufactured goods has been rapidly and consistently increasing among developed countries ever since World War II. For example, according to an estimate by Grubel and Lloyd (1975), the share of such intra-industry trade in all trade is more than 50 percent and rapidly increasing.

In view of the importance of the manufactured goods trade and the tendency toward increasing restrictions on it, various (sometimes emotional) arguments have been made on the effect of trade restrictions, and various attempts have been made to evaluate the effect of import restrictions such as the VER on the shipment of Japanese automobiles to the United States. (Several empirical studies of the VER will be reviewed in chapter 6.) However, in spite of many arguments and many empirical studies, there are few formal theoretical studies of trade restrictions which are based upon a rigorous general equilibrium framework. One of the major difficulties in rigorously modeling the manufactured goods trade results from the fact its characteristics are very different from the basic assumptions of orthodox theories of international trade, and therefore, the general equilibrium framework of orthodox trade theories cannot be easily applied.

Generally speaking, orthodox trade theories have been based upon three assumptions that are contrary to the characteristics of manufactured trade: (*a*) perfect competition, (*b*) constant returns to scale, and (*c*) homogeneous products.

First, orthodox trade theories assume that both product market and factor market are perfectly competitive. There are no imperfections (such as monopoly and oligopoly) in the product market, therefore, there is no price markup (i.e., the price of goods is always equal to marginal cost of production). The labor market is also assumed to be perfectly competitive, so there is no wage markup by the labor unions. Since, in their framework, the demand for and supply of labor are always equated through a quick change in wage rate, there is no unemployment in the economy.

Second, the orthodox trade theories often assume constant returns to scale (CRS) technology in production. Under the framework, if one dollar is needed to produce one unit of goods, the production of one million units of goods costs exactly $1 million. In other words, when an automobile plant is producing, say, 100,000 vehicles annually with the input of $1 billion, then (orthodox theories assume) anyone who invests $10,000 can produce one vehicle. According to orthodox theories, there is no setup cost when large-scale production is initiated.

Third, orthodox trade theories usually assume homogeneous products. Since all models of automobiles are assumed to be equivalent, consumers do not care which model they purchase. The choice of model is solely determined by price. For example, under the orthodox framework, if a Hyundai is one dollar cheaper than a Porsche, every consumer rushes to buy a Hyundai and nobody ever buys a Porsche. The absurdity of the assumption of homogeneous products should be clear from this example.

Manufactured goods trade seem to be better characterized by the opposite assumptions. In fact, a suitable framework for the international trade of many manufactured goods, including automobiles, seems to be as follows: (a) imperfect competition, (b) increasing returns to scale, and (c) differentiated products.

First, the product markets of many industries (such as the American automobile industry) are far from being perfectly competitive. They could be better characterized as monopolistic or oligopolistic. Instead of taking price as "given," the firm is often aware of the effect of its output decision upon price (in economic terminology, the firm is facing a downward-sloped demand curve). The labor market of some industries is also often imperfectly competitive due to the bargaining and lobbying powers of strong labor unions. Since the wage rate is "sticky," the demand for and supply of labor are not equated, and therefore we sometimes observe huge unemployment in some industries. The American automobile industry, for example, shows imperfections in both the product market and the labor market.

Second, the production of manufactured goods usually requires a large setup cost, so that the average cost decreases up to a certain level of production. According to the study by Toder (1978), for example, the minimum optimal plant scale (MOS) in the American automobile industry is 400,000 units per year, and the MOS would be much greater if multiplant, firm-level economies of scale are taken into account. But the average production level of each model of automobile in recent years was about 132,000 units, which was far below the MOS. As Toder's study suggests, when we analyze many manufacturing sectors that require huge fixed costs (such as the automobile and steel industries) a more suitable assumption would be increasing returns to scale (IRS) rather than constant returns to scale (CRS).

Third, most manufactured goods are differentiated, rather than homogeneous, products. Consumers do care about which model they are going to purchase. Through product characteristics and advertising, people readily distinguish, for example, Toyotas, Lincolns, and Yugos even though each of them is classified as an automobile. Therefore, it is absurd to assume that automobiles are homogeneous products and that consumers always purchase the cheapest model. Such product differentiation can be observed for various manufactured goods, including audio equipment, personal computers, and jewelry, to name a few.

New Theories of Trade under Imperfect Competition

Faced with the growing importance of the manufactured goods trade, for which the assumptions of orthodox trade theories are not necessarily suitable, new theories of international trade have emerged recently, and substantial efforts have been made to develop formal models of trade, especially of intra-industry trade, by distinguished economists, including Krugman, Dixit and Norman, Lancaster, and Helpman. Based upon the new framework suitable for the trade of many manufactured goods (i.e., imperfect competition, increasing returns to scale, and product differentiation), they are trying to explain why intra-industry trade among similar countries has been increasing, because the increase in (even its existence of) intra-industry trade causes theoretical difficulties to the orthodox trade theories. According to orthodox theories, international trade occurs between countries because of differences in technologies, factor endowments, or tastes, and therefore there are no trade-creating forces if countries are the same in these respects, and no country exports goods while importing the same category of goods. Actually, however, since World War II, we have observed an increasing amount of trade in similar goods among similar countries. Indeed, as mentioned above, according to Grubel and Lloyd (1975), the share of such intra-industry trade in world trade as a whole is more than half and increasing.

It has long been suggested by some prominent economists, including Balassa (1967), that increasing returns to scale would be a key factor in explaining intra-industry trade between similar countries. When production technology is characterized with increasing returns to scale (IRS), which is often the case for the production of manufactured goods, countries would be better off if each country produced, say, five models of goods and traded these models with the other rather than producing ten models and engaging in no trade. In each case, consumers can choose from ten models, but the scale of production is larger (and the average cost is smaller under IRS technology) in the former case than in the latter. In spite of this intuition, only recently has the formal theory of intra-industry trade attracted intense professional interest. Until recently, fairly unsatisfactory explanations based upon such factors as "border trade" had been given to the intra-industry trade.

One of the major reasons for the lack of a formal model of intra-industry trade based on increasing returns to scale was the well-known difficulty in modeling an economy where technology is characterized by increasing returns to scale. Namely, under increasing returns to scale the competitive equilibrium may not exist (see a textbook of microeconomics for details of this point). However, in their pioneering work, Dixit and Stiglitz (1977) overcame the theoretical difficulty involved in increasing returns to scale. They showed that a competitive equilibrium exists under increasing returns to scale and product differentiation. The essence of their argument is: consumers prefer diversity because greater diversity provides them with greater choice, while producers tend to decrease differentiation in order to exploit the economic benefit of increasing returns to scale. By these two conflicting forces the competitive equilibrium is obtained.

Krugman (1979) first applied the new framework of Dixit and Stiglitz to international trade and showed that even if countries are the same in every respect (i.e., tastes, technologies, and factor endowments) intra-industry trade will occur in order to exploit the benefit of increasing return to scale, and in fact the more similar the trading partners are, the more trade will occur. Dixit and Norman (1980) derived similar conclusions by using a two-sector general equilibrium model. Lancaster (1980) derived similar conclusions based upon his characteristics approach. Since then many studies have been published on international trade under imperfect competition. Their major contribution is the explanation of intra-industry trade in manufactured goods based upon the three realistic assumptions: (*a*) imperfect competition in the product market; (*b*) increasing return to scale; and (*c*) product differentiation.

Additional Insights into the Effect of Trade

These new theories of international trade under imperfect competition seem to give a suitable framework for the theoretical and empirical analyses of the effect of trade restrictions on automobiles and many other manufactured goods, because they are based upon three assumptions that seem to grasp the realities of those industries. The models of Krugman and of Dixit and Norman seem to be especially promising for application because their frameworks have many similarities to the neoclassical general equilibrium models on which numerous applied studies have been made.

While their frameworks are trail-blazing, a number of extensions and modifications are possible and necessary before they can be applied to the trade of automobiles and other manufactured goods. First, their models incorporated imperfect competition in the product market alone and assumed that factor markets (including the labor market) are perfectly competitive and that factors are always in full employment. As discussed above, however, the labor market is far from being perfectly competitive in many industries because of the existence of strong labor unions. It is sometimes emotionally argued, for example, that the protectionism resulting from lobbying efforts by strong labor unions like the United Auto Workers is harmful to the interests of consumers. International trade has often been blamed for being a major cause of massive unemployment in the U.S. automobile industry after the second oil crisis. While many arguments have been presented about the impact of labor unions on international trade or the impact of international trade on employment, very few formal studies have been made on the interactions between international trade problems and domestic labor problems. Therefore, it is desirable to establish a formal model that consistently incorporates imperfect competition in both markets, and thereby to analyze trade, labor unions, and unemployment.

Second, there is an important point to be improved, although it is rather technical. In their models, the elasticity of substitution among differentiated goods has been assumed to be constant. In other words, the degree of substitutability between differentiated goods is exactly the same whether the choice available to consumers is between only two types of goods or among hundreds of types of goods. It seems more plausible that goods become closer substitutes as the number of types available to consumers increases. The assumption of invariant substitutability also encounters empirical difficulties, although the assumption is useful in simplifying discussion. As was reviewed by Jacquemin (1982), for example, many empirical studies have found the following three empirical regularities (or "stylized facts" as they are fashionably called) about the effects of the opening up of trade where markets are imperfectly competitive:

1. an increase in the variety of goods available;
2. a decrease in monopolistic power;
3. a decrease in average production cost.

However (as is discussed in detail below) observations 2 and 3 cannot be well explained if we assume invariant substitutability. Therefore, we must incorporate variable substitutability as well as labor market imperfections if we are to apply the model to international trade in the real world.

In the next section, a formal general equilibrium model of international trade is established which is based upon imperfect competition, increasing returns to scale, and product differentiation. The model also incorporates labor market imperfections and the variable elasticity of substitution. In the following section, the effects of trade (and of its restrictions) are rigorously analyzed using the model. It will be rigorously shown that opening up the automobile trade (and other manufactured goods trade) can bring about various gains such as:

1. greater consumer satisfaction due to an increase in the variety of goods;
2. a decrease in the monopolistic power of domestic firms;
3. increased technical efficiency due to a decrease in the average production costs;
4. a decrease in unemployment due to reduced imperfections in the labor market;
5. a contribution to economic growth through a release of capital resources from the distorted sector.

Gains 1–3 correspond to the stylized facts on gains from trade reviewed by Jacquemin, but in addition to giving a theoretical foundation to the three stylized facts, the model gives additional insights into the effects of trade (and its restrictions). Surprisingly enough, it will be shown that opening up trade increases employment (or decreases unemployment), at least in the long run, through a decrease in the magnitude of labor market imperfections. Gain 5 would be especially relevant to developing countries where capital is a relatively scarce resource, because when less capital is necessary for the automobile industry more capital is available to the rest of the economy.

The rest of the chapter examines the mechanism of the above five gains. The intuition behind the gains from international trade is as follows: opening up trade increases consumer choice because consumers can enjoy foreign goods as well as domestic goods, and thereby substitutability between goods will be increased. Increased substitutability makes each producer face more elastic demand and decreases both the price markup and the wage markup. Decreases in the price markup and the wage markup invites more demand and consequently production increases. The increase in production and decrease in wage markup will increase employment (and decrease unemployment) at least in the long run. Further, faced with foreign competition, the market structure becomes more efficient than before. This chapter deals with qualitative analyses of such gains, and chapter 6 attempts to evaluate the magnitude of such gains with the U.S. automobile industry as an example.

MODEL IN THE CLOSED ECONOMY

The economy is assumed to consist of two sectors: the perfectly competitive sector and distorted (imperfectly competitive) sector. The former produces homogeneous products under constant returns to scale, and both product and labor markets are perfectly competitive. Thus, its characteristics are those assumed in orthodox trade theories.

The latter sector is characterized by the new assumptions discussed in detail above. More specifically, the latter sector consists of many individual firms that are producing differentiated products in a Chamberlinian monopolistic competition (a type of imperfect competition) under increasing returns to scale. In the latter sector, the labor market is also imperfect in that the labor union sets the wage rate higher than the competitive wage in the rest of the economy. Due to this wage markup, unemployment can exist in the distorted sector. The latter sector is exemplified by the automobile industry, because the framework contains various realities of the American automobile industry as discussed above.

In the following discussion, the perfectly competitive sector and the distorted sector will often be referred to as the rest of the economy and the automobile industry, respectively, in order to help intuitive understanding of the analysis. Although the distorted sector is sometimes referred to as the automobile industry for convenience, the model is intended to be general and applicable to the analysis of other manufactured goods trade.

Specifications of the Model

In order to present a rigorous analysis, rather than an emotional argument, of trade restrictions, including the voluntary export restraint on the Japanese automobiles, a general equilibrium trade model is established first. In this model, the behaviors of various economic agents (e.g., consumers, producers, and workers) are characterized by using rigorous economic theory. Therefore, the mathematics is often a little difficult and complicated. Intuitive explanations are given at each step so that readers can follow the main argument even if the mathematical expositions are skipped.

CONSUMERS

Consumers are characterized by the following individualistic social utility function:

$$U = \left(\sum_{i=1}^{N} C_i^{\beta} \right)^{\alpha/\beta} C_o^{1-\alpha}, \qquad 0 < \alpha < 1 \qquad (4\text{--}1)$$

$$\beta = \beta(N), \qquad 0 < \beta', \qquad 0 < \beta < 1 \qquad (4\text{--}2)$$

where C_i is the consumption of the ith differentiated good (or the consumption of a particular model of automobile), C_o is the consumption of goods produced by the rest of the economy, also called numeraire goods, and N is the number of types of differentiated products that consumers consider to be available to them. N is the same as n (the number of types of goods actually available to consumers) in equilibrium. The behavioral assumptions here are that consumers maximize utility, taking the prices and the number of types of products as given; and that utility is a function of the consumption of differentiated goods and numeraire goods, and the number of types of goods available.

The utility function (4–1) is similar to that of Dixit and Norman (1980), where the utility was Cobb-Douglas form in the quantity of numeraire goods and a scaler measure of consumption of differentiated products, this scaler measure being a constant elasticity of substitution (CES) function in the quantity of each product type. However, there is a crucial difference in this model: in Dixit and Norman, β is given as a constant, and therefore, the elasticity of substitution between differentiated goods $(1/(1 - \beta))$ is invariant with regard to the number of product types; in this model β is assumed to be an increasing function of the number of types of goods available to consumers (i.e., differentiated goods become closer substitutes as the variety of goods increases). In other words, unlike the Dixit and Norman formulation, here the degree of substitutability between differentiated products where the choice available to consumers is among one hundred types of goods is higher than where choice is between only two types of products. As shown in (4–2), β is an increasing function of N in the model here. Further, it seems reasonable to assume that the utility will increase as N increases even if $\sum_{i=1}^{N} C_i$ the consumption of differentiated goods) remains constant.

The society is better off in the situation where, for example, 100 units of model A and 100 units of model B are available than it is in the situation where 200 units of model A alone are available, if both models enter the social utility function symmetrically. In short, consumers are assumed to like a greater variety in consumption. As long as β satisfies those conditions for reasonable properties of the utility function, it can take any functional form. (In the empirical study in chapter 6, however, a specific functional form will be given for the purpose of estimation.)

Consumers are assumed to maximize the utility function (4–1) subject to the budget constraint

$$C_o + \sum_{i=1}^{N} P_i C_i = Y \tag{4-3}$$

where the price of the numeraire goods is set to 1 and P_i and Y are the price of the ith differentiated product and income, respectively. From this utility maximization problem, we get the following two demand functions: the demand function for numeraire goods (4–4) and the inverse demand function for differentiated products (4–5).

$$C_o = (1 - \alpha)Y \tag{4-4}$$

$$P_i = \alpha C_i^{\beta-1} \frac{Y}{Z} \tag{4-5}$$

$$Z \equiv \sum_{i=1}^{N} C_i^{\beta} \tag{4-6}$$

The elasticity of demand for the ith differentiated product (ϵ_i) is obtained by taking the derivative of (4–5).

$$\frac{1}{\epsilon_i} = -\left(\frac{\partial P_i}{\partial C_i}\right)\left(\frac{C_i}{P_i}\right)$$

$$= (1 - \beta) + \frac{\beta C_i^{\beta}}{Z} \tag{4-7}$$

Therefore, the elasticity is given by

$$\epsilon_i = \frac{1}{(1 - \beta) + \beta C_i^{\beta}/Z} \tag{4-8}$$

Note that, unlike Dixit and Norman, we are not neglecting the second term of the denominator on the right-hand side of equation (4–8), and therefore, we do not have to assume a large N. Further, because of the symmetry of the problem, (4–8) will reduce to

$$\epsilon_i = \frac{1}{1 - \beta(1 - 1/N)} \qquad (4\text{-}8)'$$

PRODUCERS

Production of numeraire goods is characterized by the following Cobb-Douglas cost function, which is an orthodox characterization.

$$TC_o = r^a W_o^{1-a} x_o, \qquad 0 < a < 1 \qquad (4\text{-}9)$$

where r is the rental rate of capital and W_o is the competitive wage rate (both of which are expressed in terms of the price of numeraire goods), x_o is the output of numeraire goods, and TC_o is the total cost.

Note that the production technology exhibits constant returns to scale, and therefore no profit exists in equilibrium. In other words, unit production cost is the same as price (set to unity here) and therefore in equilibrium

$$r^a W_o^{1-a} = 1 \qquad (4\text{-}10)$$

The demand for capital input in the numeraire goods sector can be obtained by taking the derivative of the cost function (4–9) with respect to the rental rate of capital. This technique is known as Shephard's lemma in microeconomic theory.

$$K_o = \frac{\partial(TC_o)}{\partial r}$$

$$= a r^{a-1} W_o^{1-a} x_o \qquad (4\text{-}11)$$

where K_o is the capital input in the numeraire goods sector. Similarly, labor input (L_o) is obtained by applying Shephard's lemma.

$$L_o = \frac{\partial(TC_o)}{\partial W_o}$$

$$= (1 - a) r^a W_o^{-a} x_o \qquad (4\text{-}12)$$

On the other hand, production of the ith differentiated good is assumed to be characterized by the cost function

$$TC_i = rF + r^a W_i^{1-a} m x_i \qquad (4\text{-}13)$$

where TC_i, W_i, and x_i are total cost, wage rate, and output level of the ith firm in the differentiated goods production sector, respectively.

Each firm must commit F units of capital input as a fixed cost first if it is to produce any positive amount. In the real world, a requirement for fixed cost is almost universal: we must build a plant, which requires a large amount of capital, before producing even a single automobile. In addition to the fixed cost (rF), a constant marginal cost $(r^a W_i^{1-a} m)$ is necessary thereafter. Note that the production of each differentiated good exhibits increasing returns to scale because of the fixed cost. Cost-less differentiation is assumed in the model: the firm is assumed to be able to shift its production line from type A to type B of the differentiated goods without incurring any cost. Therefore, no two firms ever produce the same types of differentiated products in equilibrium because the firm is always better off differentiating its product from the existing types to a new type. Equilibrium is given by Chamberlinian monopolistic competition: each firm tries to maximize its profit, and equilibrium profit must be zero due to free entry and exit. Whenever positive profit exists, a new entry occurs, and an exit (of firm) occurs when profit is negative. Through entry and exit, any profit or loss is eliminated at equilibrium.

The optimization (i.e., profit maximization) problem of the representative firm i in the differentiated good sector is given by

$$\text{Max } \pi_i = P_i(x_i)\, x_i - (rF + r^a W_i^{1-a} m x_i) \qquad (4\text{--}14)$$

where π_i is the profit of the ith firm. Since each firm has monopoly power for a particular type of differentiated goods, the optimization problem is essentially the same as the regular profit maximization of the monopolist. So, from (4–8) and (4–14), and noting that N (the number of product types that consumers consider to be available to them) is the same as n (the actual number of available product types) at equilibrium, we get the following profit maximizing price:

$$P_i = \frac{r^a W_i^{1-a} m}{\beta(1 - C_i^\beta / Z)} \qquad (4\text{--}15)$$

Further, due to the symmetry of the problem, (4–15) reduces to the simplified form

$$P_i = \frac{r^a W_i^{1-a} m}{\beta(1 - 1/n)} \qquad (4\text{--}15)'$$

In addition (as mentioned above) free entry and exit are assumed in the model. So, whenever there is a positive profit, entry of a new firm occurs, and therefore profit is forced to be zero (i.e., price must be the same as average cost at equiibrium)

$$P_i = \frac{rF + r^aW_i^{1-a}mx_i}{x_i} \tag{4-16}$$

By invoking Shephard's lemma again, we get factor demand functions of the ith firm as follows:

$$k_i = \frac{\partial(TC_i)}{\partial r}$$

$$= F + ar^{a-1}W_i^{1-a}mx_i \tag{4-17}$$

$$l_i = \frac{\partial(TC_i)}{\partial W_i}$$

$$= (1 - a)r^aW_i^{-a}mx_i \tag{4-18}$$

where k_i and l_i are the demand for capital and the demand for labor of the firm i, respectively.

The elasticity of derived demand for labor is obtained from the inverse demand function (4–5) and the conditional labor demand function (4–18). It can be shown by simple algebra that the elasticity of derived demand for labor η_i is reduced to

$$\eta_i = a + (1 - a)\epsilon_i \tag{4-19}$$

Note that equation (4–19) expresses the essence of the Hicks-Marshall laws of derived demand. As is widely known, the main message of the Hicks-Marshall laws is that, other things being equal, the own wage elasticity for a category of labor is high when

1. the price elasticity of demand for the product being produced is high;
2. the cost of employing the category of labor is a large share of the total cost of production;
3. other factors of production can be easily substituted for the category of labor.

First of all, it is obvious that equation (4–19) shows that the elasticity of derived demand for labor is an increasing function of the elasticity of product demand (law 1). Further, from the cost function (4–13) it is obvious that the share of the labor cost in the total variable cost is

$(1 - a)$. Therefore, equation (4–19) also shows that the more elastic the derived demand for labor, the larger the share of the labor cost (law 2). Of course, for law 2 to hold, ϵ_i must be greater than one. But, since we are assuming $0 < \beta < 1$, it is obvious that ϵ_i is always greater than 1 (see equation (4–8)′). Law 3 is not applicable as long as we use a Cobb-Douglas function, where the elasticity of substitution between the two factors is always unity. We can easily get the elasticity of derived demand for capital by doing a similar derivation, but we omit this because it is not necessary to the following discussions.

LABOR MARKET

The labor market in the differentiated goods sector (e.g., automobile industry) is assumed to be imperfectly competitive, while that in the rest of the economy is perfectly competitive. The labor market in the distorted sector is assumed to be controlled by a single labor union. This kind of labor market imperfection is easily imagined if we think of the U.S. automobile industry, for example, where the powerful United Auto Workers (UAW) exerts a strong influence in wage determination.

Although everyone would agree that the labor market is imperfectly competitive in many industries and that unions are important players, there is no consensus on the objective functions of labor unions in economic theory. While there is a high degree of consensus on the utility maximization of consumers and the profit maximization of producers, a wide variety of arguments have been made on the objective function of unions. For example, Johnson (1975) went as far as to assert that "the problem of modeling trade union behavior has proved to be virtually intractable." Some authors, including Dunlop (1944), Hieser (1970), and Johnston (1972), have argued that unions seek to maximize the total wage bill. Rosen (1970) and Calvo (1978) argued that the union seeks to maximize the difference between its members' income and what they would get under no unionization. Farber (1978) argued that unions try to maximize the expected utility of the median-aged union member, which is analogous to the median voters argument in political science.

But, in spite of the wide range of arguments, it seems that the majority would agree that the union's utility (or objective function) is a quasi-concave increasing function of wage and employment, as Oswald (1982) suggested. In the model here we will use a slightly simplified objective function (4–20) of the same functional form as that of Calvo. The behavioral assumptions in the model here are: the labor union decides the wage rate in order to maximize the objective function (4–20); firms decide the employment level, taking the wage rate set by the union as given.

$$\text{Max } V = \sum_{i=1}^{n} l_i (W_i - W_o) \qquad (4\text{--}20)$$

In other words, the union is seeking to maximize the difference between its (employed) members' income and what they would get without a union (i.e., the competitive wage rate in the rest of the economy). In some sense, the union tries to increase its importance to its members by increasing the wage markup. Note that for simplicity workers are assumed to be homogeneous in their productivity, etc., here. In empirical applications, we might have to adjust the number of workers and their wage rate in each sector according to any productivity difference.

By rearranging the first-order conditions of the maximization problem (4–20), we get the equilibrium condition

$$\frac{W_i - W_o}{W_i} = \frac{1}{\eta_i}, \qquad \text{for all } i. \qquad (4\text{--}21)$$

Equation (4–21) shows that the rate of wage markup in each firm is equal to the inverse of the elasticity of derived demand for labor of the firm, which seems to have a strong resemblance to the so-called Ramsey pricing rule in the study of industrial organization.

Note that because of the symmetry of the problem, C_i, P_i, x_i, ϵ_i, W_i, and η_i, are the same for all i. So, we shall adopt short-hand notations without subscripts in the following discussion. Further, note that the elasticity of demand for labor by the differentiated goods sector as a whole is the same as the elasticity of demand for labor by the individual firm, because each firm in the industry is assumed here to make its input decision under monopolistic competition without taking the interactions between firms into account.

Workers are assumed to allocate themselves to one of the two sectors by comparing the competitive wage in the rest of the economy with the expected wage in the automobile industry. When the risk of being unemployed exists in one of the two sectors (automobile industry), the wage rate in that sector must be higher than the other in order to compensate for the risk. This is an application of the Harris-Todaro model that was used to analyze migration of workers between the urban sector and the rural sector. The probability of workers getting a job after allocating themselves to the automobile industry is

$$P_r = \frac{L_a}{N_a} \qquad (4\text{--}22)$$

where P_r, L_a, and N_a are the probability of getting an automotive job, the amount of employment in the automobile industry, and the supply of auto workers, respectively.

Workers are assumed to be risk neutral for simplicity here, but it is easy to incorporate the risk aversions of workers. All we must do is put some measure of degree of risk aversion into the equilibrium condition (4–23). Through the movement of workers between the two industries the expected wage rate in the automobile industry will be equated with the competitive wage rate in the rest of the economy at equilibrium. Therefore, at equilibrium

$$W_o = W\left(\frac{L_a}{N_a}\right) \qquad (4\text{--}23)$$

where W is the wage rate in the distorted sector (e.g., the automobile industry). Note that we are denoting it without subscript because the wage rate in each firm turns out to be the same at equilibrium, as discussed above. Equation (4–23) can be rearranged to give

$$\frac{W - W_o}{W} = \frac{N_a - L_a}{N_a} \qquad (4\text{--}24)$$

The right-hand side of equation (4–24) is the unemployment in the automobile industry, and the left-hand side can be interpreted as the rate of wage markup in the industry, which bears a strong analogy to the Lerner index, an index of price markup often used in the study of industrial organization.

Equation (4–24) shows that the unemployment rate in the imperfectly competitive sector becomes higher as the wage markup increases. The rationale behind this is as follows: when there is a big wage difference between the two sectors, some workers tend to remain unemployed because they do not accept the lower wage job in the competitive sector, hoping for a job in the higher wage sector sooner or later. Such behavior is especially relevant for the workers who were laid off from the high wage industry. Even if there are sufficient job openings in the low wage sector, they may wait for employment in the high wage sector. Such prolonged unemployment tends to be higher, the larger the wage difference between the two sectors. From (4–21) and (4–24), we know that the (long-run) unemployment rate in the imperfectly competitive sector (e.g., the automobile industry) is a decreasing function of the elasticity of derived demand for labor.

Labor supply is assumed to be given in the model (i.e., there is no wage-leisure tradeoff). Therefore, the sum of the labor supply in both sectors is the same as the labor endowment of the economy (L)

$$N_a + L_o = L \tag{4-25}$$

Further, due to the symmetry of the problem, the amount of labor demanded by the firm is the same for all firms in the differentiated goods sector. So, the amount of labor demanded by the automobile industry as a whole (L_a) is

$$L_a = nl \tag{4-26}$$

CAPITAL MARKET AND NATIONAL INCOME

In contrast to the labor market, the capital market is assumed to be perfectly competitive in the model. Therefore, the sum of the capital demanded in both sectors is equal to the capital endowment of the economy (K) (i.e., there is no unemployment of capital resources in the whole economy).

$$K_o + \sum_{i=1}^{n} k_i = K \tag{4-27}$$

Since we are assuming that the cost function of each firm in the differentiated goods sector is identical and that each type of differentiated good enters the utility function symmetrically, (4–27) reduces to a simplified equation

$$K_o + K_a = K \tag{4-28}$$

$$K_a = nk \tag{4-29}$$

Since there are no pure profits in either sector of the economy at equilibrium, the national income is the same as the total factor payments. Note that due to free entry and free exit the profit in the monopolistically competitive sector is always reduced to zero in the long-run equilibrium. It is obvious that there are no profits in the perfectly competitive sector, where technology exhibits constant returns to scale. Therefore, the national income is

$$rK + W_o L_o + W L_a = Y \tag{4-30}$$

Equilibrium Conditions of the Model

From the above specifications of the model, we can derive eighteen independent equations for the same number of endogenous variables. The equilibrium values of the eighteen endogenous variables $(x_o, x, P, n, r, W_o, W, K_o, K_a, k, L_o, L_a, l, N_a, Y, \beta, \epsilon, \text{and } \eta)$ are obtained by solving the system of the following eighteen independent equations:

$$\beta = \beta(n), \qquad \beta' > 0, \qquad 0 < \beta < 1 \qquad (4\text{-}2)'$$

$$x_o = (1 - \alpha)Y \qquad (4\text{-}4)'$$

$$\epsilon = \frac{1}{1 - \beta(1 - 1/n)} \qquad (4\text{-}8)'$$

$$r^a W_o^{1-a} = 1 \qquad (4\text{-}10)'$$

$$K_o = ar^{a-1} W_o^{1-a} x_o \qquad (4\text{-}11)'$$

$$L_o = (1 - a)r^a W_o^{-a} x_o \qquad (4\text{-}12)'$$

$$P = \frac{r^a W^{1-a} m}{\beta(1 - 1/n)} \qquad (4\text{-}15)'$$

$$P = \frac{rF + r^a W^{1-a} mx}{x} \qquad (4\text{-}16)'$$

$$k = F + ar^{a-1} W^{1-a} mx \qquad (4\text{-}17)'$$

$$l = (1 - a)r^a W^{-a} mx \qquad (4\text{-}18)'$$

$$\eta = a + (1 - a)\epsilon \qquad (4\text{-}19)'$$

$$\frac{W - W_o}{W} = \frac{1}{\eta} \qquad (4\text{-}21)$$

$$W_o = W\left(\frac{L_a}{N_a}\right) \qquad (4\text{-}23)$$

$$N_a + L_o = L \qquad (4\text{-}25)$$

$$L_a = nl \qquad (4\text{-}26)$$

$$K_o + K_a = K \qquad (4\text{-}28)$$

$$K_a = nk \qquad (4\text{-}29)$$

$$W_o L_o + W L_a + rK = Y \qquad (4\text{-}30)$$

We now have a complete general equilibrium model for the closed economy. In the following section, the gains from international trade (or losses from trade restrictions) are analyzed by using the above system of equations. It will be shown that, when imperfect competition exists in the product and labor markets, trade restrictions are more harmful than when imperfect competition does not exist.

FIGURE 4.1 Gains from Trade in the Small Country

QUINTUPLE GAINS FROM INTERNATIONAL TRADE

In the last section, we established a rigorous general equilibrium model. This model can now be applied to theoretical and empirical analyses of international trade and its restrictions, which will bring about new insights into the effect of international trade in the real world.

Gains from Trade under the Orthodox Framework

Before applying the new model, let us briefly consider the orthodox trade theories under the Heckscher-Ohlin-Samuelson (H-O-S) framework. These orthodox trade theories derived various gains from trade, based on the three assumptions: perfect competition, constant returns to scale, and homogeneous products. A basic proposition of orthodox trade theories is that free trade is better than no trade because through the exchange of products the consumers in both trading partners have a consumption mix beyond the production capabilities in their countries under autarky. Rigorously speaking, the consumers in both countries are better off under free trade because the availability locus under free trade lies outside of the autarky production possibility frontier (PPF).

For a small country that cannot affect the terms of trade, a stronger statement can be made: free trade is the best policy. The optimality of free trade has been demonstrated in the familiar diagram (see fig. 4.1). In the free trade equilibrium of a small country the optimality condition is satisfied, because, by definition, the foreign price is given to the country, (i.e., it cannot influence its terms of trade). Since the availability locus of the small country is given by a straight line, as is depicted

FIGURE 4.2 Gains from Trade in the Large Country

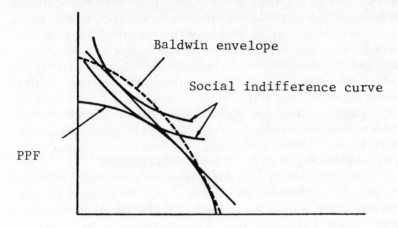

in figure 4.1, it is assured that the three marginal rates are equal: the domestic rate of substitution in consumption (*DRS*), the domestic rate of transformation in production (*DRT*), and the foreign rate of transformation in international trade (*FRT*). In other words, under the small country assumption, the optimality condition holds in equilibrium, and

$$DRS = DRT = FRT, \qquad (4-31)$$

one cannot improve welfare by deviating from the free trade equilibrium point.

For a large country, free trade may not be the best policy because the large country can influence its terms of trade by definition, but free trade is still better than no trade. This can be demonstrated by using Baldwin's famous diagram. In figure 4.2 the dashed curve is the famous Baldwin envelope, which can be derived by connecting the intersections of the foreign offer curves and social budget lines corresponding to various terms of trade. A large country may improve its welfare by imposing an optimal tariff, because the optimality condition (4–31) is not satisfied at the free trade equilibrium, where *FRT* is not equal to *DRS* or to *DRT*. However, even in the case of a large country, free trade is better than no trade, because every point on the Baldwin envelope lies outside of the autarky production possibility frontier.

Effects of Trade under Imperfect Competition

In addition to the orthodox gains from international trade, there are other sources of gains from trade liberalization in the real world, and trade restrictions would prevent the economy from realizing such gains. As discussed in the beginning of this chapter, many econometric studies have found at least threefold empirical regularities (i.e., stylized facts) on gains from trade: (a) an increase in the variety of goods in consumption; (b) a decrease in the monopolistic power of domestic producers; and (c) a decrease in the average cost of production. As discussed in detail below, the model developed in the previous section, which is based on imperfect competition in the product and labor markets, increasing returns to scale, and product differentiation, gives theoretical grounds to these three stylized facts of the effect of international trade. Further, the model also explains the gains from trade which result from a decrease in the degree of factor market imperfections.

In our theoretical analysis in this chapter, we examine the effects of international trade between two countries that are identical in taste, technology, and relative factor endowments. The sizes of the two countries are assumed to be the same for simplicity. This assumption of identical size can be easily relaxed, and in the empirical studies of chapter 6 the magnitude of gains from the U.S.-Japan automobile trade will be estimated with the size difference between the two countries taken into consideration. Based upon these assumptions, we will compare the two extreme situations: autarky and free trade. By doing so, we will try to obtain an insight into the effects of the opening up of trade (or, conversely the effects of the restrictions of trade) on the national economies. Since the two countries are assumed to be identical here, the opening up of trade is essentially equivalent to the doubling of factor endowments in the economy. By integrating the two economies, both countries can benefit from further exploitation of increasing returns to scale.

It would be convenient to solve the model before actually examining the effects of trade and its restrictions. Since we have eighteen independent equilibrium conditions in the model, the system can be solved for eighteen endogenous variables. Some simple (but tedious) algebra yields the following reduced forms:

$$x_o = (1 - \alpha)(G^{a-1} + G^a)K^a L^{1-a} \qquad (4\text{--}32)$$

$$x = \frac{FG^{a-1}(\epsilon - 1)(K/L)^{a-1}}{D^{1-a}m} \qquad (4\text{--}33)$$

$$P = \frac{D^{1-a}m}{\beta(1 - 1/n)} \qquad (4\text{--}34)$$

$$n = \frac{1 - a(1 - \alpha)(1 + G)}{F(1 + a(\epsilon - 1))} K \qquad (4\text{--}35)$$

$$r = (GK/L)^{a-1} \tag{4-36}$$

$$W_o = (GK/L)^a \tag{4-37}$$

$$W = D(GK/L)^a \tag{4-38}$$

$$K_o = K - nF(1 + a(\epsilon - 1)) \tag{4-39}$$

$$K_a = nF(1 + a(\epsilon - 1)) \tag{4-40}$$

$$k = F(1 + a(\epsilon - 1)) \tag{4-41}$$

$$l = \frac{\alpha(\epsilon - 1)L}{n(\epsilon - \alpha)D} \tag{4-42}$$

$$L_o = \frac{\epsilon(1 - \alpha)L}{(\epsilon - \alpha)} \tag{4-43}$$

$$L_a = \frac{\alpha(\epsilon - 1)L}{(\epsilon - \alpha)D} \tag{4-44}$$

$$N_a = \frac{\alpha(\epsilon - 1)L}{(\epsilon - \alpha)} \tag{4-45}$$

$$Y = (G^a + G^{a-1})K^a L^{1-a} \tag{4-46}$$

$$\beta = \beta(n) \tag{4-47}$$

$$\epsilon = \frac{1}{1 - \beta(1 - 1/n)} \tag{4-48}$$

$$\eta = a + (1 - a)\epsilon \tag{4-49}$$

where

$$D \equiv \eta / (\eta - 1), \quad \text{note that} \quad D > 1 \quad \text{and} \quad \partial D/\partial n < 0 \tag{4-50}$$

and

$$G \equiv \frac{(1 - a)(\epsilon - \alpha)}{a(\epsilon - \alpha) + \alpha}, \quad \text{note that} \quad G > 0$$

$$\text{and} \quad \partial G/\partial n > 0 \tag{4-51}$$

Although some of the above reduced forms may look extremely complicated, they are very useful for the analysis of international trade and its restrictions in the real world. By using the above reduced forms, it can be rigorously shown that international trade brings about (or conversely, that trade restrictions prevent the realization of) five additional sources of gains that orthodox trade theories have not explained:

1. a greater variety of consumption;
2. an efficiency in product market due to a decline in the monopolistic power of the domestic producers;
3. a technical efficiency of production due to a decline in the average production cost;
4. an efficiency in the labor market due to a decline in structural unemployment;
5. a contribution to economic growth due to the saving of capital resources in the imperfectly competitive sector.

In the rest of this chapter, each of the five sources is discussed in detail.

GREATER VARIETY OF GOODS IN CONSUMPTION

First, international trade provides consumers with greater satisfaction through a wider selection of goods than the selection available under autarky. For example, as the automobile trade with Japan expanded, especially since the end of the 1970s, the choices available to American consumers increased rapidly. Consumers can choose not only from domestic models but also from a variety of foreign models. Yet the current situation in automobile trade is far from free trade, and only a portion of the models available in the producing countries, such as Japan, have been introduced to the United States market.

For example, Japanese carmakers are producing very small passenger cars for the domestic market. The engine capacity of these ultra-mini models is less than half of the subcompact model available in the U.S. market. Naturally, such small cars have various advantages: they are inexpensive and extremely fuel-efficient, and they need much smaller parking spaces than most cars. These ultra-mini cars are powerful enough to run at fifty-five miles per hour on highways, although passengers in such a small car may not be very comfortable. But, some American consumers (e.g., extremely economy-conscious, with small families, living in a large city) might prefer an ultra-mini model to a standard car, although the number of these consumers may not be very large. If import restrictions on Japanese cars are totally lifted and the demand for Japanese cars in the United States further increases, some Japanese carmakers may introduce their ultra-mini models to the U.S. market and increase the choice available to American consumers.

Conversely, if Japanese imports were totally prohibited by a strict import ban, the choices open to U.S. consumers would be severely limited. They would no longer be able to choose small fuel-efficient

Japanese models. Of course, some new American models would be introduced to fill the gap. But, even after their introduction, the number of models of automobiles available to American consumers would probably be below the current level under partially opened trade (under the Japanese voluntary export restraint).

The effect of trade on the variety of goods is rigorously shown by using equation (4–35) above. By differentiating (4–35) we can show that $\partial n/\partial K > 0$ and that $\partial^2 n/\partial K \partial K < 0$. Namely, the number of types of differentiated goods (n) increases as the capital endowment of the economy (K) increases, although the rate of increase in n is less than proportional to the increase in K. The opening up of trade between the two countries is essentially equivalent to doubling the factor endowment, which can be used in an integrated fashion. In the closed economy neither country can exchange goods with the other, but both countries can benefit from an international division of labor under the open economy. The opening up of trade between the two countries means the doubling of K available to the larger integrated economy. The doubling of K, in turn, increases the number of types of differentiated goods, which is the same as the number of firms (or plants) due to the assumption of costless differentiation, as explained in the previous section. Further, note that as the social utility function (4–1) shows, an increase in the number of types of goods will increase utility even if the quantity of differentiated goods in consumption remains constant. Hence, trade liberalization will increase consumer satisfaction in both countries through the greater variety of goods in consumption, which is brought about by the increase in the size of the integrated economy. Conversely, trade restrictions would decrease consumer satisfaction to the extent that such restrictions reduce the effective size of the integrated economy.

However, note that the increase in the number of types of goods is less than proportional to the increase in the size of the economy (i.e., the number of firms in each country after the opening up of trade is lower than before trade). Because of foreign competition in the open economy, some of the domestic plants (or some types of differentiated goods) would be forced out of business, although consumer choice is still wider in the open economy because they have access to both foreign and domestic goods. This last point will become important when we analyze other losses from trade restrictions below.

The intuitive rationale of the above gain from trade, or loss from its restriction, is as follows: Since consumers prefer a greater variety to a limited choice, from a consumer's point of view the ideal situation would be one in which the choice is so large that all consumers can purchase custom-built cars with their exact specifications. Production technology prevents this almost infinite differentiation. Producing each particular type of goods requires a certain amount (probably large) of capital as a fixed cost. Therefore, from the viewpoint of production efficiency, the best policy is to produce only one type of good in order to minimize the necessary fixed cost. The equilibrium amount of product differentiation in the market is given by these two conflicting forces, as shown by Dixit and Stiglitz (1977). Integration of the two economies by international trade effectively increases the capital endowment, which can now be employed over both economies, although the sum of the amounts of capital endowments in the two countries remains unchanged. The increase in the integrated capital endowment makes it possible to increase the number of types of goods available to the integrated economy. Note that the capital utilized as a fixed cost in the integrated economy is less than the sum of the capital for fixed costs of the two countries before trade. Although the number of types of goods available after trade liberalization is less than the sum of the number of types in the two countries before trade, the number of types available to consumers in both countries increases through the economic integration. Hence, trade liberalization enables society to enjoy a greater variety in consumption with lower fixed costs in production, and various restrictions on trade would prevent such a gain.

This first gain from trade, greater variety in consumption, has been analyzed in previous studies, including Dixit and Norman (1980). But, since they assumed invariant elasticity of substitution as well as perfect competition in the labor market, the gains from trade stop here. In fact, international trade brings about additional gains, as discussed below.

MARKET EFFICIENCY—DECREASE IN MONOPOLISTIC POWER

Stylized fact 2 above asserts that trade liberalization decreases the market power of domestic producers. Many empirical studies have been done on the relationship between the degree of foreign competition (usually expressed as the import ratio of the industry) and the market power of domestic producers (usually measured by profit margins in the industry). Most studies seem to agree that import competition reduces market power. For example, Jacquemin, De Ghellinck, and Huveneers (1980) found a negative relationship between import ratios and profit margins in Belgian manufacturing industry.

Generally, theoretical explanations given to this stylized fact have been based on two firms (foreign and domestic) producing homogeneous goods under a duopoly framework. New trade theories based upon the three basic assumptions above have had greater difficulty in explaining this stylized fact. For example, in the monopolistic competition model of Dixit and Norman (1980), the elasticity of demand for each differentiated good is invariant with regard to the degree of foreign competition. This assumption is not very realistic in the actual situation, and if we assume variable substitutability (as is assumed in our model) the effect of trade on market power is well explained.

A commonly used measure of market power is the Lerner index (*L.I.*), which is defined as

$$L.I. \equiv \frac{P - MC}{P},\qquad(4\text{--}52)$$

where *MC* stands for marginal cost. From equation (4–13) above, we know that the marginal cost of each firm in the automobile industry is $r^a W^{1-a} m$. Substituting $MC = r^a W^{1-a} m$ and equation (4–34) into equation (4–52), we get

$$L.I. = 1 - \beta(1 - 1/n),\qquad(4\text{--}53)$$

where β is an increasing function of *n* as is shown in equation (4–2). We know from the discussion above that trade liberalization would increase *n* through an increase in the integrated capital endowment. Hence, equation (4–53) shows that trade liberalization reduces the market power of the domestic firm, which is expressed here as the Lerner index, or the rate of price markup.

Intuitively, trade liberalization increases the number of types of differentiated goods through the increase in the market size of the integrated economy. The increased variety of goods available to consumers gives them a wider selection than before. Since the range of selection is widened, goods become closer substitutes than before, and each firm faces a more elastic demand for its products. The price markup by monopolistic firms is lessened, because if a firm increases price, it loses more customers than before, and the firm's profits would become lower than they were before trade liberalization. Conversely, trade restrictions encourage the firm to increase the price markup because the firm faces a less elastic demand curve without foreign competition, and therefore these restrictions increase market inefficiency due to the monopolistic power of domestic producers. In this sense, international trade plays the role of an antitrust policy.

TECHNICAL EFFICIENCY IN PRODUCTION

International trade often becomes a catalyst for more efficient production. First, import competition forces domestic firms to reorganize their production lines in a more efficient way. Many empirical studies have found a negative relationship between protection and technical efficiency: Block (1974) found that tariff protection in Canada has contributed to inefficient industrial structures; Carlsson (1972) found that the reduction of import competition by tariff protection increased the number of inefficient producers in Sweden; Jacquemin, De Ghellinck, and Huveneers (1980) found a similar relationship for the case of Belgium. Second, the expansion of market size by the creation of an export market after trade liberalization contributes to technical efficiency through exploitation of the benefits of increasing returns to scale (IRS) technology. Scherer (1975), for example, found a positive relationship between technical efficiency and the export fraction of total shipment in six industrialized countries.

The impact of trade restrictions on technical efficiency can be rigorously shown. The production level of each firm (x) is given by equation (4–33) above. By differentiating (4–33) we can show that $\partial x/\partial n > 0$. Further, we already know that trade liberalization increases n. Hence, after trade liberalization the production level of each firm increases. Since the technology of the differentiated goods sector is characterized by increasing returns to scale (IRS), the average cost of production is decreased by trade liberalization. The positive relationship between the liberalization of trade and technical efficiency is rigorously proved.

Further, trade liberalization also contributes to the decrease in average cost through another channel. Due to free entry and exit, pure profit is forced to zero in the long run, or the average cost (AC) must be equal to the unit price (P). So, from equation (4–34) we can obtain

$$AC = P = \frac{D^{1-a}m}{\beta(1 - 1/n)} \qquad (4\text{–}54)$$

From (4–10) and (4–13) we know that the numerator of the right-hand side of equation (4–54) is equal to the marginal cost of production, which is an increasing function of D. Dividing equation (4–38) by equation (4–37) we obtain

$$D = \frac{W}{W_o} \qquad (4\text{–}55)$$

Namely, D turns out to be the degree of wage markup in the differentiated goods sector where the labor market is imperfectly competitive. By differentiating D, we can show that $\partial D/\partial n < 0$. This means that the marginal cost is decreased by a decline in wage markup after trade liberalization. It can be shown that rental rate (r) also declines after trade liberalization. Hence, from (4–54), trade liberalization brings about a decline in average cost (i.e., technical efficiency) through two channels: further exploitation of IRS technology and the decline in wage markup. Note that in spite of the decrease in W the total wage of auto workers (WL_a) increases after the liberalization of trade because the increase in employment more than offsets the wage decline. We can show that $\partial^2(WL_a)/\partial K \partial K > 0$ by using (4–38) and (4–44).

Intuitively, the opening up of trade increases the market size and enables each firm to capture more customers in the world market. The increased production level of each firm results in a decrease in average cost (technical efficiency), because each firm has to put in a certain amount of capital as a fixed cost regardless of the level of production. In other words, trade liberalization reduces the fixed cost per product. In addition, due to increased competition, the firm faces more elastic demand than before, which in turn makes the derived demand for labor more elastic. Faced with a more elastic demand for labor, the wage markup by the union is lessened, and the production cost of differentiated goods decreases further. Conversely, trade restrictions contributes to a higher average cost (technical inefficiency) through both these channels.

EFFICIENCY IN THE LABOR MARKET

The theoretical explanations of gains from trade liberalization given above all concern the product market. In addition to the triple gains in the product market, trade liberalization brings about another important effect through a change in the degree of labor market distortion.

As shown in equation (4–24), unemployment can exist even in the long-run equilibrium if union power creates a sectoral wage differential and the degree of wage markup in the imperfect sector is high when the elasticity of labor demand is low, as shown in (4–21). In fact (4–21) and (4–24) yield the equilibrium condition

$$\frac{W - W_o}{W} = \frac{N_a - L_a}{N_a} = \frac{1}{\eta} \tag{4–56}$$

Note that $(N_a - L_a) / N_a$ is the unemployment rate in the automobile industry, as explained in the previous section. From (4–48) and (4–49), it can be shown that the elasticity of demand for labor (η) is an increasing function of n,

$$\frac{\partial \eta}{\partial n} > 0 \tag{4–57}$$

Hence, from (4–56) and (4–57), trade liberalization, which increases n

in the integrated economy, decreases unemployment. Trade restrictions increase unemployment, at least in the long run. Note that the unemployment considered here must be distinguished from unemployment in the usual sense, which results from short-run macroeconomic disturbances. The unemployment considered here results from the workers' free choice. In this sense, it could be argued that this unemployment is "voluntary." However, to the society, voluntary (or structural) unemployment resulting from the imperfect labor market structure is clearly a loss because it means the underutilization of the factor.

The above findings may be a little surprising because proponents for trade restrictions often argue that such restrictions are necessary in order to reduce unemployment. Actually, however, trade liberalization decreases unemployment through correcting distortions in the labor market. As shown above, trade liberalization increases the variety of goods available to consumers. The increase in variety makes goods closer substitutes for each other. Demand for each type of differentiated good becomes more elastic. When demand for a product becomes more elastic, the derived demand for labor in each firm also becomes more elastic (Hicks-Marshall laws of derived demand). An increase in the elasticity of derived demand for labor in each firm will decrease the wage markup by the union. Faced with a lower wage markup, producers of differentiated goods will hire more workers in order to substitute labor for capital, because labor becomes cheaper than before. In addition, the demand for products is increased by the decrease in price. Employment in the differentiated goods sector will, therefore, increase for two reasons: a higher demand for products due to lower price markups; and the factor substitution toward more labor input due to a lower wage markup. Further, as the difference in wage rate between the automobile industry and the rest of the economy declines, workers would be faster to take a lower-paid job when they are laid off from the higher-wage industry. Through this multistep mechanism trade liberalization increases employment and reduces unemployment, and trade restrictions have the opposite effect.

One caveat is necessary here. The above finding is based upon comparative statics, and therefore, it is true only in the long-run equilibrium after every variable has been fully adjusted. The analysis does not necessarily preclude possible gains from trade restrictions in the adjustment period. (This point will become clearer when we examine the effect of trade restrictions in the asymmetrical short-run case in the next chapter).

CONTRIBUTION TO ECONOMIC GROWTH

International trade may bring about an additional gain that is especially relevant to developing countries where capital is relatively scarce.

As shown below, under trade restrictions the differentiated goods sector tends to take more capital input from the rest of the economy than it does under free trade, although capital is a very important resource for economic growth.

By differentiating equation (4–40), we can show that

$$\frac{\partial^2 K_a}{\partial K \partial K} < 0, \tag{4–58}$$

where K_a is the input of capital in the differentiated good sector (e.g., the automobile industry) and K is the capital endowment of the economy. Equation (4–58) shows that input of capital into the automobile industry in each country decreases after trade liberalization. Further, from (4–33) and (4–35) we can show that

$$\frac{\partial^2 (nx)}{\partial K \partial K} > 0, \tag{4–59}$$

where n is the number of firms in the automobile industry, which is the same as the number of types of automobiles because of the assumption of costless differentiation. Equation (4–59) shows that automobile production in each country after trade liberalization is larger than in autarky. Hence, from (4–58) and (4–59), after trade liberalization, the automobile industry in each country requires less capital, although the production of automobiles in each country increases. Conversely, under trade restrictions, the automobile industry in each country requires more capital input for a lower production of automobiles.

Intuitively, integration of two economies of the same size increases the number of types of differentiated products, but not by 100 percent. Therefore, the fixed cost per unit in the automobile industry declines. The decrease in fixed cost per unit, in turn, decreases the capital requirement in the automobile industry, and releases capital resources to the rest of the economy. Where capital is scarce but very important to economic development (this situation probably holds for many developing countries), the release of capital to the rest of the economy could be counted as an additional gain from trade liberalization.

Quintuple Gains from Trade—A Summary

The mechanism of the quintuple gains from international trade proved above is briefly summarized in figure 4.3.

First, the opening up of trade increases the number of types of dif-

FIGURE 4.3 Mechanism of Quintuple Gains from Trade

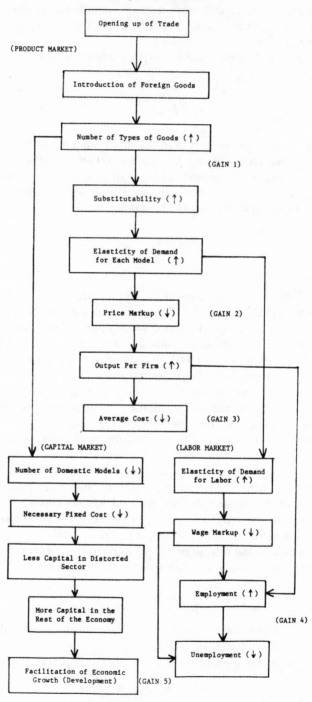

ferentiated goods available to consumers through the introduction of foreign goods. This increase in the types of goods available pleases consumers, who like variety in consumption (gain 1). This gain has been pointed out by previous studies, for example, Krugman (1979) and Dixit and Norman (1980). However, since they assumed invariant elasticity of substitution and perfect competition in the labor market, for mathematical simplification, their analysis on gains from trade often stops here. But, our model, which incorporates variable substitutability and imperfect competition in the labor market, gives additional insights into the gains from trade.

Second, due to the increase in the number of types of differentiated goods after the opening up of trade, the goods become closer substitutes, and the demand for each type of goods becomes more elastic. Due to the increase in the elasticity of demand, the price markup by monopolistic firms will decline (gain 2). In this sense, international trade can be regarded as a kind of antitrust policy.

Third, due to the decline in price and the expansion of the market size, the production of each firm increases. Since the technology in many manufacturing industries is characterized by increasing returns to scale (IRS), the average cost of production will decrease (gain 3).

Fourth, the opening up of trade will bring about an important gain concerning the labor market. By the Hicks-Marshall laws of derived demand, the elasticity of derived demand for labor increases when the elasticity of product demand increases. Hence, after the opening up of trade the derived demand for labor becomes more elastic, and therefore the wage markup by the labor union decreases. Due to the decrease in the wage markup and the increase in production, employment in the distorted sector (e.g., the automobile industry) increases and unemployment goes down, at least in the long run (gain 4).

Fifth, there is another gain that is important for developing countries. Although the number of models available to consumers increases after trade, the number of domestic models declines due to foreign competition. Each firm must expend a certain fixed cost for each type of differentiated product. A decline in the number of domestically produced types of goods implies a decrease in the capital resources necessary for the fixed costs of the distorted industry. Therefore, after the opening up of trade, consumers in both countries enjoy greater variety and a greater quantity of differentiated goods with lower capital resources required in the distorted sector. This saving of capital resources would aid further economic growth.

Of course, the above findings are applicable only in the long-run symmetric equilibrium. The analyses for the short-run asymmetric case are given in the next chapter, where the U.S.-Japan automobile trade is carefully analyzed under a rigorous model.

CHAPTER FIVE

Political Economy of the U.S.-Japan Automobile Trade—Theory

IN CHAPTER 4 we developed an analytical framework of international trade which is based upon three new assumptions: (*a*) imperfect competition in both the product and the labor markets; (*b*) increasing returns to scale due to (high) fixed costs; and (*c*) product differentiation. These new assumptions are more suitable than those of orthodox trade theories for analyzing the intra-industry trade of manufactured goods, which has become more and more important in world trade. By using the rigorous framework, we have derived five additional sources of gains from international trade which the orthodox trade theories have often overlooked.

In this chapter, the new framework is applied to a more specific trade problem: the U.S.-Japan automobile trade. In addition to the problems discussed in chapter 2, orthodox trade theories encounter other difficulties when applied to the U.S.-Japan automobile trade. Surprisingly enough, the orthodox theories do not readily explain even the pattern of the U.S.-Japan automobile trade. As is discussed in detail below, the orthodox trade theories based upon the Heckscher-Ohlin-Samuelson framework cannot explain, for example, why Japan has a strong comparative advantage in the automobile trade or why both labor and management in the American automobile industry strongly support import restrictions on Japanese automobiles. However, the new theory based upon imperfect competition in both product and labor markets gives some insights into these phenomena.

In the following discussion, first, three paradoxes in the orthodox trade theories when applied to the U.S.-Japan automobile trade will be examined. Second, the basic general equilibrium model developed in chapter 4 will be extended to include additional realities of the U.S.-Japan automobile trade, such as the productivity difference and the differences in the labor markets of the two countries. Third, the pattern and the effect of the U.S.-Japan automobile trade (and of its restrictions) will be rigorously analyzed with the extended model. This chapter is, however, confined to theoretical analyses. Empirical analyses with the actual data are presented in chapter 6. At the end of this chapter, the relative factor endowments (K/L) in the United States and Japan are examined in order to verify the validity of one of the key assumptions of our model: that the United States and Japan are very similar in terms of relative factor endowments. As in chapter 4, detailed nonmathematical explanations with intuitive appeal are given in every step of the analysis for those readers who skip mathematical proofs.

One qualification of the model should be pointed out. In this chapter, as well as in the last, our framework of analysis is a two-country model. In reality, the United States is importing automobiles from many countries as well as from Japan, although the Japanese share of total U.S. imports is overwhelming. (For example, in 1984, the share of Japanese imports in the U.S. market was 18.3 percent while the share of other imports was only 5.1 percent.) But, we should remember that our model, too, is only an approximation of reality.

ORTHODOX TRADE THEORIES AND THE U.S.-JAPAN AUTOMOBILE TRADE—THREE PARADOXES

Our major motivations in developing a new theory of international trade under imperfect competition were that the three basic assumptions of orthodox trade theories are not very realistic when applied to international trade in various manufactured goods and that they cannot explain intra-industry trade between similar industrialized countries at all. The orthodox trade theories based upon the Heckscher-Ohlin-Samuelson framework encounter the following three additional difficulties when we apply them to the recent U.S.-Japan automobile trade.

Japanese Comparative Advantage

First, the Heckscher-Ohlin-Samuelson (H-O-S) theorem encounters difficulty when it is applied to the pattern of the recent U.S.-Japan automobile trade. The essence of the H-O-S theorem is that a capital-abundant country exports capital-intensive goods and imports labor-intensive goods, while the trade pattern of a labor-abundant country is just the opposite. As is shown in table 5.1 below, automobiles are undoubtedly capital-intensive goods, whose capital-labor ratio is more than two times higher than the economy-wide capital-labor ratio in both the United States and Japan. As is well known, Japan has a strong comparative advantage in automobiles over the United States. For example, in 1986, Japanese exports of passenger cars to the United States were about 2.5 million units, while the U.S. exports to Japan were about three thousand units. Therefore, the H-O-S theorem would predict that the economy-wide capital-labor ratio in Japan (the net exporter of capital-intensive automobiles) must be much higher than that of the United States (the net importer of the capital-intensive goods). However, that is not the case in the U.S.-Japan automobile trade.

As will become clearer when we examine the data on the relative factor endowments, the data show that the economy-wide capital-labor ratio of the Japanese economy is almost the same as that of the United States. As is shown in figure 5.1 below, the economy-wide capital-labor ratio of Japan was about 94 percent of that of the United States in 1980. In view of the continuously higher saving rate (and higher investment rate) of the Japanese economy, the capital-labor ratio of Japan is considered to be the same as (or, even to exceed) that of the United States in recent years.

This figure may surprise many observers, especially the development economist, because the common belief is that Japan is a relatively labor-abundant country and that the Japanese capital-labor ratio (K/L) is much lower than that of the United States. In the 1960s, in fact, the K/L in Japan was much lower than that in the United States. For example, the Japanese K/L in 1965 was only 17.8 percent of that of the United States. But, since the end of the 1960s, Japan has caught up dramatically by heavy investment, and in the 1980s the two figures are almost equal. Thus, Japan is certainly not a highly capital abundant country in comparison with the United States; in fact, the two countries are very similar to each other in terms of relative factor endowments (i.e., the economy-wide capital-labor ratio). Hence, the prediction of the orthodox trade theories based on the H-O-S framework fails to explain the actual pattern of the U.S.-Japan automobile trade (i.e., the strong comparative advantage of Japan in the production of capital-intensive automobiles).

Ricardian theory, a conventional trade theory that emphasizes technological differences between trading partners, might be able to explain the pattern of the U.S.-Japan automobile trade. Technological differences between the Japanese automobile industry and its U.S. counterpart would be one of the major factors that contribute to the Japanese advantage because, as many studies suggest, Japan seems to have superior technology, at least in the production of small cars. In addition, the higher wage rate of American autoworkers supported by their strong labor union (i.e., the difference in the degree of labor market imperfections in the two countries) would help explain the Japanese advantage. We show in the following discussion that an asymmetry of labor market imperfection alone can generate a substantial difference in the competitive edge. Further, while the Ricardian theory can explain the first paradox (i.e., the Japanese comparative advantage), it cannot give satisfactory explanations to the following two paradoxes. The new theory developed here gives consistent explanations to all three paradoxes.

Higher Wage Rate in the U.S. Automobile Industry

The second paradox concerns the relative wage rate of the auto-workers in the United States and Japan. Orthodox trade theories based upon perfect competition in the labor market tell us that factor reward is determined according to its marginal productivity, and it is normally assumed that productivity is a decreasing function of the input of the factor if the inputs of other factors remain constant (The law of decreasing productivity of labor). In other words, the wage-rental ratio (W/r) is higher, the higher the capital-labor ratio (K/L).

When applied to the U.S.-Japan automobile trade, orthodox trade theories would predict that the K/L in the Japanese automobile industry should be much lower than that of the United States, because the wage rate of Japanese autoworkers (in terms of the relative wage level against the economy-wide wage rate in the same country) is much lower than that of their U.S. counterparts. The prediction must hold, according to orthodox trade theories, since the economy-wide K/L's in both countries are similar and the industrial differentials of rental rate in both countries are less extreme than the difference in wage rate. However, the prediction of the orthodox theories contradicts the actual K/L of the automobile industries in both the United States and Japan.

Since the relationship between K/L and the relative wage rate is important for understanding the automobile trade conflict between the United States and Japan, let us examine in some detail the capital-labor ratios of the automobile industries in the two countries. While the economy-wide capital-labor ratios in the two countries are very similar to each other, those in the automobile industry are very different. Table 5.1 shows the K/L of the automobile industries in the two countries in 1980. Since data on capital stock in the Japanese automobile industry were not available, the table shows the figure for the transport equipment manufacturing sector of Japan. As the U.S. data suggest, K/L in the automobile industry seems to be higher than that in other industries in the transport equipment manufacturing sector.

Table 5.2 shows that the weight of the automobile industry in the transport equipment manufacturing sector as a whole is much higher in Japan than it is in the United States. Therefore, if we compare K/L in the Japanese transport equipment sector (63.5 thousand dollars per worker) with that in the United States (41.0 thousand dollars per worker), the difference would be overestimated. But, if we compare

TABLE 5.1.
Capital-Labor Ratio in the Auto Industry

	Japan	U.S.
	(×$1,000 per worker)	
Transport equipment	63.5	41.0
Motor vehicle and parts	N.A.	47.2
Other	N.A.	33.7
Whole economy	20.7	22.0

Source: Compiled from data in *Survey of Current Business, Employment and Earnings, Japan Yearbook of Statistics.*
Note: Data are for 1980.

K/L in the Japanese transport equipment sector with K/L in the U.S. automobile industry (47.2 thousand dollars per worker), the difference is probably underestimated. The true difference lies between these extremes. In other words, the Japanese automobile industry K/L is 35–55 percent higher than its American counterpart.

One of the reasons for the high K/L in the Japanese automobile industry seems to be the number of small suppliers in Japan. In Japan, relatively small firms supply parts to big auto companies whose main work is to assemble these parts into a car. In the United States the degree of vertical integration in the auto industry is higher. Data on K/L in the automobile industry and related industries in Japan suggest that, except for the primary metal industry, K/L in such related industries is lower than that of the automobile industry. For example, the capital-labor ratios in the electric machinery, fabricated metal products, general machinery, and primary metal industries in Japan are 27.1, 27.7, 48.1, and 167.7 (thousand dollars per worker), respectively. These figures should be compared with that of the transport equipment manufacturing sector (63.5 thousand dollars per worker). Therefore, when

TABLE 5.2.
Relative Size of Auto Industry in Transport Equipment Sector

	Japan	U.S.
	(%)	(%)
Transport equipment	100.0	100.0
Motor vehicle and parts	71.2	53.9
Other	28.8	46.1

Source: Compiled from the data in *Employment and Earnings*, and *Japan Yearbook of Labor Statistics.*
Note: Data are for employment in 1980.

capital-labor ratios of the related industries are taken into consideration, the difference in K/L of the automobile industries in the two countries would be smaller than the figure in table 5.1.

In spite of the above qualification, K/L in the Japanese automobile industry seems to be much higher than that of its U.S. counterpart, although the wage rate in the American automobile industry is much higher. This constitutes an apparent paradox for orthodox trade theories, in which the wage rate is considered to be an increasing function of labor productivity, and labor productivity is, in turn, an increasing function of K/L.

The difference in labor market imperfections presents a possible explanation for the apparent paradox. As discussed above, there are various reasons to believe that (a) the wage rate in the Japanese industry is determined much more competitively than in the U.S. industry and (b) the higher wage rate supported by the United Auto Workers (UAW) contributes to the American disadvantage in the automobile trade between the two countries. A rigorous theoretical analysis will be given below in this chapter, to show how the labor market imperfection constitutes a source of comparative disadvantage through higher labor cost. Empirical supports for the theoretical analysis are given in the next chapter.

Ubiquitous Protectionism by both Labor and Management in the American Automobile Industry

Orthodox trade theories based on the H-O-S framework encounter a third difficulty when applied to the U.S.-Japan automobile trade, which may not be as crucial as the others. According to Bhagwati and Srinivasan (1983), for example, the Stolper-Samuelson theorem (one of the most important propositions under the orthodox framework) implies that a decline in the relative price of the importable good will unambiguously reduce the real return to the factor intensively employed therein and increase the real return to the other factor when incomplete specialization obtains in production. In simpler words, when capital-intensive goods (e.g., automobiles) are imported from abroad at a cheaper price than before, the return to capital (rental rate) will decline, while the return to labor (wage rate) increases. When applied to the U.S.-Japan automobile trade, the theorem would predict that imports of automobiles from Japan would hurt capital holders and benefit workers in the United States, because the automobile is a capital-intensive good. American autoworkers should benefit from the Japanese competition through an increase in the wage rate under free trade. Therefore, according to the theorem, American autoworkers should support free trade in automobiles and be against import restrictions.

In reality, that is not the case. In addition to the management of the American automobile industry (who may be regarded as representing the interests of capital holders), American autoworkers also strongly favor restrictions (or a ban, if possible) on imports of Japanese automobiles. For example (as discussed in chapter 2), the United Auto Workers (UAW) submitted a petition for import relief to the United States International Trade Commission (ITC) in 1980, and various statements calling for maintaining the voluntary export restraint (VER) on Japanese cars were enthusiastically made by American union leaders. The Stolper-Samuelson theorem would have difficulty in explaining this attitude because, according to the theorem, international trade should benefit American autoworkers through an increase in their wage rate.

Of course, conventional trade theories based on the sector-specific factor model, such as the study by Jones (1971), would partially explain the attitude of American autoworkers toward protection. If both factors are specific to the sector (i.e., if there is no mobility of labor between the automobile industry and the rest of the economy), both factor holders (i.e., labor and management) would oppose a free trade regime where foreign-made automobiles might flood the U.S. market.

The new theory based on imperfect competition gives a reasonable explanation for the protectionist attitude of the American autoworkers, even though labor mobility between the automobile industry and the rest of the economy exists. The new theory gives consistent explanations for all three paradoxes, and it contributes to the understanding of the effect of trade (and of its restriction) on employment and unemployment. The details of the analysis using the new model are given below.

THE NEW THEORY AND THE UNITED STATES–JAPAN AUTOMOBILE TRADE

Twofold Extension of the Basic Model—"Sticky" Product Differentiation and Asymmetry

Before applying the new framework of international trade to the U.S.-Japan automobile trade in a rigorous way, the basic model developed in chapter 4 (called the first model in the following discussions) must be extended in two important ways in order to incorporate additional realities of the U.S.-Japan automobile trade. Note that the quintuple gains from trade (and corresponding losses from trade restrictions) in the last chapter were derived from examination of the symmetric case in the (very) long run, where all variables are fully adjusted. However, when we look at the actual U.S.-Japan automobile trade, we notice that some of the variables are very slow to adjust (i.e., "sticky") and that asymmetry exists between the automobile industries in the two countries.

First, the number of domestic automobile models does not seem to change very much (at least in the short run) while other variables adjust fairly quickly. This stickiness in product differentiation must be incorporated in the extended model, (called the second model hereafter). As the data in the United States show, the price and quantity of automobiles and labor input in the automobile industry seem to adjust fairly quickly to market conditions. Although less quickly, the wage rate in the automobile industry has also adjusted to the market situation, even in the United States after the second oil crisis, as discussed above. On the other hand, as the report on the U.S. automobile industry by Altshuler et al. (1984), for example, pointed out, automobiles are such a sophisticated product that it takes several years to bring a new model to the market after starting the designing process. This sluggishness in introduction of new models is also verified by the fact that the total number of domestic automobile models does not change very much from year to year. Therefore, the stickiness of product differentiation should be incorporated in the extended model.

Second, asymmetry exists between the Japanese and the U.S. automobile industries, such as differences in technology and labor market imperfections, and therefore asymmetry must be incorporated in the model. As various authors, including Bhagwati (1982), pointed out, there is good reason to believe that Japan has a technological advantage over the United States, at least in the production of small cars. In addition (as was examined in detail in chapter 3) the labor market in the American automobile industry seems to be much less competitive than its Japanese counterpart, and the wage markup of the American autoworkers over average American workers is fairly large, while in Japan this is not observed.

In view of the above, the basic model is extended to incorporate sticky product differentiation and asymmetry in the following discussions. Using the extended model, the following three points will be rigorously shown:

1. Labor market imperfections create a higher wage rate in the industry (an explanation to paradox 2 above).
2. The wage markup created by labor market imperfections constitutes a source of comparative disadvantage, and therefore, even if the two countries are similar in relative factor endowments, a

one-sided trade pattern of automobile is possible (an explanation to paradox 1 above).
3. When asymmetry in labor market imperfections exists, both labor and management in the industry of the country where the labor market is more imperfect will benefit from protection (an explanation to paradox 3 above).

Symmetry Case—Pure Profit

First, let us introduce one element of our extensions, the stickiness of product differentiation. Although both extensions are necessary to understand the pattern and effects of the U.S.-Japan automobile trade, we shall add them individually. In this section, therefore, the two countries are still assumed to be identical in every respect, and it is also assumed that trade restrictions by one country invite immediate retaliation by the trading partner. Note that, as in chapter 4, we mean a total ban on imports by "trade restriction", and therefore, we are comparing free trade with autarky. Under the extended symmetry framework, we examine the effects of trade (and its restriction) in the situation where the number of domestic models is so sticky that it does not change at all (at least in a reasonable length of time). Therefore, when trade restrictions are imposed, the number of models of automobile available to consumers will be reduced to exactly half of those available under free trade (because they have no longer access to foreign models). In the following discussion, we compare the autarky case with the initial long-run equilibrium under free trade in order to examine the effects of trade restrictions under sticky product differentiation.

EQUILIBRIUM CONDITIONS OF THE EXTENDED MODEL

Formal analysis of the symmetric sticky product differentiation case is very similar to the analysis in chapter 4, and therefore, we can use most of the equilibrium conditions developed there, which are listed again for the reader's convenience. The new equilibrium conditions (which include the equations in chapter 4) are as follows:

$$\beta = \beta(n), \quad \beta' > 0, \quad 0 < \beta < 1 \tag{5-1}$$

$$x_o = (1 - \alpha)Y \tag{5-2}$$

$$\epsilon = \frac{1}{1 - \beta(1 - 1/n)} \tag{5-3}$$

$$K_o = ar^{a-1}W_o^{1-a}x_o \tag{5-4}$$

$$L_o = (1 - a)r^a W_o^{-a} x_o \tag{5-5}$$

$$r^a W_o^{1-a} = 1 \tag{5-6}$$

$$k = F + ar^{a-1} W^{1-a} mx \tag{5-7}$$

$$l = (1 - a)r^a W^{-a} mx \tag{5-8}$$

$$P = \frac{r^a W^{1-a} m}{1 - 1/\epsilon} \tag{5-9}$$

$$\pi = Px - (rF + r^a W^{1-a} mx) \tag{5-10}$$

$$\eta = a + (1 - a)\epsilon \tag{5-11}$$

$$\frac{W - W_o}{W} = \frac{1}{\eta} \tag{5-12}$$

$$W_o = W \frac{L_a}{N_a} \tag{5-13}$$

$$N_a + L_o = L \tag{5-14}$$

$$L_a = nl \tag{5-15}$$

$$K_o + K_a = K \tag{5-16}$$

$$K_a = nk \tag{5-17}$$

$$W_o L_o + W L_a + rK + n\pi = Y \tag{5-18}$$

The above equations are exactly the same as those for the equilibrium conditions in chapter 4 with two exceptions, (5–10) and (5–18). In the long-run analyses in the last chapter, we used a "zero profit equation" (4–16)' instead of the "profit equation" (5–10), because in the (very) long run when all variables, including the number of models of automobile, are adjusted, profit is always forced to be zero through entry and exit of the firms. However, the possibility of new entry to fill the gap is excluded here in the short-run analysis, and positive or negative profits can be made by incumbent firms. Therefore, the profit equation (5–10) is more relevant here. In addition, in the analysis in chapter 4, national income consists of factor payments alone, because profits are always forced to be zero in equilibrium through entry and exit. But, in the sticky product differentiation case, pure profits can exist, and therefore the national income identity (5–18) consists of profits as well as factor payments.

EFFECT OF TRADE RESTRICTIONS UNDER SYMMETRY

In order to analyze the effects of trade restrictions in the short-run case (i.e., under sticky product differentiation) we must examine what happens to various endogenous variables when the number of types of goods (n) is halved. (Note that the number of types of goods in this case is smaller than the long run equilibrium value of n under autarky in chapter 4.)

Effects on Prices and Wage. By inspecting the above equilibrium conditions we easily find the effects of trade restriction on prices and wages in the automobile industry. From equation (5–3), after restrictions are imposed, ϵ decreases, or demand for each model becomes less elastic than before, and price markup (degree of monopolistic power of the domestic firms) increases (see equation (5–9)). Similarly, from equation (5–11) we know that the elasticity of derived demand for labor in the automobile industry also declines, and therefore, wage markup increases (see equation (5–12)). Thus, qualitative effects on price and wage in the automobile industry are exactly the same as the long-run case of the last chapter, and the intuitive rationale behind these increases in price and wage is exactly the same as the long-run case (see chapter 4 for details).

Reduced Forms in the Symmetric Case. On the other hand, the effects on profit (π), output (x), and labor input (L_a) in the automobile industry are more complicated to analyze than the effects on price and wage. Therefore (as was the case in chapter 4) it is useful to obtain reduced forms before analyzing the effects on these variables. Simple (but tedious) algebra yields the following simplified expressions for all endogenous variables:

$$x_o = (1 - \alpha)(H^{a-1} K + H^a L + n\pi) \tag{5–19}$$

$$x = \frac{(K - nF) - a(1 - \alpha)((K - nF) + HL)}{aH^{1-a}nD^{1-a}m((1 - \alpha)E + 1)} \tag{5–20}$$

$$P = \frac{D^{1-a}m}{1 - 1/\epsilon} \tag{5–21}$$

$$\pi = \frac{(K - nF) - a(1 - \alpha)((K - nF) + HL)}{aH^{1-a}n((1 - \alpha) + 1/E)} \tag{5–22}$$

$$r = H^{a-1} \tag{5–23}$$

$$W_o = H^a \tag{5–24}$$

$$W = DH^a \tag{5–25}$$

$$K_o = a(1 - \alpha)(K + HL + H^{1-a}n\pi) \tag{5-26}$$

$$K_a = K - a(1 - \alpha)(K + HL + H^{1-a}n\pi) \tag{5-27}$$

$$k = \frac{K - a(1 - \alpha)(K + HL + H^{1-a}n\pi)}{n} \tag{5-28}$$

$$l = \frac{L - (1 - a)(1 - \alpha)(K/H + L + H^{-a}n\pi)}{nD} \tag{5-29}$$

$$L_o = (1 - a)(1 - \alpha)(K/H + L + H^{-a}n\pi) \tag{5-30}$$

$$L_a = \frac{L - (1 - a)(1 - \alpha)(K/H + L + H^{-a}n\pi)}{D} \tag{5-31}$$

$$N_a = L - (1 - a)(1 - \alpha)(K/H + L + H^{-a}n\pi) \tag{5-32}$$

$$Y = H^{a-1}K + H^aL + n\pi \tag{5-33}$$

$$\beta = \beta(n) \tag{5-34}$$

$$\epsilon = \frac{1}{1 - \beta(1 - 1/n)} \tag{5-35}$$

$$\eta = a + (1 - a)\epsilon \tag{5-36}$$

where

$D \equiv \eta/(\eta - 1)$, note $D > 1$ and $\partial D/\partial n < 0$,

$E \equiv 1/(\epsilon - 1)$, note $E < 1$ and $\partial E/\partial n < 0$,

$$H \equiv \frac{(1 - a)(K - nF)}{aL}$$

Note that H is unchanged when K, L, and n are doubled or halved. Although the reduced forms look complicated, they are very useful for analyzing the short-run effects of trade and its restriction in the following discussions.

Effect on Profit. The impact on the profit of each firm is easily analyzed by examining equation (5–22) above. Since we are assuming that the two countries are identical in every respect, imposition of trade restriction is equivalent to halving the values of K, L, and n. Note that the value of H is unchanged by halving K, L, and n, and that E is a decreasing function of n. The numerator of (5–22) becomes exactly half under trade restriction while the denominator declines by more than half, so the value of π is increased by trade restriction. Namely, incumbent firms are able to earn pure profit in the short-run (sticky product differentiation) case when the possibility of new entry is excluded.

The intuitive argument follows. After restriction of automobile trade, the demand for each type of automobile becomes less elastic because of the decrease in the number of types available. With a less elastic demand, producers in both countries can increase the price markup, and profit increases. This result suggests that producers would be enthusiastic about protection even if there were no asymmetry between the two countries.

Effect on Output. The impact of trade restriction on domestic output (x) is more complicated, because two conflicting forces influence the output level of each domestic firm. Namely, while trade restriction tends to increase the output of domestic firms through an increase in domestic demand for their products, restriction tends to decrease output because domestic firms lose their export market (note that we are examining symmetric trade restriction here). The net effect depends on the relative magnitude of these two conflicting forces, and it can be rigorously shown that the latter force is stronger than the former. By differentiating (5–20) we can show that x declines when K, L, and n become half, or that the output of each domestic firm is decreased by trade restriction. However, note that (as shown above) domestic producers can increase profit in spite of a decline in output by an increase in price.

Effect on Labor Demand. Similarly, the impact on labor demand in the automobile industry is easily analyzed by examining equation (5–31). By differentiating (5–31) we can show that L_a declines after trade restriction. This result seems to be obvious. As shown above, the wage rate of the automobile industry (W) increases and domestic output decreases after the imposition of trade restriction. In other words, under trade restriction, substitution effect and scale effect work together to reduce the demand for labor in the automobile industry. Thus, in the symmetric case where trade restriction by one country always invites retaliation by the trading partner, trade restriction decreases domestic employment.

Overall Effects in the Symmetry Case. The analyses of the effects on prices, wage, profit, output, and employment suggest that, if there were no asymmetries between the United States and Japan, automobile trade restriction would have the following effects in the short run.

1. Consumers would be hurt because the price of automobiles increases and the number of available models of automobiles declines.
2. Producers in the automobile industry would benefit because they can earn greater profits.
3. The position of the autoworkers would be ambiguous because the

amount of employment declines while the wage rate increases.

In reality, however, various asymmetries exist between the United States and Japan, and therefore, the analysis in the next section is more relevant to the actual U.S.-Japan automobile trade and restriction on it. The analysis in this section, however, is a necessary stepping stone toward the asymmetry case in the next section.

Asymmetry Case—Possible Explanations of the Three Paradoxes

TWO ASYMMETRIES—TECHNOLOGY AND LABOR MARKET

Nature of Asymmetry. Asymmetry between the two countries is introduced in this section to our analysis of the U.S.-Japan automobile trade. Although the economy-wide capital labor ratios are similar, a number of differences exist between the United States and Japan, such as the size of the economy, automotive production technology, and the degree of imperfect competition in the labor market.

First, the Japanese economy is less than half the size of the United States economy. Due to its bigger market size, the American auto industry could enjoy the benefit of increasing returns to scale more than its Japanese counterpart could *under autarky*. As explained below, however, the difference in the size of the economy cannot constitute a comparative advantage in the open economy, since we are assuming that tastes and capital-labor ratios are the same in the two countries and that there are no transportation costs. The effects of market size disappear as soon as the two economies are integrated by free trade and producers in both countries face the same integrated market. Therefore, without loss of generality, we can ignore the difference in economy size between the United States and Japan in the following analysis.

On the other hand, differences in technology and labor market imperfections affect the competitive edge even after the opening up of trade, and they must be included in the formal analysis. As many authors, including Bhagwati (1982), have pointed out, the Japanese automobile industry seems to have superior technology (at least for small cars) over its U.S. counterpart. Further (as discussed in detail in chapter 3) there are a number of reasons to believe that the labor market of the U.S. automobile industry is much less competitive than that of Japan, and that the U.S. wage rate is determined much less competitively than Japan's. In view of this, asymmetry in technology and labor market imperfections are incorporated in the formal analysis of the U.S.-Japan automobile trade below.

A Simplifying Assumption. In the following discussion of the asymmetry case, a simplifying assumption will be made in order to keep the analysis manageable. If we maintain the complete general equilibrium framework in the analysis of the asymmetry case, we must deal with 72 (18 × 4) nonlinear equations. In order to avoid this complexity, we assume in this chapter, that the interest rate (r), the wage rate in the rest of the economy (W_o), and the national income (Y) are unchanged by the opening up of the automobile trade. Essentially, we are adopting an approach that has been commonly used in the study of industrial organization (i.e., an industry analysis where the industry concerned is separately analyzed without introducing various interactions with the rest of the economy). This approach is justified if the industry concerned is relatively small. Although it may be debatable whether the automobile industry is small enough to justify this assumption, we believe that its use contributes a great deal to our understanding of the U.S.-Japan automobile trade.

Under the simplifying assumption, in the formal analysis below, we will extend the model by introducing asymmetry in technology and labor market imperfections. Note that (as explained above) we can ignore asymmetry in economy size without loss of generality. The analysis using the extended model will give us insights into the following three stylized facts:

1. Why Japan is overwhelmingly a net exporter in the automobile trade although the economy-wide capital labor ratios in Japan and the United States are similar;
2. Why the wage rate of American autoworkers is much higher than that of their Japanese counterparts;
3. Why both management and labor in the American automobile industry are very enthusiastic about restriction on imports of Japanese automobiles.

EQUILIBRIUM IN THE CLOSED ECONOMY

The following is a formal analysis of the pattern and effects of automobile trade in the asymmetry case, where cost functions (i.e., technologies) are different and the labor market in one country (country I) is imperfectly competitive in the sense of the above analysis, while that in country II is perfectly competitive. The method of analysis is as follows: (*a*) first the long-run equilibrium values of endogenous variables in the two countries are calculated for the closed economy; (*b*) equilibrium values of the endogenous variables in the open economy are calculated under the sticky product differentiation case; and (*c*) the two equilibria are compared.

In the analysis of chapter 4, the representative firm in the imperfectly competitive sector (e.g., the automobile industry) was characterized by the cost function (4–13), and it was assumed that all firms in the two countries have the same technology. This cost function (4–13) is

$$TC = rF + r^a W^{1-a} m x \tag{5-37}$$

In this chapter, we allow different cost functions in the two countries (although all firms in the same country are still assumed to have the same technology), so that the superiority of production technology in the Japanese automobile industry can be incorporated into the model. Therefore, the cost function of the representative firm in country II is expressed by

$$TC^* = rF + r^a W^{*1-a} m^* x^* \tag{5-38}$$

In the asymmetry analysis of this section, a superscript * indicates values for country II. When country II has superior technology over country I, m^* is smaller than m (in this case we might wish to regard country I and country II as the United States and Japan, respectively).

Note that we are assuming that the interest rate (r) and the wage rate in the rest of the economy (W_o) are the same in both countries. Actually, however, both r and W_o are somewhat lower in Japan than in the United States. So, Japan seems to have more reasons for its competitive edge beyond those analyzed in this section. Further, note that when m^* is smaller than m, the total cost of country II (TC^*) is smaller than that of country I (TC) even if other variables (wage rate, rental rate, and output) are the same in the two countries. In this case, we conclude that the technology of country II is superior to that of country I. The rF term in equations (5–37) and (5–38) is the fixed cost (which is invariant to the production level), and the second terms ($r^a W^{1-a} m$ and $r^a W^{*1-a} m^*$) are the marginal costs. We characterize the difference in technology as a difference in marginal cost.

The extreme case of the difference in labor market imperfections is incorporated in the formal model. The labor market in country I is imperfectly competitive in the sense discussed in chapter 4. The labor market imperfection in country I results from the existence of a single union in the distorted sector (e.g., the American automobile industry) which maximizes the objective function (5–39). (This equation is identical with (4–20) in chapter 4. For details of its implication, see the discussion in chapter 4.)

The objective function of the labor union is

$$\text{Max } V = \sum_{i=1}^{n} l_i (W_i - W_o) \tag{5-39}$$

The labor union is seeking to maximize the difference between (employed) members' income and what they would get without a union. By manipulating the first-order conditions of the maximization problem, we get

$$W = DW_o$$

$$D \equiv \frac{\eta}{\eta - 1} \tag{5-40}$$

note

$$D > 1$$

On the other hand, it is assumed that the labor market in country II is perfectly competitive and that the wage rate in the automobile industry is determined competitively as in the rest of the economy. Therefore, the wage rate in the automobile industry is the same as that in the rest of the economy,

$$W^* = W_o \tag{5-41}$$

With these two exceptions (i.e., differences in technology and labor market imperfections), the characterization of the model is the same as that in chapter 4, and we can use most of the equilibrium conditions in chapter 4. Therefore, the equilibrium conditions in the closed economy are as listed below.

In country I (imperfect labor market)—

$$\beta = \beta(n) \tag{5-42}$$

$$\epsilon = \frac{1}{1 - \beta (1 - 1/n)} \tag{5-43}$$

$$x = \frac{\alpha Y}{Pn} \tag{5-44}$$

$$P = \frac{\epsilon r^a W^{1-a} m}{\epsilon - 1} \tag{5-45}$$

$$0 = Px - (rF + r^a W^{1-a} mx) \qquad (5\text{--}46)$$

$$\eta = a + (1 - a)\epsilon \qquad (5\text{--}47)$$

$$K_a = n(F + ar^{a-1} W^{1-a} mx) \qquad (5\text{--}48)$$

$$L_a = n(1 - a)r^a W^{-a} mx \qquad (5\text{--}49)$$

$$W = DW_o \qquad (5\text{--}50)$$

$$W_o = W\left(\frac{L_a}{N_a}\right) \qquad (5\text{--}51)$$

where

$$D \equiv \frac{\eta}{\eta - 1} \qquad (5\text{--}52)$$

In country II (perfect labor market)—

$$\beta^* = \beta(n^*) \qquad (5\text{--}53)$$

$$\epsilon^* = \frac{1}{1 - \beta^*(1 - 1/n^*)} \qquad (5\text{--}54)$$

$$x^* = \frac{\alpha Y}{P^* n^*} \qquad (5\text{--}55)$$

$$P^* = \frac{\epsilon^* r^a W_o^{1-a} m^*}{\epsilon^* - 1} \qquad (5\text{--}56)$$

$$0 = P^* x^* - (rF + r^a W_o^{1-a} m^* x^*) \qquad (5\text{--}57)$$

$$\eta^* = a + (1 - a)\epsilon^* \qquad (5\text{--}58)$$

$$K_a^* = n^*(F + ar^{a-1} W_o^{1-a} m^* x^*) \qquad (5\text{--}59)$$

$$L_a^* = n^* (1 - a) r^a W_o^{-a} m^* x^* \qquad (5\text{--}60)$$

$$W^* = W_o \qquad (5\text{--}61)$$

Note that n is equal to n^* in equilibrium for the following reasons. Substituting equations (5–45) and (5–46) into (5–44), we obtain equation (5–62).

$$n = \frac{\alpha Y}{rF\epsilon} \qquad (5\text{--}62)$$

Similarly, substituting equations (5–56) and (5–57) into (5–55), we obtain

$$n^* = \frac{\alpha Y}{rF\epsilon^*} \qquad (5\text{–}63)$$

Note that ϵ is a monotonously increasing function of n and that ϵ^* is a monotonously increasing function of n^*. Further, the functional forms of ϵ and ϵ^* are identical. Therefore, from equations (5–62) and (5–63) we know that $n = n^*$ and $\epsilon = \epsilon^*$.

We are assuming that national income (Y) is the same in both countries in addition to assuming the equality of interest rates and tastes in the two countries. If the national income of country II is smaller than that of country I, n^* is smaller than n in autarky. Since ϵ and ϵ^* are increasing functions of the number of types of differentiated goods, the autarky demand of country II is less elastic than that of country I if n^* is smaller than n. Therefore, if the price markup due to inelastic demand is large enough to override the effects of differences in technology and labor market imperfections, then the autarky price of differentiated goods in country II can be higher than that in country I, if the national income of country II is smaller than that of country I. However, as explained above, the effect of the size difference on prices disappears as soon as the two economies are integrated by free trade, because under free trade all producers in the two countries face an integrated market of the same size. For this reason, we assume, without loss of generality, that the national incomes of the two countries are the same.

Because n is the same as n^* and ϵ is the same as ϵ^*, it follows that $\beta = \beta^*$. We will use a simplified notation (without superscript *) for these variables in the following discussions. Dividing (5–45) by (5–56) and noting that ϵ is equal to ϵ^*, we get

$$\frac{P}{P^*} = D^{1-a} \frac{m}{m^*} \qquad (5\text{–}64)$$

D is the degree of wage markup due to the labor market imperfection in country I ($D > 1$), and m/m^* is the degree of technical inefficiency of the automobile industry in country I relative to that in country II.

Therefore, equation (5–64) shows that the degree of labor market imperfection and technological inefficiency contributes to a higher autarky price in country I (relative to that in country II). Note that differences in technology and labor market imperfections do not disappear immediately after the opening up of trade. Thus, it is predictable that a difference in autarky price would constitute a source of comparative (dis)advantage at least in the short run, as discussed in detail in the next subsection.

In addition, it is important to note that, even if m is equal to m^* (i.e., the technologies of the automobile industries in the two countries are the same), the labor market imperfection in country I alone can generate a competitive disadvantage in country I. Further, the wage rate in the automobile sector in country I (W) is higher than that in country II (W^*), which is clear from inspection of equations (5–50) and (5–61). Namely, the wage rate in country I is higher than that in country II due to the labor market imperfection in the former.

EQUILIBRIUM IN THE OPEN ECONOMY

When international trade is opened up between country I and country II, the number of models of differentiated products available to consumers in both countries increases. Since the number of existing models is assumed to be unchanged (due to the assumption of the sticky product differentiation), the number of available models after the opening up of trade becomes exactly double. (Note that we found in the above analysis that n is equal to n^*.) So, equilibrium conditions after trade are obtained by putting $2n$ in place of n in the above equilibrium conditions.

The demand equations for each differentiated product become complicated because x_i is no longer the same for all i. Not that x^* is bigger than x in the closed economy, too. Demand for each differentiated good produced in country I is expressed by the following inverse demand function. (Compare with equation (5–9) above.)

$$\hat{P}_i = \frac{2\alpha \hat{x}_i^{\hat{\beta}-1} Y}{\left(\sum_{i=1}^{n} \hat{x}_i^{\hat{\beta}} + \sum_{i=n+1}^{2n} \hat{x}^{*\hat{\beta}} \right)} \tag{5–65}$$

where the symbol ˆ indicates the values of variables after the opening up of trade. Without loss of generality, models produced by country I are numbered from 1 to n, and models produced by country II are numbered from $n + 1$ to $2n$. Since all firms in the same country are symmetric, $\hat{x}_i$ is the same for all models produced in country I and $\hat{x}_i^*$ is the same for all models produced in country II. Therefore, (5–65) reduces to

$$\hat{P} = \frac{2\alpha Y \hat{x}^{\hat{\beta}-1}}{n(\hat{x}^{\hat{\beta}} + \hat{x}^{*\hat{\beta}})} \tag{5–66}$$

The inverse demand function for each model produced in country II is expressed as

$$\hat{P}^* = \frac{2\alpha Y \hat{x}^{*\hat{\beta}-1}}{n(\hat{x}^{\hat{\beta}} + \hat{x}^{*\hat{\beta}})} \tag{5-67}$$

Except for demand functions, equilibrium conditions after the opening up of trade are obtained by putting the symbol ^ on each of the endogenous variables in the equilibrium conditions of the closed economy. Hence, equilibrium conditions after the opening up of trade are expressed by the following sixteen equations:

$$\hat{\beta} = \beta(2n) \tag{5-68}$$

$$\hat{\epsilon} = \frac{1}{1 - \hat{\beta}(1 - 1/(2n))} \tag{5-69}$$

$$\hat{P} = \frac{2\alpha Y \hat{x}^{\hat{\beta}-1}}{n(\hat{x}^{\hat{\beta}} + \hat{x}^{*\hat{\beta}})} \tag{5-70}$$

$$\hat{P}^* = \frac{2\alpha Y \hat{x}^{*\hat{\beta}-1}}{n(\hat{x}^{\hat{\beta}} + \hat{x}^{*\hat{\beta}})} \tag{5-71}$$

$$\hat{P} = \frac{\hat{\epsilon}\hat{D}^{1-a}m}{\hat{\epsilon} - 1} \tag{5-72}$$

$$\hat{P}^* = \frac{\hat{\epsilon}m^*}{\hat{\epsilon} - 1} \tag{5-73}$$

$$\hat{\pi} = \hat{P}\hat{x} - rF - r^a\hat{W}^{1-a}m\hat{x} \tag{5-74}$$

$$\hat{\pi}^* = \hat{P}^*\hat{x}^* - rF - m\hat{x}^* \tag{5-75}$$

$$\hat{\eta} = a + (1 - a)\,\hat{\epsilon} \tag{5-76}$$

$$\hat{K}_a = n(F + ar^{a-1}\,\hat{W}^{1-a}m\hat{x}) \tag{5-77}$$

$$\hat{K}_a^* = n(F + ar^{a-1}\,W_o^{1-a}\,m\hat{x}^*) \tag{5-78}$$

$$\hat{L}_a = n(1 - a)r^a\hat{W}^{-a}m\hat{x} \tag{5-79}$$

$$\hat{L}_a^* = n(1 - a)r^aW_o^{-a}m\hat{x}^* \tag{5-80}$$

$$\hat{W} = \hat{D}W_o \tag{5-81}$$

$$W_o = \hat{W}\left(\frac{\hat{L}_a}{\hat{N}_a}\right) \tag{5-82}$$

$$\hat{D} = \frac{\hat{\eta}}{\hat{\eta} - 1} \tag{5-83}$$

The pattern and effects of trade can be rigorously analyzed by comparing the above equilibrium conditions with the equilibrium conditions of the closed economy. But, first note that the wage rate of the automobile industry in country I (W) is higher than that in country II ($W^* = W_o$) both under free trade and under autarky. From (5–81) we know that, the higher the wage markup resulting from the imperfect labor market (D), the greater the difference between the wage rates in the two countries.

This gives some insights into why the American auto wage is higher than its Japanese counterpart. Since (as discussed in detail in chapter 4) the labor market in the American automobile industry has been less competitive than that in Japan, the American autoworkers have achieved their higher wage rate through the power of their labor union (an explanation to paradox 2 above). Unfortunately, however, this wage markup constitutes one of the sources of the U.S. disadvantage in automobile trade, as is examined in detail below.

PATTERN OF TRADE—SOURCES OF JAPANESE ADVANTAGE

We have said that orthodox trade theories based on the Heckscher-Ohlin-Samuelson (H-O-S) framework cannot explain the Japanese advantage over the United States in the automobile trade, but the new theory based on the imperfect competition in the labor market can. Even if the relative factor endowments (i.e., the economy-wide capital labor ratio) of the two countries are similar, differences in technology and labor market imperfections can generate differences in autarky prices and competitiveness between the two countries. Further, even if the technologies were the same in the two countries, asymmetry in labor market imperfections alone can generate a difference in competitiveness.

The logical argument follows. First, when the technology (cost function) of one country differs from that of the other, the autarky price of that category of goods in the technologically efficient country is lower, even if the relative factor endowments and factor prices are exactly the same in the two countries. Second, when the wage rate of the distorted sector in one country is higher than that in the other country due to a difference in labor market imperfections, the autarky price in the high-wage country is higher than that in the other country even if factor prices in the economy as a whole are the same in the two countries. A difference in autarky prices and a competitive edge resulting from asymmetry in technology and labor market imperfections allows one country to be a net exporter (or importer) of a category of goods even if there are no differences in relative factor endowments.

The formal analysis of the difference in competitiveness generated by differences in technology and labor market imperfections follows. First, the ratio of imports to exports in country I (or, equivalently, the ratio of exports to imports in country II) is equal to the ratio of the total output of the differentiated good of country II to that of country I. Further, this relationship does not depend on the assumption the national economies are the same size in the two countries. This relationship is expressed by

$$DQ^I = \frac{IM^I}{EX^I} = \frac{EX^{II}}{IM^{II}} = \frac{n^*\hat{x}^*}{n\hat{x}} \tag{5-84}$$

where IM and EX are imports and exports, respectively. The larger the value of DQ^I (disadvantage in terms of quantity), the bigger the competitive superiority of country II over country I. In order to determine the value of DQ^I, we must determine the value of $\hat{x}^*/\hat{x}$. Substituting equation (5–72) into equation (5–70), we obtain

$$\frac{\hat{\epsilon}\,\hat{D}^{1-a}m}{\hat{\epsilon}-1} = \frac{2\alpha Y\hat{x}^{\hat{\beta}-1}}{n(\hat{x}^{\hat{\beta}} + \hat{x}^{*\hat{\beta}})} \tag{5-85}$$

Similarly, substituting (5–73) into (5–71), we obtain

$$\frac{\hat{\epsilon}m^*}{\hat{\epsilon}-1} = \frac{2\alpha Y\hat{x}^{*\hat{\beta}-1}}{n(\hat{x}^{\hat{\beta}} + \hat{x}^{*\hat{\beta}})} \tag{5-86}$$

Dividing (5–85) by (5–86) and rearranging, we get

$$\frac{\hat{x}^*}{\hat{x}} = \hat{D}^{(1-a)/(1-\hat{\beta})}\left\{\frac{m}{m^*}\right\}^{1/(1-\hat{\beta})} \tag{5-87}$$

Substituting (5–87) into (5–84) and noting that $n = n^*$, we get

$$DQ^I = \frac{IM^I}{EX^I} = \frac{EX^{II}}{IM^{II}} = \hat{D}^{(1-a)/(1-\hat{\beta})}\left\{\frac{m}{m^*}\right\}^{1/(1-\hat{\beta})} \tag{5-88}$$

Equation (5–88) shows that the difference in competitive edge (or, equivalently, the net export-import position) depends on the wage markup due to an imperfect labor market and on the technological difference. When the labor market is imperfectly competitive only in country I and when the technology in country I is less efficient than that in country II, country I becomes a net importer of the differentiated goods even if its economy-wide capital labor ratio is the same as that of country II. Further, the net import position of country I increases as a function of the difference in the wage markup and technology. It is important to note that, even if the technologies of the two countries were the same (i.e., $m = m^*$), the imperfect labor market structure of country I alone could generate its disadvantage.

While equation (5–88) shows the net import position of country I in terms of quantity, a similar relationship can be expressed in terms of values. Multiplying both sides of equation (5–88) by $\hat{P}^*/\hat{P}$, and substituting (5–72) and (5–73) into it, we obtain

$$DV^I = \frac{\hat{P}^* IM^I}{\hat{P} EX^I} = \frac{\hat{P}^* EX^{II}}{\hat{P} IM^{II}} = \hat{D}^{\hat{\beta}(1-a)/(1-\hat{\beta})} \left\{ \frac{m}{m^*} \right\}^{\hat{\beta}/(1-\hat{\beta})} \tag{5–89}$$

Although DV^I (disadvantage in terms of value) is smaller than DQ^I because $\hat{P}$ is greater than $\hat{P}^*$, the same argument is applicable. Namely, country I becomes a net importer of the differentiated goods because of its less efficient technology and the wage markup resulting from its labor market imperfections.

The above analysis gives a possible explanation to the pattern of the U.S.-Japan automobile trade. Regard the United States as country I and Japan as country II in the analysis. As pointed out in various studies, there are a number of reasons to believe that the Japanese automobile industry has a technology superior to the United States, at least for small cars. Further (as discussed in detail in chapter 3) the labor market of the American automobile industry is less competitive than the Japanese. For these reasons, among others, the Japanese automobile industry has a competitive edge over its U.S. counterpart, and the United States has been net importer of automobiles (an explanation of paradox 2 above).

EFFECT OF TRADE

We have just examined the pattern of trade when asymmetries in technology and labor market imperfections exist between the two trading partners. Within this framework, the effects of trade and its restriction are also easily analyzed by comparing the two sets of equilibrium conditions (in the closed economy and in the open economy). We now examine the effects of trade on various economic agents (i.e., consumers, producers, and workers) in the two countries. This examination gives some insights into why both management and labor in the American automobile industry are very enthusiastic about protection.

Effects on Consumers. It is predictable that even in the asymmetry case opening up trade will benefit consumers in both countries. Opening up trade increases the number of types of goods available to consumers in both countries and the prices of the differentiated goods decline through the increased elasticity of demand. Thus, international trade benefits consumers in two ways, an increase in variety for consumption and a decrease in prices.

The formal proof of the consumer gains is trivial. First, opening up trade increases the number of types of goods available to consumers from n to $2n$. Second, by comparing (5–45) to (5–72), and by comparing (5–56) to (5–73), we know that $\hat{P} < P$ and $\hat{P}^* < P^*$. Thus, international trade gives unambiguous gains to consumers in both countries through greater a variety for consumption and lower prices, even in the asymmetry case.

Effects on Producers. In the symmetric case above, producers of the differentiated goods in both countries benefit from trade restrictions through an increase in pure profits. But, it is suspected that trade may hurt the producers in one country and benefit those in the other, if there is a difference in competitiveness resulting from asymmetries in technology and labor market imperfections. As rigorously shown below, this is indeed the case; output level and profit in country I decrease after the opening up of trade, while in country II both output and profit increase.

First, let us examine what will happen, after the opening up of trade, to the domestic output level of the differentiated goods in country I where technology is less efficient and the labor market is imperfectly competitive. Substituting equation (5–87) into (5–71), we obtain

$$\hat{x} = \frac{2\alpha Y}{\hat{P}n(1 + AB)} \tag{5–90}$$

where

$$A \equiv D^{\hat{\beta}(1-a)/(1-\hat{\beta})}, \qquad A > 1$$

and

$$B \equiv \left(\frac{m}{m^*}\right)^{\hat{\beta}/(1-\hat{\beta})}, \qquad B > 1$$

Further, dividing (5–90) by (5–44), we obtain

$$\frac{\hat{x}}{x} = \left(\frac{P}{\hat{P}}\right)\left(\frac{2}{(1 + AB)}\right) \tag{5–91}$$

Note that $2/(1 + AB)$ is less than 1 because both A and B are greater than 1. Therefore, $\hat{x}/x$ is less than 1 unless $\hat{P}$ (price after trade) is very much smaller than P (autarky price). Although the value of $P/\hat{P}$ depends on the specification of β, it is not very big in almost all reasonable cases, as shown below. Thus, in almost all reasonable cases, the domestic output of the differentiated goods in country I will decline after the opening up of trade.

Second, let us examine the profits of the producers of the differentiated goods in country I. From equations (5–46) and (5–74), we obtain

$$\frac{\hat{\pi} + rF}{rF} = \left(\frac{\epsilon - 1}{\hat{\epsilon} - 1}\right) \left(\frac{\hat{D}^{1-a}\hat{x}}{D^{1-a}x}\right) \tag{5–92}$$

Note that if the left-hand side of equation (5–92) is less than 1, then $\hat{\pi}$ is less than zero, which means that the profit of the producers in country I declines after the opening up of trade (also note that the profit level in the initial autarchy equilibrium is zero). Since $\hat{\epsilon} > \epsilon$ and $\hat{D} < D$, then whenever $\hat{x}/x$ is less than 1, π is less than zero. This is obvious. We already found that the price of the differentiated goods declines after the opening up of trade. Therefore, whenever domestic output declines, profit also declines. Since in almost all cases output declines after trade (as explained above), profit also declines. Thus, domestic producers in country I are hurt after the opening up of trade through declines in output and profit, and they may well be against free trade and argue for protection.

Third, in country II output will unambiguously increase after trade. Substituting (5–87) into (5–71) and rearranging, we obtain

$$\hat{x}^* = \frac{2\alpha Y}{\hat{P}^* n(1 + 1/(AB))} \tag{5–93}$$

Dividing (5–93) by (5–56), we obtain

$$\frac{\hat{x}^*}{x^*} = \left(\frac{P^*}{\hat{P}^*}\right) \left(\frac{2}{1 + 1/(AB)}\right) \tag{5–94}$$

Since $P^* > \hat{P}^*$ and $2/(1 + 1/(AB)) > 0$, $\hat{x}^*$ is unambiguously greater than x^* (i.e., the output in country II will increase after the opening up of trade). This is not surprising because even in the symmetric case domestic output is increased after the opening up of trade. In the asymmetric case here, country II has an competitive advantage over country

I through its superior technology and perfectly competitive labor market, and therefore, it is natural that output of the differentiated goods in country II increases after the opening up of trade.

Fourth, the effect of trade on profit in country II is determined as follows. From equations (5–57) and (5–75), we obtain

$$\frac{\hat{\pi}^* + rF}{rF} = \left(\frac{\hat{P}^* - m^*}{P^* - m^*}\right)\left(\frac{\hat{x}^*}{x^*}\right) \tag{5–95}$$

Thus, profit in country II will increase unless the decline in price after the opening up of trade is large enough to override the increase in domestic output. This also depends on the specifications of β, but (as will be shown below) profit in country II increases after the opening up of trade in almost all cases.

In view of the above analyses, if we regard the United States as country I and Japan as country II, the attitude of management in the automobile industries of the two countries toward the automobile trade (and its restriction) is easily understood. The American auto producer is against free trade because both output and profit are decreased by Japanese competition. On the other hand, the Japanese auto producers prefer free trade to restrictions, because both their output and profit increase after trade.

Effects on Workers. Workers are greatly influenced by developments in wage rate and employment level. So, if both wage rate (W) and employment (L_a) in the imperfectly competitive sector (e.g. the American automobile industry) are decreased by foreign competition after the opening up of trade, workers in the sector would be against free trade.

First, let us examine the effects of trade on autoworkers in country I. Dividing equation (5–81) by (5–50), we obtain

$$\frac{\hat{W}}{W} = \frac{\hat{D}}{D} \tag{5–96}$$

Since $\hat{D} < D$ holds, $\hat{W} < W$ follows. The wage markup in the distorted sector in country I is decreased through the increased elasticity of derived demand for labor (η), that, in turn, results from the increase in the elasticity of demand for product (ϵ) caused by the increase in the number of types of available goods after the opening up of trade.

The effect of employment in the distorted sector in country I is obtained by dividing (5–79) by (5–49), which gives

$$\frac{\hat{L}_a}{L_a} = \left(\frac{W^a}{\hat{W}^a}\right)\left(\frac{\hat{x}}{x}\right) \tag{5-97}$$

As (5–97) shows, if the output level is decreased by foreign competition after trade and if the scale effect is not dominated by the substitution effect due to the decline in the wage rate, then the amount of labor demanded (L_a) declines after the opening up of trade. Again, this depends on the specifications of β, but in almost all cases the labor demand in country I declines after the opening up of trade (as is shown in the next subsection). Thus, in country I, where technology is less efficient and the labor market is imperfectly competitive, both wage rate and employment in the distorted sector decline after trade. Therefore, workers in the distorted sector would be against free trade and in favor of protection.

On the other hand, in country II, where the labor market is perfectly competitive, labor demanded is unambiguously increased by the increase in domestic output after trade. This is obvious when we compare equation (5–80) with (5–60).

A Note of Sufficient Conditions. The above results on the effects of trade on producers and workers in the two countries depend on the specifications of β, as suggested above. In fact, in almost all cases, sufficient conditions for the above results are satisfied.

First, although β is expressed in a general functional form β(n), it must satisfy certain conditions to give the utility function (4–1) reasonable properties. One of these reasonable properties is that consumers prefer variety in consumption. In other words, it seems reasonable that, if the number of available types of differentiated goods increases and even if the total amounts of differentiated goods consumed are unchanged, then the social welfare expressed by equation (4–1) increases. Namely, the society will be better off when, say, 100 types of automobiles are available than when only, say, 10 models are available. It can be shown that the necessary condition for such a property of the utility function reduces to the inequality

$$\hat{\beta} \leq \frac{\log 2 + \log n}{\log 2 + \log n/\beta} \tag{5-98}$$

In the following discussion, we will assume that condition (5–98) is satisfied because it must hold for the utility function to have reasonable properties.

From (5–98), if we choose some value of β and n, the maximum allowable $\hat{\beta}$ is determined. Maximum allowable $\hat{\beta}$ in turn, determines

TABLE 5.3.
Satisfactory Combinations of n and ϵ (I)

	$(a = 0.1)$	$(a = 0.255)$	$(a = 0.5)$
$\epsilon = 1.1$	3	4	7
$\epsilon = 1.2$	2	2	4
$\epsilon > 1.3$	2	2	2

the maximum allowable $W/\hat{W}$, $P/\hat{P}$ and so on. Further, for any given β, $\hat{\beta}$ is an increasing function of n. Therefore, for any given ϵ (or β), we can determine the minimum value of n that satisfies the sufficient condition. Note that there is a one-to-one correspondence between β and ϵ for any given n.

Of the three sufficient conditions (i.e., conditions for decreases in output, profit, and labor demand), the sufficient condition for the decrease in labor demand is the most restrictive. If the sufficient condition for the decrease in labor demand after trade is satisfied, the other two sufficient conditions are also satisfied. Table 5.3 shows various combinations of ϵ and n which satisfy the sufficient condition for the decrease in labor demand after trade in country I. As this table shows, if the elasticity of demand for each type of differentiated goods is greater than 1.3, any n greater than or equal to 2 satisfies the condition. As will be examined in detail in the next chapter, the elasticity of demand for each model of automobile (ϵ) is about seven in the long run, and about 3.5 in the short run, and fifty to one hundred models of automobiles are available to consumers in many industrialized countries. Therefore the above sufficient conditions for the decrease in labor demand in country I after trade are almost always satisfied. We can conclude that in almost all cases, output, profit, and labor demand in country I will decrease after the opening up of trade.

Similarly, table 5.4 shows satisfactory combinations of ϵ and n for an increase in profit in country II after the opening up of trade. In this case, virtually any combination of ϵ and n satisfies the sufficient condition.

TABLE 5.4.
Satisfactory Combinations of n and ϵ (II)

	$(a = 0.1)$	$(a = 0.255)$	$(a = 0.5)$
$\epsilon = 1.1$	2	2	2
$\epsilon = 1.2$	2	2	2
$\epsilon > 1.3$	2	2	2

From the above results, we can safely say that in almost all reasonable cases in the automobile trade, the values of the three major endogenous variables (i.e., domestic output, profit, and labor demand) are decreased in country I after the opening up of trade, while in country II all of these variables are increased. In other words, while some of the earlier analyses depend on the functional forms of the endogenous variables, we can safely conclude that the results of those analyses hold in all reasonable cases in the real world.

POLITICAL ECONOMY OF THE U.S.-JAPAN AUTOMOBILE
TRADE—A SUMMARY

In this chapter, we have examined the pattern and effects of trade in the short-run asymmetry case, where product differentiation is too sticky to change and where asymmetries exist in technology and labor market imperfections between the two trading partners. The major findings are as follows:

1. Even if the relative factor endowments (i.e., economy-wide K/L) are the same in the two trading partners, other asymmetries, such as those in technology and labor market imperfections, can generate a difference in competitiveness, and therefore one of the countries can become a net importer of that category of goods. Further, even if the production technology were the same, asymmetry in labor market imperfections alone can generate a substantial difference in competitiveness.
2. A difference in labor market imperfections in a particular industry can generate a difference in the wage rate of the distorted industry. Namely, the wage rate in the country where the labor market is imperfect is higher than that of the country where the labor market is perfectly competitive (other things being equal, of course).
3. When a difference in competitiveness is generated by a difference in technology and/or labor market imperfections, opening up trade hurts both producers and workers in the distorted industry in the disadvantaged country through decreases in domestic output, profit, wage rate, and employment, while it benefits consumers through a greater variety and lower prices.

As examined in detail in the next section, while the economy-wide K/L in the United States is very similar to that of Japan, the United States has been a net importer of automobiles because of (among other things) less efficient technology and a higher degree of imperfect competition in the labor market. (An explanation of paradox 1 above.)

Second, due to the stronger power of the U.S. labor union, the wage rate of American autoworkers relative to average American workers is much higher than that in Japan, in spite of the fact that the Japanese automobile industry is more capital-intensive. (An explanation of paradox 2 above.)

Third, management in the American automobile industry is very enthusiastic about trade restrictions on Japanese automobiles because their profits are smaller under free trade than under restrictions. Similarly, American autoworkers also strongly favor restrictions, because their wage rate and employment are smaller under free trade. (An explanation of paradox 3 above.)

It may be too early to conclude that these three implications explain the recent U.S.-Japan automobile trade, because we have confined ourselves to the theoretical analysis. Empirical verifications are given in the next chapter.

RELATIVE FACTOR ENDOWMENTS IN THE UNITED STATES AND JAPAN

Similarity in Economy-wide Capital Labor Ratio

In previous subsections of this chapter, it has been shown that, even if other things, such as tastes and relative factor endowment (K/L), are the same in the United States and Japan, asymmetry in technology and in the degree of labor market imperfection can generate a difference in the competitive edge in many industries, including the automobile industry. Further, it has been shown that, even if technologies are the same, the difference in the labor market imperfections alone can generate a competitive disadvantage. In the theoretical analyses, we have argued that the above framework captures the reality of the U.S.-Japan automobile trade without showing the validity of the underlying assumptions of the model.

Some of these underlying assumptions, however, might be debatable. So, before using the model to estimate the effects of a voluntary export restraint on the shipment of the Japanese automobiles to the U.S. market, we must verify the key assumptions that might be controversial: (*a*) the wage rate in the American automobile industry is determined less competitively than that in the Japanese automobile industry, and (*b*) Japan and the United States are the same (or at least very similar) in terms of their relative factor endowments.

The validity of the first assumption (labor market imperfections) was examined in detail in chapter 3. Here, therefore, we will examine the relative factor endowments (i.e., economy-wide capital labor ratio) in

FIGURE 5.1 Japanese Capital-Labor Ratio

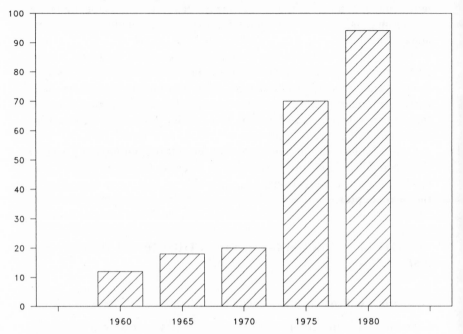

Source: Prime Minister's Office of Japan, *Statistical Yearbook of Japan;* U. S.
Department of Commerce, *Survey of Current Business.*
Note: United States = 100.

the United States and Japan to verify the second key assumption of the
model. The examination will be more detailed than necessary for ver-
ification of the assumption because we believe that previous studies of
this problem are very few, and that the following examination is important and interesting for its own sake.

The popular belief (at least among development economists) on the
relative factor endowments in the two countries would be that Japan is
a much more labor-abundant country than the United States. But, no
major studies compare the data on the capital labor ratio of the two
countries in recent years. Most studies have examined the capital-labor
ratio (K/L) in the 1950s or 1960s. Since the middle 1960s, Japan has
invested heavily and achieved high economic growth, and obviously the
current situation in Japan is very different from the situation in the 1950s
or the 1960s.

In view of the above, we will examine the data on capital stock (K)
and labor supply (L) in the United States and Japan in order to compare
K/L in the two countries. While data on labor supply are readily avail-

able, comparable data on capital stock are difficult to obtain, because the coverage of the data in the two countries differs. We have made various attempts to adjust the data so that the coverage of the data of the two countries becomes comparable.

Figure 5.1 is the result of adjusted estimates. The capital-labor ratio here is the value of the capital stock in the nonfinancial, private, corporate business sector divided by the total labor force of each country. Although we have made various adjustments to make the coverage in the two countries comparable, there are still many differences in the data from the two countries, such as the treatment of depreciation allowances. Therefore, figure 5.1 is not an accurate comparison, and it is intended only to give a rough idea of the relative factor endowments of the two countries in recent years.

Since the data on American capital stock were expressed in U.S. dollars and the Japanese data were expressed in Japanese yen, we have converted the Japanese figures into dollars by using the average exchange rate in each year. Figure 5.1 shows the trend of the Japanese *K/L* relative to that of the United States since 1960.

The finding may be somewhat surprising. The current picture of the capital labor ratio in the two countries is very different from that in the 1960s. As figure 5.1 shows, the U.S. capital-labor ratio in the 1960s was more than five times that of Japan. So, if we consider the economic relationship of the two countries in those days, Japan can be characterized as a labor-abundant country and the United States as a capital-abundant country. However, since the early 1970s, Japan has caught up dramatically. The Japanese *K/L* relative to that of the United States increased from 20.5 percent in 1970 to 71.6 percent in 1975 and 94.1 percent in 1980.

Thus, the relative factor endowment of Japan has been almost the same as that of the United States in recent years. Therefore, the basic assumption of the model (i.e., *K/L* is the same in the United States and Japan) is supported by actual data when we analyze the effects of the Japanese auto VER on the U.S. economy after 1981.

Sources of the Japanese Catch-up

What are the main reasons for Japan's dramatic catch-up? Obviously, the comparison of *K/L* in the two countries is affected by at least three things: (*a*) the exchange rate of the two currencies, (*b*) the relative size of the capital stocks of the two countries (*K*), and (*c*) the relative size of the labor force in the two countries (*L*).

First, changes in the exchange rate of the two currencies greatly affect the relative positions of the two countries. Until the Breton Woods

FIGURE 5.2 Capital-Labor Ratio

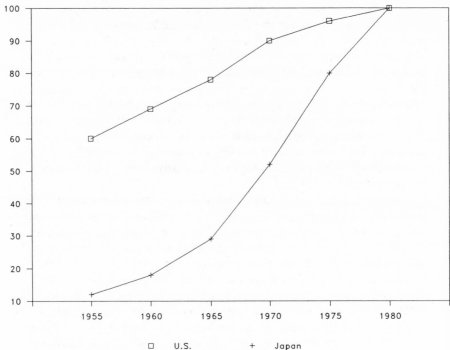

□   U.S.   +   Japan

Source: Prime Minister's Office of Japan, *Statistical Yearbook of Japan;* U.S.
Department of Commerce, *Survey of Current Business.*
Note: Index 1980 = 100.

system collapsed in the early 1970s, the exchange rate of the two currencies was 360 yen per dollar. But, after the middle 1970s, the Japanese
yen appreciated dramatically, and the annual average exchange rate in
1980 was 226 yen per dollar. This drastic change in the exchange rate
may give a wrong impression of the change in the Japanese K/L relative
to that in the United States. It is possible that the Japanese K/L (relative
to its U.S. counterpart) until the early 1970s is underestimated because
of the undervaluation of the Japanese currency. The effects of the change
in the exchange rate must be removed to correctly evaluate the change
in the relative magnitude of K/L in the two countries.

   Figure 5.2 serves this purpose. In the figure, the indices (1980 = 100)
of K/L in the two countries are plotted to remove the effects of the
change in the exchange rate. Even with the exchange rate effect is
removed, the rate of increase in the Japanese K/L is dramatic. For
example, from 1970 to 1980, the K/L in Japan almost doubled while in
the United States the increase was only 11 percent.

FIGURE 5.3 Real Capital Stock

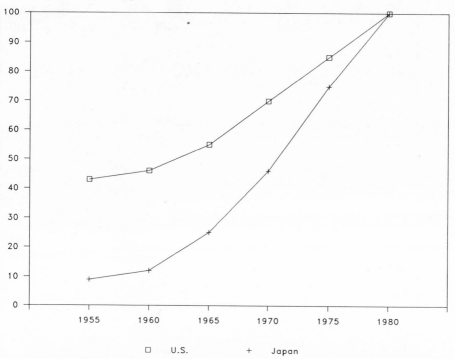

□   U.S.   +   Japan

Source: Prime Minister's Office of Japan, *Statistical Yearbook of Japan;* U.S.
Department of Commerce, *Survey of Current Business.*
Note: Index 1980 = 100.

Second, the change in K/L is affected by the relative growth of K
and L. Figure 5.3 shows the change in capital stock while figure 5.4
shows the change in labor force in the United States and Japan. These
figures suggest that both capital growth and labor growth in the two
countries have contributed positively to the Japanese catch-up. As figure
5.3 shows, real capital stock in Japan has grown more rapidly than that
in the United States. For example, Japan's real capital stock in 1980 is
more than seven times that in 1960, while in the United States real
capital stock has grown by only 100 percent in the same period. This
may not be surprising because the saving rate in Japan has been much
higher than that in the United States.

Contrary to the growth in capital stock, the growth in the labor force
in Japan was less rapid than that in the United States, as figure 5.4
shows. The growth in the labor force in the United States was remarkable, especially in the 1970s, partly because of immigration and the
increasing participation of women in the labor market. From 1970 to

FIGURE 5.4 Civilian Labor Force

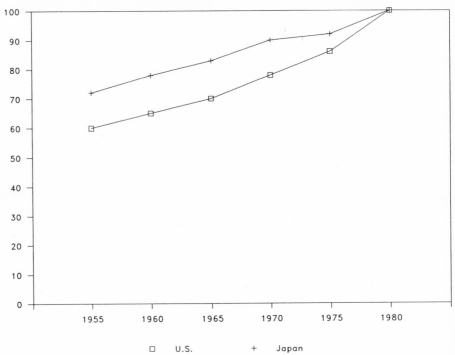

□   U.S.   +   Japan

Source: Prime Minister's Office of Japan, *Statistical Yearbook of Japan*; U.S.
Department of Commerce, *Survey of Current Business*.
Note: Index 1980 = 100.

1980, the American labor force has grown by 27 percent, while the
Japanese labor force has increased by only 9 percent. The slower growth
of the Japanese labor force along with the rapid growth of capital stock,
has contributed to the rapid increase in the economy-wide capital-labor
ratio in Japan.

In chapters 4 and 5, we have established a new general equilibrium
trade model that incorporates imperfect competition in both the product
and the labor markets, and we have used the model for theoretical
analyses of the U.S.-Japan automobile trade. In the next chapter, we
will use the model to estimate the magnitude of various effects of trade
(and of trade restriction), taking the U.S.-Japanese automobile trade
as an example. (Note that, as pointed out above, the model is general
and can be applied to many industries in many countries.)

CHAPTER SIX

Cost of Automobile Trade Restrictions—Estimations

IN CHAPTERS 4 and 5, we established a formal model that is based on: (*a*) imperfection competition in both product and labor markets, (*b*) increasing returns to scale technology in production, and (*c*) product differentiation. This new framework is more suitable than orthodox theories for the analysis of manufactured goods trade and restrictions on it, because the model incorporates various realities in world trade. Using the model, we did theoretical analyses on gains from international trade (or, equivalently, losses from trade restrictions) both in the long run and in the short run. The main conclusions from these analyses were: in many cases, a weakness in international competitiveness in the domestic industries often results from imperfections in the product and labor markets; when such imperfections are the main cause of the weak competitiveness, trade restriction cannot save the domestic industries and the jobs of domestic workers, and the cost of the restrictions to consumers is very large; trade restrictions often encourage further imperfections in the domestic market, and all parties concerned lose from the restrictions at least in the long run.

While chapters 4 and 5 dealt with theoretical analyses based on comparative statics, in this chapter we will conduct an empirical analysis of gains from trade and losses from trade restrictions using the rigorous model. Although we will apply the model to the U.S.-Japan automobile trade in our empirical analysis, the model is not confined to the special case study of the automobile trade. The model is intended to capture various realities of the manufactured goods trade so that it can be applied to many industries in many countries.

In the previous analyses, we have verified that the key assumptions of our model seem to capture the realities of the manufacturing trade between industrialized countries, including the U.S.-Japan automobile trade. In this chapter, first the long-run gains from the automobile trade are estimated for the United States using the long-run symmetry model (the first model) developed in chapter 4. Estimates of the effects of the

VER on the Japanese automobile shipments are then made using the short-run asymmetry model (the second model) developed in chapter 5.

ESTIMATION I—LONG-RUN GAINS FROM THE AUTOMOBILE TRADE

First, let us examine the long-run gains from trade (or, equivalently, losses from trade restrictions). In the theoretical analysis in chapter 4, we showed that international trade would bring about the following five gains in the long run, and that the restrictions would prevent the economies from enjoying the benefit of the five gains. Specifically, by using a rigorous general equilibrium trade model, we derived the following sources of gains from trade in the long run:

1. The satisfaction of consumers increases because they have a greater variety of differentiated goods to choose from.
2. Market efficiency is encouraged because the price markup of each firm is lowered by a decrease in the monopolistic power of domestic firms.
3. Technical efficiency in production (in the sense of decline in the average production cost) is encouraged because domestic firms can further exploit the benefit of increasing returns to scale technology when the demand for each type of differentiated goods increases due to the decline in price markup.
4. Structural unemployment declines because the imperfect competition in the labor market is, to some extent, corrected by increased foreign competition, because the wage markup that results from labor market imperfections in the distorted sector is decreased.
5. The economic growth of the country is encouraged because of the savings in capital resources used as a fixed cost in the imperfectly competitive sector. (Capital resources saved in the imperfectly competitive sector can be used in the rest of the economy to facilitate further economic growth.)

In this section, the magnitude of these five gains from trade (or losses from restrictions on trade) are calibrated by using the American automobile trade in 1986 as an example.

Method of Estimation

As shown in chapter 4, when the parameter values in the first model are determined, the equilibrium values of eighteen endogenous variables in the model (equations listed as equilibrium conditions in chapter 4) can be obtained. So, the parameter values in the model are first determined by using data from various sources. The system of eighteen equations is then solved with the evaluated parameters to obtain equilibrium values of the eighteen endogenous variables for the American automobiles market.

The current American car market is restrictive in the sense that various barriers exist to the free international flow of automobiles, but it is not a closed economy because the United States imports and exports automobiles. It might be called a "partially opened trade" regime. In view of this, the model is solved first to get the predicted values of the endogenous variables in the current real-world situation (partially opened trade regime). The model is then solved for changed parameter values so that the values of the endogenous variables in the two hypothetical situations (autarky and no trade barriers) are obtained. Finally, the values of the endogenous variables in the real-world case are compared with those under autarky and those under no trade barriers in order to evaluate the gains from trade (and from trade barriers).

Note that, in the estimation for the no-trade-barrier case, we are comparing the actual (partially opened) situation in 1986 with the situation in which the existing automobile-producing countries are totally integrated, without artificial barriers (such as the voluntary export restraint on Japanese automobile) or natural barriers (such as transportation costs) to trade. Therefore, it should be pointed out first that there are problems of both overestimation and underestimation in the figures in table 6.3. On one hand, the figures are an overestimation of the real losses from trade restrictions because we are comparing the current partially opened situation with the situation where neither artificial nor natural barriers to automobile trade exist. Obviously, even after total integration of the world economy, some natural barriers (such as transportation costs) exist. On the other hand, the figures in table 6.3 are an underestimation of losses from trade restrictions in the long run, because we are considering only the current auto production in each country. Obviously, over time, some developing countries will start producing automobiles while others further expand their production. If we consider potential auto production, the size of the integrated economy (and the gains from economic integration) becomes greater than the size of the economy on which the figures in table 6.3 are based.

As is clear from the specifications of the model in chapter 4, the model can be solved easily and the effects of trade (and of its restrictions) can be easily evaluated by simulation, if the values of all parameters are determined. Unfortunately, because most parameters are not observable, their values are calculated indirectly. The detailed method for the indirect calculations is discussed below.

First, a specific functional form should be given to the general form of β in equation (4–2). Since β must satisfy various conditions to give reasonable properties to the utility function (4–1), the permissible functional form of β is limited. Among the limited choices, one possibility is

$$\beta = 1 - \frac{\gamma}{\log N + \gamma} \qquad 0 < \gamma \qquad (6\text{–}1)'$$

In the following estimation the functional form of (6–1)′ is given to β for the purpose of estimation.

Second, α in the utility function

$$U = \left(\sum_{i=1}^{N} C_i^{\beta} \right)^{\alpha/\beta} C_o^{1-\alpha}, \qquad 0 < \alpha < 1 \qquad (4\text{–}1)$$

must be identified. Since the utility function is of Cobb-Douglas functional form, α turns out to be the same as the share of differentiated products (in this case the share of automobiles) in the total consumption expenditure. (For a proof of this, refer to a textbook of microeconomics). Table 6.1 shows the trend in the share of expenditures on new passenger cars in total personal consumption of American consumers. Since automobiles are durable goods, the expenditure share fluctuates substantially depending on economic conditions (e.g., in recessionary years consumers tend to defer the purchase of a new car until their income increases). Therefore, it is reasonable to use an average value. We took the average value since 1971 and set α equal to 0.034.

Third, since the cost function of the numeraire goods producing sector

$$TC_o = r^a W_o^{1-a} x_o, \qquad 0 < a < 1, \qquad (4\text{–}9)$$

is also of Cobb-Douglas form, a similar argument can be made (i.e., $(1 - a)$ in the cost function (4–9) is equal to the labor share of total output of the national economy).

Strictly speaking, the above statement is not correct because only the rest of the economy, which does not include the automobile industry,

TABLE 6.1.
Share of New Autos in Total Consumption Expenditures

Year	Share (%)
1971	4.2
1972	4.3
1973	4.2
1974	3.1
1975	3.0
1976	3.5
1977	3.7
1978	3.6
1979	3.3
1980	2.8
1981	2.7
1982	2.7
1983	3.0
1984	3.2
1985	3.3
1986	3.6

Source: Bureau of Economic Analysis, U.S. Department of Commerce.

exhibits constant returns to scale (CRS). However, since the share of the automobile is only 3.4 percent of the total consumption, CRS in the whole economy may be assumed here for the purpose of estimation. It is widely known that the percentage of labor share in the national economy is very stable over a long period of time (see Douglas (1976), for example). This stability of the labor share is also verified by the recent data in table 6.2. Therefore, it is reasonable to use the average of recent data (here from 1970 to 1986) and set $(1 - a)$ equal to 0.745 ($a = 0.255$).

Fourth, γ in equation (6–1) above must be determined. Since it is extremely difficult to estimate γ directly, a different approach is taken. Namely, γ is calculated by using the actual values of the endogenous variable β and n. Once we evaluate ϵ, then β can be calculated by using equation (4–8)′. Therefore, the estimate of γ can be derived from the actual values of n (the number of automobile models available to U.S. consumers) and ϵ (the elasticity of demand for each model). We obtained $\gamma = 0.6722$ by using values of ϵ and n which were obtained in the following way.

The number of models ($n = 91$) was calculated from the data in 1983 (in *Automotive News*) after adjusting for the effective availability of imports. We neglected models that had a very small volume of sales (i.e., less than 10 percent of the average sales *of each model* here). In 1983 a strict VER on Japanese automobiles was in effect, and it was

TABLE 6.2.
Share of Compensation to Workers in the National Income

Year	Share (%)
1970	75.5
1975	75.1
1977	74.3
1978	73.9
1979	74.1
1980	75.6
1981	74.7
1982	76.2
1983	74.3
1984	73.1
1985	73.4
1986	73.2

Source: Survey of Current Business.

common for consumers to wait many months to get an automobile from Japan. Some customers might have chosen to relinquish a Japanese import in favor of a less satisfactory domestic model. In these circumstances, the Japanese models were effectively not available to these customers. Therefore, we estimated the number of foreign models that were effectively available by dividing the total quantity of foreign imports by the average number of sales of each domestic model.

The value of β was obtained by substituting $\epsilon = 7.06$ into equation (4–8)'. As explained above, ϵ is the elasticity of demand for each type of differentiated product (in this case each model of automobile in the U.S. market). The estimated value of ϵ used in this section is an estimation by Cowling and Cubbin (1971). Several attempts to estimate the elasticity of demand for each model have been made, including those of Hunker (1983) and Toder (1978). Hunker's estimate is a short-run elasticity and Toder's estimates vary widely depending on the regression equation specifications. Therefore, we used the estimate by Cowling and Cubbin. (Interested readers might wish to see Goto (1986) for the estimation of the cost of protection of automobile trade based on the estimated values of ϵ by Hunker and Toder).

Fifth, parameters F and m in the cost function

$$TC = rF + r^a W^{1-a} mx \qquad (6\text{–}2)$$

must be evaluated. Note that, different from (4–13), subscript i's are omitted here because of the symmetry of the problem (see chapter 4 for details).

TABLE 6.3.
Gains from Automotive Trade in 1986 (U.S.)

	Autarky	Current Situation	No Trade Barrier
Available models: foreign and domestic (*n*)	69	91	213
Domestic models (*n₁*)	69	65	54
Production in each plant (*x*)*	91.1	100.0	126.7
Total domestic production (*n₁x*)*	96.3	100.0	105.1
Price (*P*)**	12,117	11,837	11,213
Relative wage (*W/W_o*)	1.240	1.221	1.180
Auto employment (*L_a*)*	97.3	100.0	106.4
Supply of autoworkers (*N_a*)*	98.8	100.0	102.7
Unemployed (*N_a − L_a*)*	105.7	100.0	86.0
Capital in auto industry (*a*)*	102.0	100.0	95.3
Lerner index ((*P − MC*)/*P*)	0.16	0.14	0.12

Source: Author's estimate. For method of estimation, see the text.
*Index (current situation = 100.0).
**Current dollars (1986).

$F = 229.157$ million and $m = 8,753$ were estimated using a technique similar to that used in estimating γ— the actual average price of each car (P) and the average number of automobiles produced by each firm (x) were substituted into equations (4–15)' and (4–16)' above. For mathematical simplification, but without loss of generality, the rental rate (r) and the competitive wage rate in the rest of the economy (W_o) in 1986 are set to unity by the choice of units of endowments of capital (K) and labor (L). Note that the costs considered here include the normal profit of the firms that is to be distributed to the owners of the capital. Finally, the values of K and L were calculated to make the factor prices (r and W_o) in the current situation unity.

Result of Estimation

With values for all parameters (obtained as above), the model can be solved for the eighteen endogenous variables. Table 6.3 is the result of estimations for selected endogenous variables. The second column of table 6.3 shows the predicted values of the selected endogenous variables in the actual situation (i.e., partially opened trade) of the United States in 1986. The third column shows the predicted values of the same endogenous variables under the hypothetical situation in which all barriers to automobile trade were removed, while the first column is the autarky situation in which no automobile trade is allowed.

As explained in chapter 4, trade liberalization is essentially the same as an increase in factor endowments in the integrated economy. Therefore, the size of the integrated economy is calculated to evaluate gains from automobile trade (and losses from trade barriers). In order to get the share of the passenger cars produced in the United States in the total car output of the world, the figure is adjusted to take into account the degree of openness of the current U.S. market.

By inspecting table 6.3, the real-world case (or partially opened trade case) in the United States can be easily compared to the hypothetical cases in order to determine the magnitude of the five gains from trade under imperfect competition: (a) a greater variety of goods; (b) increased market efficiency; (c) increased technical efficiency; (d) decreased structural unemployment; and (e) possible contributions to economic growth.

GAIN 1: GREATER VARIETY OF GOODS

Trade liberalization gives consumers greater satisfaction through a wider selection of goods, because they have greater access to foreign goods than before. According to our estimate, if all trade barriers were removed, the number of automobile models available to U.S. consumers would increase from the current 91 to 213 due to a dramatic inflow of foreign automobiles, and consumer satisfaction would increase because consumer prefer a greater variety in consumption. Conversely, American consumers are now obliged to be content with less choice due to various trade barriers such as the Japanese VER.

Note that the number of models available to consumers after trade liberalization (213) is fewer than the sum of currently available models in each country. As detailed in chapter 4, although the number of domestic models in each country is decreased by increased foreign competition, consumers enjoy greater variety because more foreign models are introduced through the economic integration. On the other hand, if all current imports are banned, the choices of American consumers would be reduced to 69. Note that the number of domestic models in autarky (69) is greater than the current number of domestic models (65). This is because, if imports of foreign automobiles were prohibited, domestic carmakers would introduce some new models to fill the gaps.

GAIN 2: MARKET EFFICIENCY

When trade barriers exist, market distortion in the domestic economy is increased. As discussed in detail in chapter 4, many empirical studies found that the degree of foreign competition is positively correlated with the degree of market power of domestic producers. Trade restrictions encourage domestic firms to increase their price markup because foreign competition is weakened by the restrictions. Here, we used the Lerner index (percentage price markup) to measure the market power of the domestic firms. As shown in table 6.3, according to our estimation, the Lerner index would be decreased from 0.14 to 0.12 by the removal of current trade barriers. The monopolistic power of domestic producers would be lessened by increased foreign competition after the removal of trade barriers. Thus, international trade might be considered to be a type of antitrust policy.

GAIN 3: TECHNICAL EFFICIENCY

The most interesting point of the estimation in this section is probably the effect of trade (and its restriction) on the prices of automobiles in the U.S. market. As pointed out earlier, international trade often catalyzes a price markdown through more efficient production by domestic producers. According to our estimate, the average price of an automobile in the U.S. market would decrease from the current $11,837 to $11,213 (or become $624 cheaper) if all existing trade barriers were removed. Note that this price reduction is a net gain to the U.S. economy as a whole (not a mere transfer of income from producers to consumers), because (as discussed in detail in chapter 4) the price is equal to the average cost of production in the long run due to free entry to and exit from the market. Therefore, when this price reduction ($624) is multiplied by the number of automobiles sold in the U.S. market, we obtain the total cost of existing trade barriers to the U.S. economy as a whole. In other words, because of the various barriers to automobile trade, the United States is losing more than $6 billion every year.

GAIN 4: DECLINE IN STRUCTURAL UNEMPLOYMENT

The effect of trade barriers on the labor market is also substantial. If all trade barriers were removed, structural unemployment in the United States would decline greatly. Note that in this estimation the long-run equilibria are compared, and the unemployment considered here (structural unemployment) must be distinguished from cyclical unemployment resulting from short-run macroeconomic disturbances. As explained in chapter 4, structural unemployment exists even in the long-run equilibrium due to the wage markup in the imperfectly competitive labor market.

It is often pointed out that structural unemployment in the U.S. economy has increased since the early 1970s, which corresponds to the widening of the gap between the average wage in the U.S. economy as a whole and the wage in certain industries (such as the automobile and steel industries). This phenomenon seems to support the validity of our model, in which the structural unemployment rate is an increasing function of the wage markup in the imperfectly competitive industry. Using the model, the relative wage of autoworkers in the United States is estimated to be 1.221, (i.e., autoworkers are paid 22.1 percent more than the average American worker due to labor market imperfections. According to our estimate, the wage markup would decline from the current 22.1 percent to 18.0 percent when foreign competition is intensified after the removal of existing trade barriers.

According to labor statistics, the relative wage of autoworkers is more than 50 percent above average. But, this wage differential seems to include wage differences due to the productivity differences of workers (caused by, for example, education, skills, and experience). The figure of 22.1 percent in table 6.3 should be interpreted as a pure wage markup due to imperfect competition in the labor market. It is estimated here that due to the decrease in wage markup and the increased demand for automobiles, structural unemployment in the U.S. automobile industry would be decreased by 14.0 percent if all existing trade barriers were removed. In other words, trade barriers present obstacles to a reduction in structural employment, and the U.S. economy suffers another inefficiency due to insufficient factor utilization.

GAIN 5: POSSIBLE CONTRIBUTION TO ECONOMIC GROWTH

Finally, due to the decrease in the necessary fixed cost in the automobile industry after the removal of trade barriers (note that the number of domestic automobile models available decreased from the current 65 to 54 after the removal of trade barriers), some capital resources (4.7 percent of the total capital in the U.S. automobile industry) are released from the automobile industry to the rest of the economy, even though the total production of domestic automobiles is increased by 5.1 percent. Although the higher economic growth might not be too important to the United States, this release of capital from the imperfectly competitive sector would be very important to many developing countries.

As summarized above, the magnitude of the quintuple gains from automobile trade, which were analyzed theoretically in chapter 4, is fairly substantial. While the United States is losing more than $6 billion every year due to various barriers to the automobile trade, it can be shown that under the general equilibrium framework based on the realistic assumptions, including the assumption of imperfect competition in both product and labor markets, other losses from trade barriers are also substantial. In particular, it is a little surprising to find that the removal of trade barriers could decrease the amount of structural unemployment in the U.S. industry by as much as 14 percent in the long run (when the degree of imperfect competition in the labor market is corrected to some extent by the increased foreign competition). Thus, in some sense, international trade is not only an antitrust policy to break up imperfect competition in the product market, but also a remedy for labor market imperfections.

ESTIMATION II—EFFECT OF THE VER ON THE U.S. ECONOMY

The estimation in this section concerns short-run asymmetric effects. The estimated gains in the last section concerned how much the United States could benefit from expanded automobile trade if all barriers, both artificial and natural, were removed and all of the world's existing automobile producers were able to operate in an integrated economy. The estimated gains of the last section are realized only in a (very) long-run equilibrium, and therefore represent the upper limit of the U.S. gains from unrestricted automobile trade. Further, the automobile industries in all countries were assumed to be the same in various respects including production technology. But, when the trade policies of a country are discussed, people are often more concerned with the short-term effect rather than the very long-term effect.

Further, in the short term, various asymmetries exist between automobile industries in different countries. For example, there are a number of reasons to believe that the Japanese automobile industry has a technological advantage over its U.S. counterpart, at least in the production of smaller cars, and that the labor market in the U.S. automobile industry is much less competitive than that in its Japanese counterpart.

In view of the above, in this section, the short-term effect of automobile trade (and of its restrictions) is estimated by using the short-run asymmetric model developed in chapter 5 (the second model), which assumes that the trading partners are different in technology and in the degree of imperfect competition in the labor market. More specifically, we shall examine the effects of the Japanese voluntary export restraint (VER) on automobile exports on U.S. consumers, auto producers, and autoworkers.

The estimation of the short-run effect is made for the U.S. market in 1984. Although the U.S. demand for automobiles recovered in 1984 due to the general recovery of the U.S. economy, sales of Japanese automobiles could not expand because the severe VER was in effect; and therefore, the impact of trade restriction was very evident in that year. But, before estimating the effect of the Japanese VER, previous studies on it will be briefly examined.

Existing Estimates of the Effect of the Japanese VER

Under the VER on Japanese automobiles, the American automobile industry began its recovery at the end of 1982, as the U.S. economy as a whole began its recovery. Production and employment in the U.S. automobile industry increased, but at the same time the price of automobiles in the U.S. market increased. In 1984, the American Big Three, General Motors, Ford Motor Company, and Chrysler, earned record profits due to the increases in both sales volume and prices. Faced with these circumstances, some people (even in the United States) began to argue that the Japanese VER hurt consumers too much and that the VER may not have been necessary to save the American automobile industry. At the same time, various attempts were made to measure the effects of the VER on the U.S. economy.

In February 1985, the U.S. International Trade Commission (ITC) published a fairly comprehensive study of the effect of the Japanese automobile VER on the U.S. economy. Based on the assumption that a 4 percent reduction in the import share of the market results in 1 percent increase in domestic price, they estimated that, without the Japanese VER, the price of a domestic car in the United States in 1984 would have been $660 lower. Using various elasticities for demand for and supply of automobiles, they estimated that, without the VER, the domestic production of passenger cars would have been 618,000 units lower. Assuming that the production of fourteen cars creates one job in the U.S. automobile industry, they estimated that the Japanese VER saved 44,000 jobs in the year. They also estimated that the total cost to U.S. consumers of the Japanese VER in 1984 amounted to as much as $8.52 billion.

Crandall (1984), using projections of his regression results of many regressors in the right-hand side of his estimation equations, estimated that without the Japanese VER the price of an American car in 1984 would have been $829 below the actual price. He also estimated the effects of the VER on domestic production and employment to be 445,000–712,000 vehicles and 46,200 jobs, respectively.

Feenstra (1984) estimated the effects of the Japanese VER by using his hedonic regression, which takes into consideration the quality change of Japanese cars under the VER. His estimate of the effect of the VER on the price of domestic automobiles is 3.1 percent in 1981. His estimates on the effects of production and on employment are much smaller than those of the ITC or Crandall. According to his estimate, the effect of the VER on the production of U.S. cars was only 53,000 units. Assuming that the production of 9.5 cars creates one job in the American automobile industry, he estimated that the VER saved only 5,600 jobs of U.S. autoworkers.

Tarr and Morkre (1984), using a technique similar to the ITC's, estimated the cost of the Japanese VER on the U.S. consumers at \$1.1 billion. According to their estimate, in spite of the huge loss to consumers, only 4,600 jobs in the American automobile industry were saved by the Japanese VER.

With so many studies on the effects of the Japanese VER on the U.S. economy, readers might question our rationale for adding another estimate. There are three reasons. First, while other studies assume that a fixed number of workers is necessary to produce one automobile (i.e., the labor input coefficient is invariant according to the level of production), our model allows the labor input coefficient to vary. Second, our model explicitly incorporates imperfect competition in the labor market as well as in the product market, and very few major studies incorporate labor market imperfections. In view of the importance of the labor union in the American automobile industry, we believe the impact of labor market imperfections should be included in estimates of the effect of the Japanese VER. Third, unlike the above studies, our model is based on a general equilibrium (rather than a partial equilibrium) framework that includes explicit specifications of the behaviors of consumers, producers, and workers in the whole economies of both countries. In this sense, we believe, our estimate has a firm micro foundation.

Method of Estimation

BASIC STRATEGIES OF ESTIMATION

The basic strategies of estimation here are very similar to those used to estimate the long-run effect in the last section. After evaluating the model's parameters, we solved the model with the parameters for the two situations, the current situation with the Japanese VER and the hypothetical situation without it, and we compared the values of the endogenous variables in the two situations to get the effects of the VER.

First, by the method used for the long-run estimation above, parameter values are estimated for the United States in the base year. We used 1979 as a base year because the adverse impact of the second oil crisis on the American automobile industry was not very serious in 1979. Since it is very difficult to directly estimate the demand elasticity of each automobile model, we borrowed the elasticity value from previous studies. While in the long-run case the value of 7.06 (Toder's estimate) was used, for the short-run effect of the Japanese VER, the value of 3.5

(Hunker's estimate) is used. We used 3.5 (i.e., approximately half of 7.06) here, because it is widely believed that the short-run elasticity of automobiles as a whole (about one) is half of the long-run elasticity (about two).

Second, parameter values for Japan in the same base year (1979) were estimated, taking into account differences between the United States and Japan in the size of the national economy, the degree of imperfect competition in the labor market, and production technology. While the labor market in the American automobile industry is assumed to be imperfect in the sense discussed in chapters 4 and 5 (a wage markup due to union power and the unemployment due to the wage markup), the labor market in the Japanese automobile industry is assumed to be perfectly competitive, because (as shown in chapter 3) there is very little wage markup in the Japanese automobile industry. The technological difference in the automobile industries of the two countries is represented by the difference in the marginal cost of production of a passenger car. Our estimates of the marginal costs of automobile production in the United States and in Japan turned out to be $5,495 and $3,493, respectively (in 1984). In other words, the marginal cost of the United States is about $2,000 (or 60 percent) higher than that of Japan. Note that the difference in marginal cost of production reflects the difference in both technology and labor cost: the production cost in the American automobile industry is higher than that in the Japanese industry not only because the United States has less efficient technology, but also because of the wage markup in the U.S. automobile industry resulting from imperfect competition in the labor market.

Third, by using the obtained parameter values, the model is solved for two situations: (a) the current situation with the Japanese VER, where the share of the Japanese automobiles in the U.S. market is 18.3 percent (i.e., actual market share of Japanese imports in 1984); and (b) the hypothetical situation without the VER, where the share of Japanese imports is 32.1 percent (i.e., our estimate of the share of Japanese imports, explained in the next subsection).

When solving the model for the situation with the Japanese VER, we allowed the price of Japanese (and American) cars to differ in the U.S. and Japanese markets. Note that in the theoretical analysis in chapter 5, the price of Japanese (and American) cars is assumed to be the same in the two markets for simplification. The assumption of price discrimination in the two markets seems to be more realistic, because under the import restriction, which is in effect only for the U.S. market, the price of a particular car in the American market would be higher than in the Japanese market. Faced with a scarcity of Japanese automobiles in the early 1980s, some American consumers were willing to

TABLE 6.4.
Share of Japanese Cars in the U.S. Market

Year	Actual (%)	Predicted (%)
1966	0.5	0.2
1967	0.9	1.6
1968	1.6	2.6
1969	2.5	3.2
1970	4.2	3.8
1971	5.9	4.3
1972	5.7	5.1
1973	6.2	6.0
1974	6.7	7.2
1975	9.3	8.6
1976	9.2	10.2
1977	12.0	12.1
1978	12.2	14.2
1979	16.6	16.6
1980	21.3	19.3
1981	21.8	22.1
1982	22.6	25.2
1983	20.9	28.6
1984	18.3	32.1

Sources: Actual values from the U.S. Motor Vehicle Manufactures Association;
predicted values are author's estimate (for method see discussion in the text).

pay a premium (i.e., a price above the sticker price) to get a Japanese car. Finally, the predicted values of the endogenous variables in the two situations (with and without the Japanese VER) are compared to determine the effect of the VER on the U.S. market.

PREDICTED MARKET SHARE OF JAPANESE IMPORTS WITHOUT
THE VER

The predicted share of Japanese automobiles in the U.S. market in the hypothetical situation (i.e., without the Japanese VER) was obtained by a method similar to that used in the ITC study cited above. First, the share of Japanese imports from 1966 to 1981 (before the Japanese VER) was regressed on various functional forms of time trends with adjustment for the serial correlation. The regression coefficient (R^2) in that regression was as high as 0.97, and the bias from the serial correlation was removed (the Durbin-Watson value was 1.94). By using the estimated coefficients in the regression equation, the Japanese share was projected for the years after 1982.

Table 6.4 shows the actual and predicted values of the Japanese share for 1966–84. Using this projection, we estimated the hypothetical value

TABLE 6.5.
Effects of the VER on the U.S. Market

	No VER	Current	(Total Ban)
Japanese share (%)	32.1	18.3	0
Number of Japanese imports (millions)	3.753	1.906	0
Price of U.S. car ($)	10,632	10,998	11,239
Price of Japanese car ($)	7,329	7,459	—
U.S. production (millions)	7.453	7.773	8.157
U.S. autoworkers (thousands)	644.0	667.8	698.3

Source: Author's estimate. For method of estimation, see discussion in the text.
Note: Data and estimates are for 1984.

of the Japanese share without the VER in 1984 to be 32.1 percent. The big difference between the actual and the predicted values after the imposition of the VER is justified in view of the fact that the Japanese share was increasing dramatically during the period between the outbreak of the second oil crisis in 1979 and the imposition of the Japanese VER in 1981.

The Effect of the Japanese VER on the U.S. Market

Using the method described above, the effect of the Japanese voluntary export restraint was estimated for the United States in 1984. Table 6.5 shows a summary of the estimation results for selected variables, and it is one of the most important and interesting tables in this book. The second column in the table shows the equilibrium values of the selected endogenous variables in the current situation (with the Japanese VER), while the first column shows the estimated values of the same variables for the hypothetical situation (without the VER). The third column shows another (unlikely) hypothetical situation, in which Japanese imports are totally excluded from the U.S. car market.

SUBSTANTIALLY HIGHER PRICE OF AMERICAN CARS

As is shown in table 6.5, it is estimated that if there had been no VER in 1984, the average price of the American passenger car would have been $10,632 instead of the actual price of $10,998. In other words, American consumers were paying $366 more for each domestic car. Faced with a scarcity of Japanese automobiles, created by the voluntary export restraint, the American automobile producers could increase the price of their cars, because Japanese and American cars are (imperfect) substitutes. The Japanese automobile producers could also increase the price of their cars, due to the scarcity under the VER. When the impact of the price increase of Japanese cars is taken into account, the cost of the Japanese VER to American consumers in 1984 is more than $3 billion. Our estimate of the cost to consumers lies between the ITC estimate ($8.52 billion) and the Tarr and Morkre estimates ($1 billion). Note that American consumers incur this cost every year that the VER continues.

SMALL EFFECT ON U.S. PRODUCTION

Since the alleged rationale for promoting trade restrictions on automobile, including the Japanese VER, is that restrictions are necessary to save the firms and workers in the American automobile industry, an examination of the effect of trade restrictions on domestic output and employment is very important. Our results suggest that the effect of the Japanese VER on the output of U.S. car producers is not as large as protectionists argue.

As table 6.5 shows, according to our estimate, due to the Japanese VER, the number of Japanese cars imported was reduced by 1.84 million units to 1.91 million units in 1984. In other words, if there had been no VER in 1984, there would have been well over 3 million Japanese-made automobiles in the U.S. market. In spite of the severe restrictions on Japanese imports, the production of American automobiles was estimated to increase by only 0.32 million cars in 1984. The price markups resulting from the increased market power of domestic firms under the Japanese VER discouraged domestic sales, and therefore the increase in domestic production due to the VER was much smaller than the suppressed number of Japanese imports.

The estimate of the effect of the VER on domestic production under our model, which explicitly incorporates imperfect competition in both product and labor markets and product differentiation, is smaller than that of most previous studies (with the exception of the Feenstra study). When the market structure is imperfectly competitive, trade restriction is more harmful because it increases the imperfect competition (i.e., monopolistic firms at home further increase the price markup, as observed in the U.S. automobile market), and thereby further weakens the international competitiveness of the domestic industry.

Our estimate of the effect of a total ban on Japanese automobiles is interesting. Our estimate suggests that, even if Japanese imports were totally banned from the U.S. market, the production of American automobiles would increase by only 0.38 million units, because such a restriction would enable the domestic producers to increase their prices by another $241 to $11,239 in 1984, and the increase in prices would further discourage domestic consumption. Thus, when the weakness of the domestic industry results, at least in part, from an imperfect market structure, trade restrictions tend to worsen, rather than improve, the problem.

MUCH SMALLER EFFECT ON EMPLOYMENT

Most of the previous studies used a fixed labor input coefficient in production. For example, in the ITC study the input of one more worker is necessary and sufficient to produce another 14 automobiles, while in Feenstra's study 9.5 automobiles are produced per worker. While in their studies the labor input coefficient is invariant with respect to other variables, in our model the impact of the VER on employment is estimated in the general equilibrium framework, which incorporates imperfect competition in the labor market. Therefore, we do not have to assume an a priori coefficient, and our estimate can take into consideration various effects resulting from a change in market imperfections under the VER.

As shown in table 6.5, our estimate of the effect of the Japanese VER on employment in the American automobile industry was 23,800 jobs in 1984. In other words, due to the increase in domestic production under the VER, the number of jobs for American autoworkers increased by 23,800 (3.6 percent) to 667,800 in 1984. Our estimate is smaller than those of the ITC and Crandall but larger than those of Feenstra and Tarr. In our model the VER (and any form of trade restriction) is considered to have increased imperfect competition in both the product and the labor markets, and such an increase in the market structure tends to decrease the level of employment in the distorted sector (as discussed in earlier chapters). Thus, the favorable effect of trade restrictions on domestic employment seems to be much smaller than protectionists often argue.

The Case for Free Trade

According to our estimate, due to the Japanese VER, American consumers had to pay more than $3 billion while 23,800 jobs in the American automobile industry were saved in 1984. Of course, it is very difficult to evaluate the cost to consumers of the increased employment opportunities. But, several things must be taken into consideration when we discuss the costs and benefits of trade restrictions, such as the Japanese VER.

First, (as shown in chapter 3) American autoworkers are paid a much higher wage than average American workers, while in Japan this difference is almost nonexistent. As examined in detail in the theoretical part of this book, it is suspected that this higher wage rate (i.e., the wage markup) is a (greater) source of competitive disadvantage for the American automobile industry in comparison with its Japanese counterpart. Another estimation using our model suggests that if all restrictions on automobile trade between the United States and Japan were removed, the Japanese share in the U.S. market would reach 46 percent (the current share is 18 percent) while the American share in the Japanese market would be only 5 percent (the current share is less than 1 percent). This one-sided advantage of the Japanese automobile industry over its U.S. counterpart results from differences in technology and wage rates in the auto industries of two countries. Another estimate based on our model suggests that, even if American technology is assumed to be the same as the Japanese, the difference in labor market imperfections alone would generate a substantial difference in competitiveness: in this case, the Japanese share in the U.S. market would be 36 percent, and the U.S. share in the Japanese market, 21 percent.

Second, even before the second oil crisis, when the share of Japanese automobiles in the U.S. market was smaller, the level of employment in the American automobile industry fluctuated widely according to general economic conditions. As examined above (see chapter 3 for details), since the wage rate in the American automobile industry was inflexible, the adjustment to the decline in sales was made mostly through a reduction in employment, and therefore, we observed huge layoffs of autoworkers in recessionary years. For example, in the recession of the first oil crisis (1974–75), when the share of Japanese automobiles was a mere 6–9 percent, the number of American autoworkers decreased by 138,900. Further, in the recession after the second oil crisis the number of U.S. autoworkers declined by more than 200,000. These figures can be compared with the above estimate of 23,800. In other words, the number of jobs saved by the severe VER was only 10 percent of the number lost during the second oil crisis.

Third, we may divide $3 billion (i.e., the cost to consumers) by 23,800 (the number of jobs saved) to get the cost to consumer per job saved under the VER:

$$\$3,000,000,000 \ / \ 23,800 \ = \ \$126,050$$

American consumers had to pay more than $126,000 to save each job in the American automobile industry under the Japanese VER. This loss to consumers per job saved may be compared with the average annual wage of American autoworkers ($37,000 in 1984) in order to appreciate the magnitude of the loss. Even when compared with the autoworker's wage rate, which is 50 percent higher than that of average

U.S. workers, the cost to consumers seems to be very large.

Finally, the long-term effect of trade restrictions must be noted. Even if restrictions were initially intended to be temporary, in an attempt to given an umbrella to domestic industries during an adjustment period, they tend to continue for a long period of time. Although the U.S. government is claiming that the "official" VER it requested was terminated in March 1985, the "unofficial" VER is still in effect and is expected to continue. In fact, almost a decade has passed since the Japanese government announced voluntary export restraints on automobile shipments to the United States in 1981. As discussed in chapter 4, trade restrictions hurt all parties concerned, including American autoworkers, because the restrictions further encourage market imperfections in the importing country. In the long run, where technology becomes similar and restrictions invite retaliation, the conclusions from the analysis in chapter 4 become valid. When the long-run symmetric model was applied, trade restrictions, including a perpetual Japanese VER, decrease domestic employment as well as domestic production through increased imperfect competition in both the product and the labor markets in the importing country. Thus, a perpetual VER on Japanese automobiles is harmful not only to American consumers but also to American autoworkers in the long run.

CHAPTER SEVEN

Foreign Direct Investment and Domestic Employment

FOREIGN DIRECT INVESTMENT BY JAPANESE FIRMS

In the previous chapters, we have examined the interrelationship of international trade problems and domestic labor problems, taking the U.S.-Japan automobile trade in recent years as an example. It was shown that the weakness in international competitiveness of the American automobile industry was created, at least in part, by less efficient technology and by imperfect competition in the labor market. Due to the big difference in competitiveness between the Japanese and the U.S. automobile industries, there is a huge imbalance in the automobile trade, in spite of the fact that the export of Japanese automobiles to the U.S. market is severely restricted by a VER while Japan does not impose any tariffs or quotas. The difference in competitiveness between the two countries is not confined to automobiles. In many manufactured goods trade, Japan seems to have a competitive advantage over the United States. As a result, the trade gap between the United States and Japan has recently become very large (see table 1.1 for details).

As is well known, Japan's huge trade surplus brought about a dramatic appreciation of the Japanese yen and trade conflicts between Japan and other countries (most notably the United States). The appreciation of the yen and the trade conflicts, in turn, have encouraged the outflow of Japanese capital in recent years. For example, a massive outflow of Japanese firms to other Asian countries is occurring because, due to the sharp appreciation of the Japanese yen, it is often cheaper to produce in these Asian countries than in Japan even when productivity differences are taken into account. Further, (as examined in detail in later sections) Japanese carmakers are building plants in the United States because, due to the perpetual VER, that is the only way to increase sales of Japanese automobiles in the United States.

As the rapid outflow of Japanese firms continued on a large scale, many people in Japan expressed their concern about a possible adverse impact on Japanese employment. The possibility of *Sangyo Kudoka* (deindustrialization) is one of the hottest current issues among Japanese economists. Many discussions have been held on how many domestic employment opportunities are and will be lost due to the outflow of Japanese firms, and quite a few estimates are available on the impact of capital outflow on domestic jobs. Most of these estimates seem to involve methodological shortcomings, as explained in detail below. So, in view of the shortcomings of the existing studies, a new estimate is presented in this chapter on the effect of capital outflow on Japanese workers. In our empirical study, the elasticity of domestic employment with respect to capital outflow will be estimated directly.

In this chapter we briefly discuss the current situation and various views on deindustrialization in Japan and the United States. A method of estimation is presented and used to estimate how many domestic job opportunities in Japan are (and will be) lost due to the outflow of Japanese capital. One of the major findings in this chapter is that the number of jobs lost in the Japanese economy as a whole is at most around 300,000. Although our estimate also involves imperfections, we will present a new estimate of the effects of possible deindustrialization, since there are very few solid econometric estimates in spite of the heated debates on the problem in Japan.

Foreign Direct Investment and Deindustrialization

Since the Japanese yen started dramatically appreciating after the fall of 1985, discussions on possible deindustrialization of the Japanese economy have become very popular in Japanese business and labor. Frequent outflow of Japanese firms in the automobile and consumer electronics industries has been reported in the Japanese press. Many Japanese argue that large-scale outflow of Japanese firms will have an adverse impact on the production and employment of Japanese industries, and that the Japanese economy will be *deindustrialized* in the near future unless the outflow is contained.

In spite of frequent discussions of deindustrialization, its exact definition is not very clear, and therefore the discussions have not been very systematic or consistent. While most agree that deindustrialization involves a decline in production and employment in the manufacturing sector, resulting from foreign direct investment and imports from Japanese-owned plants abroad, the perceived signs of deindustrialization vary: a reduction in employment as a whole; a decline in the quality of domestic jobs due to the weakening of the manufacturing sector in the national economy; stagnation in innovation due to lack of R&D investment.

While agreement on the definition of deindustrialization in Japan is far from unanimous, two main elements can be pointed out. First, the term is used for "deindustrialization" in the narrow sense. When many Japanese manufacturing firms build plants overseas, exports of manufactured goods from Japan may decrease while imports of these goods from abroad, including Japanese plants located abroad, may increase. As a result, the domestic manufacturing sector might be weakened, and the Japanese economy might be *deindustrialized*. As for the impact on domestic employment, the concerns are whether the service sector can absorb the workers displaced from the shrinking manufacturing sector and whether the jobs created in the service sector are as good as those lost from the manufacturing sector.

Second, the term implies the *hollowing* of the Japanese manufacturing sector. Namely, as firms in the Japanese manufacturing sector build many plants abroad, most of the production capability of the Japanese manufacturing firms may be transferred to foreign countries. As a result, the firms located in Japan might specialize in management or marketing, where few employment opportunities are available, while the labor-intensive part of the firm moves to Japanese plants located in foreign countries.

Probably, discussions on the possible deindustrialization of the national economy started in the United States, where many multinational corporations have been engaging in production in foreign countries. It seems, at least in Japan, that many U.S. economists and labor leaders are deploring the deindustrialization of the American economy. As is well known, in the United States, major industries, including automobiles and consumer electronics, have been conducting large-scale production abroad especially since the middle 1960s. Labor unions in the United States fear that the expansion of production in foreign countries may result in the loss of job opportunities in the United States.

The fear of job loss resulting from deindustrialization in the United States became very strong in the 1980s, when the weakness of major industries in international competition seemed evident and a dramatic increase in imports and unemployment occurred after the second oil crisis. For example, in June 1980, a sensational cover story appeared in *Business Week* emotionally emphasizing the fear of deindustrialization of the American economy resulting from foreign deployment of American multinational corporations. After examining detailed time series data on production and employment in the U.S. economy, Blueston and Harrison (1982) concluded that the increase in production by American firms abroad cause many domestic plants to close down, producing massive layoffs of American workers. Labor leaders consistently expressed the fear of lost domestic jobs due to the outflow of American multinationals. For example, in the Senate Foreign Relations Committee in 1984, R. Oswald of the AFL-CIO asserted that foreign direct investment by American firms was equivalent to the export of the employment opportunities of American workers.

The U.S. government seems to take issue with the concern about deindustrialization of the American economy. For example, the Economic Report of the President of 1986 asserted that the U.S. economy is sound and far from being de-industrialized because, although employment in the manufacturing sector is declining, many other indicators (e.g., productivity, wage rate, capital stock in the U.S.) show the soundness of the U.S. manufacturing sector. Lawrence (1984) examined detailed data on the U.S. manufacturing sector, and concluded that the U.S. economy is not deindustrializing although it is in a temporary slump. He argued that, when the shipments from various sectors are compared in real terms (i.e., in constant price), the share of the manufacturing sector in the total U.S. economy is not declining at all, and that the growth of exports of manufactured goods (in constant price) far exceeded the growth of imports from 1970 to 1980. The U.S. economy looks unsound simply because incidents in a limited number of American industries, such as the automobile industry, are being sensationally reported by the press.

Thus, there are two very different views on the possible deindustrialization of the U.S. economy. But, both sides agree, to some extent, that the competitiveness of American industries has been weakened in the 1980s. So, let us examine the data on U.S. trade in order to get an insight into the relationship between the outflow of American capital and the alleged weakening of the U.S. economy.

First, it can be easily observed that the trade deficit of the United States (especially the trade deficit against Japan) has become extremely large in the 1980s. As examined in some detail in chapter 1, the imbalance in U.S.-Japan trade is very large. For example, in 1986, the value of Japanese exports to the United States ($81.3 billion) was three times that of American exports to Japan ($29.2 billion).

Second, the composition of exports and imports shows a notable trend: the weight of manufactured goods in exports is declining while that in imports is increasing over time. Figure 7.1 shows the composition of American exports and imports by major categories of goods in 1965 and 1984. When we compare the figures in 1965 and in 1984, it is apparent that manufactured goods have become increasingly important in U.S. trade partly because the composition of the world trade as a whole has moved from primary products to more sophisticated manufactured goods, reflecting economic development worldwide.

But, closer examination of figure 7.1 reveals that in the United States

FIGURE 7.1 U.S. Trade by Commodities (by percentage)

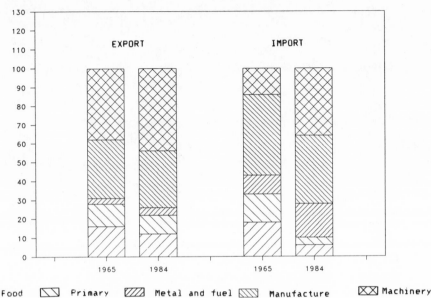

Source: U.S. Department of Commerce, *Survey of Current Business*.

the change in the composition of exports is very different from that of imports. While the share of manufactured goods (including machinery and transport equipment) in total U.S. imports increased by 16 percent (from 56 percent in 1965 to 72 percent in 1984), the share of the same categories of goods in total U.S. exports grew only by 4 percent to reach 72 percent in 1984. As a result, surprisingly enough, in the United States the share of manufactured goods in imports is the same as the share in exports. In other words, the United States is no longer a net exporter of manufactured goods, which are, generally speaking, more capital-intensive than primary products. Faced with the growing share in U.S. imports of manufactured goods, including machinery and transport equipment, protectionists in the United States have deplored the critical situation of U.S. industries, which, they argue, resulted in part from the massive outflow of American firms in the 1960s and 1970s.

When we examine the validity of arguments on the possible dein-dustrialization of the U.S. economy, the long-term trend of foreign investment should be taken into consideration. As explained above, argument is that the national economy is deindustrialized as a result of massive transfer of domestic production bases to foreign countries

FIGURE 7.2 Foreign Direct Investment (U.S.)

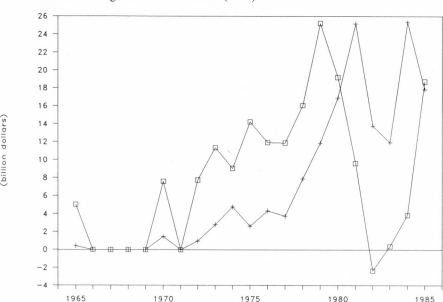

□ Outflow of US firms   +   Inflow from abroad

Source: U.S. Department of Commerce, *Survey of Current Business*.

through foreign direct investment. But, the data suggest that the weakened international competitiveness of American industries has been brought about not so much by the outflow of U.S. capital as by imperfect competition in both the product and the labor markets (as explained in detail in the previous chapters).

We can observe an interesting trend in American foreign direct investment in figure 7.2, which shows time-series data on outflow (i.e., direct investment by U.S. firms into foreign countries) and inflow (i.e., direct investment by foreign firms into the United States) since the middle 1960s. As figure 7.2 shows, until the end of the 1970s the United States was a net exporter of production capital, then the United States turned into a net capital importer in the 1980s. The outflow of U.S. firms declined dramatically in the 1980s when the United States was suffering from a huge trade deficit. In other words, the weakened international competitiveness of U.S. industry coincides with capital *inflow* rather than outflow.

While it is often pointed out, especially by Japanese economists and business leaders as well as American labor leaders, that the recent weakness of the U.S. economy has been brought about by the massive outflow of production capacities of American industry, we cannot find hard evidence to support their argument. Rather, the weaker positions in international competition of certain industries, such as the automobile and steel industries, result from other causes, such as inefficient market structures and labor market imperfections.

Japanese Foreign Direct Investment—An Overview

DRAMATIC INCREASE IN THE OUTFLOW OF JAPANESE CAPITAL

A dramatic increase in Japanese foreign direct investment (FDI) contributed a great deal to the emergence of concern about possible deindustrialization of the Japanese economy. Faced with a rapid increase in the outflow of Japanese firms on a large scale, both business and labor began to fear that the employment opportunities of Japanese workers might be endangered by such transfer of production capacity to foreign countries. Indeed, the increase in Japanese foreign direct investment is dramatic in the 1980s.

Figure 7.3 shows yearly levels of Japanese foreign direct investment (FDI) since 1975. While the FDI from Japan was insignificant in the 1960s, it started to increase in the early 1970s. The Japanese FDI exploded in the 1980s, as Japan accumulated a hugh trade surplus and as the Japanese yen sharply appreciated. While the Japanese FDI was $4.7 billion in 1980, it doubled to $8.9 billion the next year. The rapid increase in the Japanese FDI continued, and it reached $22 billion in 1986, spurred by a sharp appreciation of the Japanese yen after September 1985.

QUOTA-JUMPING INVESTMENT

A new trend can be observed in the deployment of Japanese foreign direct investment (FDI) in the 1980s: from "low wage–seeking" FDI to "quota-jumping" FDI. Figure 7.4 shows the trend in Japanese FDI by destination. As this figure shows, until the end of the 1970s, most of the Japanese FDI was directed to developing countries, such as countries in Asia and Latin America. Japanese firms had established plants in these countries in order to exploit their much lower wage rate (and therefore lower production costs) than that in Japan. In the 1980s, the preferred destination has shifted toward countries in North America and Europe, where the wage rates are often higher than those in Japan. For example, as figure 7.4 shows, while two-thirds of the Japanese FDI was directed to developing countries in 1976, the emphasis was shifted toward developed countries in 1985 when two-thirds was directed to developed countries.

Figure 7.3 Foreign Direct Investment (Japan)

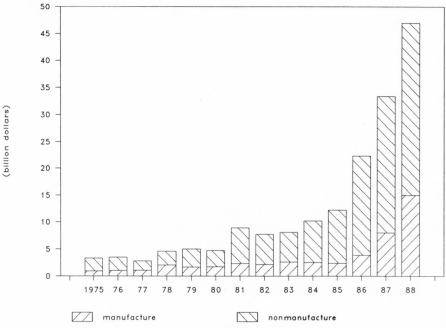

Source: Japanese Ministry of International Trade and Industry.

Trade conflicts between Japan and other industrialized countries seem to greatly influence the shift in destination of Japanese FDI toward developed countries. Figure 7.5 summarizes the results of a survey by the Japanese government (Ministry of International Trade and Industry) on the reasons for the establishment of plants in foreign countries. Most of the Japanese firms that built their overseas plants in the 1970s did so because of the cost advantage of production in foreign countries (mostly in developing countries where wage rates were far below the Japanese level). But, in the 1980s the reasons are quite different. The Japanese firms must build their plants in foreign countries (mostly in developed countries) because without doing so they could not increase their sales in those foreign countries due to various trade restrictions. As figure 7.5 shows, in the 1980s most of the Japanese firms in the manufacturing sector (including machinery, automobiles, and consumer electronics) gave trade conflict as a reason for their decision to build plants overseas. In the next subsection, the Japanese automobile-production plants in the United States are briefly discussed as an example of a quota-jumping investment.

FIGURE 7.4 Japanese FDI by Destination

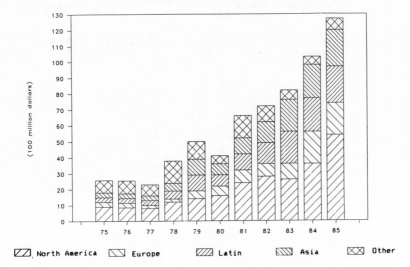

Source: Japanese Ministry of International Trade and Industry.

Japanese Automobile Plants in the United States

RESHAPING THE US AUTO MARKET

A typical example of a quota-jumping investment is the establishment of Japanese automobile plants in the United States in the 1980s. When imports of Japanese automobiles were severely restricted by the VER started in 1981, the interests of the three parties concerned (the Japanese auto producers, the U.S. auto producers, and American autoworkers) coincided to some extent to encourage the building of Japanese auto plants in the United States. In the early 1980s, management and labor in the American automobile industry insisted that the Japanese should build their cars in the United States, hoping that the strong Japanese competitiveness would be weakened when they had to produce their cars with union labor and with various inefficiencies, such as the high absenteeism of American workers. Japanese automakers also wanted factories in the United States, because production in America seem to be the only way to increase the sales of cars with Japanese name tags under the severe VER.

FIGURE 7.5 Reasons for Foreign Direct Investment

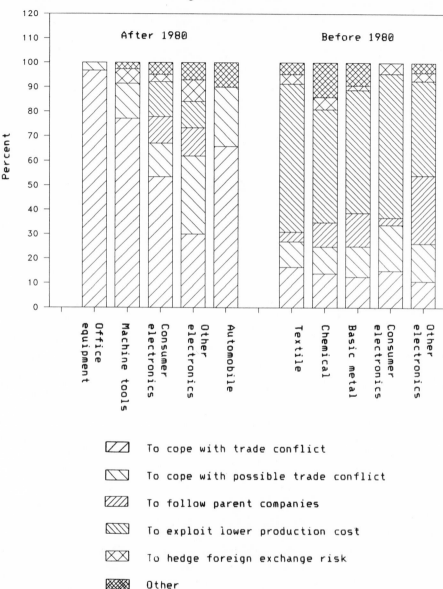

Source: Japanese Ministry of International Trade and Industry.

TABLE 7.1.
Japanese Auto Plants in the United States

Company(ies)	Location	Start Date	Capacity (vehicles)	Employment	Union
Toyota & GM	Fremont (California)	12/84	300,000	3,400	yes
Mazda	Flat Rock (Michigan)	9/87	240,000	3,400	yes
Mitsubishi & Chrysler	Normal (Illinois)	9/88	240,000	2,900	yes
Fuji (Subaru) & Isuzu	Lafayette (Indiana)	9/89	120,000	1,700	no
Honda	Marysville (Ohio)	11/82	510,000	8,000	no
Nissan	Smyrna (Tennessee)	6/83	440,000	5,100	no
Toyota	Georgetown (Kentucky)	7/88	200,000	3,500	no
Total			2,050,000	28,000	

Source: *Business Week* (August 1989).

Note: Production and employment are planned figures. Data on unionization are as of September 1989.

Honda was the first Japanese automaker to start building cars in the United States. In November 1982, Honda completed its factory in Ohio and began to produce Honda Accords for the U.S. market. Since then, most of the other Japanese automakers have followed Honda's approach and built factories in the United States.

Table 7.1 summarizes the current status of Japanese auto plants in the United States. As the table shows, by the end of 1989, seven Japanese automobile factories (including joint ventures with American automakers) were operating in America. The total production capacity of these factories exceeds two million vehicles per year, and more than twenty thousand workers are employed there. The Japanese cars made in America sold quite well, and their share in the total U.S. auto production has increased consistently. In 1989, about 15 percent of cars made in America were produced in these Japanese factories, and the share of these Japanese cars seems to be increasing. Due to the expansion of the Japanese plants in the United States, domination of the U.S. auto market by Detroit seems to be challenged.

IMPACT ON THE LABOR MARKET

The expansion of the Japanese auto plants is also affecting the labor market of the U.S. automobile industry. The U.S. automakers and the United Auto Workers (UAW) have lived together comfortably with adversary bargaining for many years. Almost all of the American autoworkers had been organized under the UAW. Under imperfectly competitive market structures, both in the product and the labor markets, they could achieve huge price markups and wage markups at the expense of the U.S. consumers, as discussed in the previous chapters. But, the strong market powers of the Big Three and of the UAW are dwindling: the market power of the Big Three is weakening because they are losing market share, and the UAW is losing its power in the labor market of the American automobile industry because it has not been very successful in unionizing the Japanese auto plants in the United States.

Of the seven Japanese auto plants in the United States listed in table 7.1, the UAW has succeeded in organizing only the three plants where Japanese companies build automobiles with or for U.S. automakers. The three unionized plants are New United Motor Manufacturing Inc. (NUMMI) in California, Diamond-Star Motors in Illinois, and Mazda in Michigan. NUMMI is a joint venture by GM and Toyota, where GM brand cars and Toyota brand cars are being produced. Diamond-Star Motors is a joint venture by Chrysler and Mitsubishi, where both brands of car are produced. Eighty percent of the cars produced in the Mazda plant in Flat Rock, Michigan are Ford brand cars. Except for these three plants, the UAW has not been able to organize Japanese auto plants in the United States. Even at the three unionized plants, the UAW accepted a Japanese-like union contract that allows managers to deploy workers more flexibly and more cheaply than in most American auto plants.

Obviously, the UAW attempted to unionize the Japanese plants to maintain its dominant power in the labor market of the U.S. automobile industry. It first tried to organize Honda's Ohio factory in 1985. But, fearing an apparent defeat, the UAW withdrew the petition for an organizing election just a few weeks before the vote was to be taken by the workers there. Confrontation between the UAW and the Japanese carmakers culminated in the summer of 1989 when the UAW attempted to organize the Nissan plant in Smyrna, Tennessee. Although both sides expended substantial energy and resources there, the result of the election was an astonishing defeat of the UAW. During the election campaign, the companies emphasized that the wage rate at the Nissan plant was equivalent to the industry average and that the plant had been operating without a single layoff ever since it opened in 1983. The workers at the Nissan plant rejected the UAW's bid to represent workers there by a 2-to-1 margin.

In addition to the nonunion atmosphere, more and more American workers in the Japanese auto plants have accepted a Japanese-like work style. For example, in those Japanese plants, detailed job classifications have disappeared, so managers can deploy workers to different positions according to labor input needs. Further, generally speaking, worker absenteeism in the Japanese auto plants is much lower than that in their U.S. counterparts. For example, before the GM and Toyota joint venture (NUMMI) started, the old GM factory in Fremont, California had about 20 percent absenteeism. Recent figures in *Business Week* (14 August 1989) show that absenteeism in the NUMMI Fremont factory was less than 2 percent. Thus, foreign direct investment in the United States by the Japanese auto industry seems to have affected the labor market of the American automobile industry in various ways.

IMPACT ON DOMESTIC EMPLOYMENT IN JAPAN

Lessons from the Color Television Trade

In the last section, we briefly discussed how Japanese foreign direct investment (FDI) affected the labor market in the United States. Since FDI is a transfer of production capabilities to foreign countries, it involves a transfer of employment opportunities from the sending country to the receiving country. Therefore, if a large surplus of labor exists, the outflow of production capabilities might bring about a serious unemployment problem in the sending country.

As shown in figure 7.3, the rate of increase in Japanese FDI has been dramatic in the 1980s. In view of this, the fear of possible deindustrialization has been expressed by business and labor leaders in Japan. They argue that, although the current unemployment rate in Japan is lower than those in most countries, the dramatic outflow of production capabilities may cause a serious unemployment problem in the future. Discussion of possible deindustrialization of the Japanese economy is so wide-spread that Japanese newspapers frequently carry articles on the problem, and many estimates have been made of the impact of Japanese FDI on domestic employment in Japan. However, the magnitude of the effect of FDI on domestic employment depends upon such factors as how much the overseas production replaces the export of the same category of goods and how much export of related products the FDI induces. (For example, when Japanese automakers build cars in the United States, they ship many parts from Japan.) Therefore, an

FIGURE 7.6 Production, Export, and Employment (Japanese color TVs)

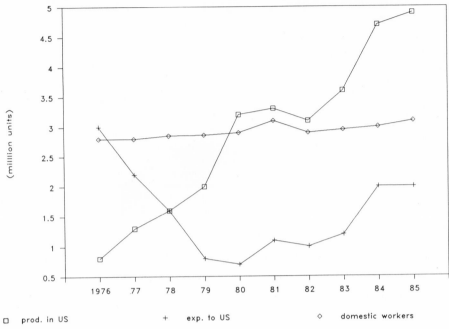

□   prod. in US   +   exp. to US   ◇   domestic workers

Source: Japanese Ministry of Labor; Japanese Ministry of International Trade and Industry.

increase in overseas production does not necessarily mean a reduction in domestic employment.

Development of overseas production and domestic employment in the color television industry gives a good example of the ambiguous effect of FDI on employment. Figure 7.6 shows various indicators in the Japanese color television industry since the middle 1970s: the number of color TVs exported to the United States, the number of Japanese color TV produced in the U.S., and the number of workers in the consumer electronics industry in Japan. As discussed in detail in Chapter 2, when exports of Japanese color television sets to the United States increased dramatically (150 percent increase from 1975 to 1976!), management and labor in the U.S. industry strongly urged the U.S. government to take severely restrictive measures against the Japanese imports. After intense negotiation, the Japanese agreed on the orderly market agreement (OMA) on their shipment of color television sets to the United States. Further, the agreement contained a clause that encouraged Japanese firms to build their plants in the United States. As a result, after 1977 Japanese exports of color TV sets declined dramatically while the production of Japanese color TV sets in the United States rapidly increased. But, (as shown in figure 7.6) employment in the Japanese consumer electronics industry did not decline at all, because the Japanese firms switched their production lines to the production of VCRs and because they increased their shipments of color TV sets to the European market. Thus, the effect of overseas production on domestic employment is ambiguous, and the direction and magnitude of such an effect should be estimated before we emphasize fears of deindustrialization of the Japanese economy.

Estimation of the Employment Effect

AVAILABLE ESTIMATES

As Japanese FDI became a hot issue for business and labor in Japan, various estimates were attempted on the impact of the outflow of Japanese capital on domestic employment in Japan (interested readers might wish to refer to Goto (1988) for summaries of these estimates). Probably the most comprehensive of these empirical studies is the one by the Japan Institute of Labor (1984). It classified the effect on domestic employment into three sub-effects: (*a*) a decline in employment opportunities due to the decline in exports replaced by overseas production; (*b*) a decline in employment opportunities due to imports from Japanese plants located overseas; and (*c*) an increase in employment opportunities due to increased exports of parts and materials to Japanese plants overseas. Adding up the three sub-effects, the study concluded that due to Japanese FDI to the United States the employment opportunities of Japanese workers were decreased by 10,000 to 200,000 jobs and that due to FDI to Asian countries, they were decreased by 120,000 to 300,000 jobs. The wide range in this estimate should be noted. This is because the study *assumes* a certain percentage of replacement ratio on how many exports would be replaced by an increase in production overseas. More specifically, it assumes two sets of replacement ratios (100 percent replacement and one-third replacement) instead of estimating the magnitude of such replacement.

ON METHODOLOGY

The methodology of available estimates on the employment effect of FDI is very similar to that used by the Japan Institute of Labor. First, the value of overseas production by Japanese firms is computed. Second, it is assumed that the decline in exports after FDI is proportional to the value of overseas production. For the replacement ratio of exports by FDI, rather arbitrary figures (e.g., one-third, one-half, or 100 percent)

TABLE 7.2.
Elasticity of Exports with respect to Foreign Direct Investment

	Elasticity	Time Lag (year)	R^2	t	D.W.
Food & tobacco	−0.51786	2	0.9372	−2.22	1.4563
Textiles & clothing	−0.16606	1	0.9794	−1.59	1.9282
Chemicals	−0.19168	3	0.9755	−1.88	1.8457
Metal & metal products	−0.32349	3	0.9775	−2.06	2.1169
Machinery	−0.21536	1	0.9948	−1.12	1.1937
Electric machinery	−0.28305	2	0.9954	−1.78	2.1192
Transport equipment	−0.17135	3	0.9944	−1.36	1.9966
Other manufacturing	−0.14774	1	0.9888	−1.84	0.9773

Source: Author's estimate. See text for method of estimation.
Note: Estimation period is 1965–85.

are used for the purpose of estimation of the employment effects. As the authors of such studies themselves admit, the figure used for the replacement ratio is arbitrary, and therefore, they cannot decide which figure is most likely. Third, after obtaining the effect on domestic production, the employment effect is calculated by using the labor input ratio.

We attempted an estimate by directly measuring the elasticity of exports (or domestic production) with respect to FDI. Table 7.2 summarizes the elasticities by major industries. In the estimate, the logarithm of the value of exports was regressed on the logarithm of the value of accumulated FDI and on time trend. Since a time lag is likely to exist between FDI and a decline in exports, lagged variables are used on the right-hand side of the regression equation.

More specifically, we used the estimation equation

$$\ln(EXP) = \beta_o + \beta_1\ln(INV_{t-a}) + \beta_2 T + \beta_3 T^2$$

where EXP = value of exports

INV = foreign direct investment (accumulated)

T = time trend

a = time lag.

In view of the high values of R^2 and t (given in table 7.2), the result in table 7.2 seems to be fairly reliable. But, as shown in table 7.2, the value of the elasticity varies from industry to industry.

Given the estimated values of elasticity of exports with respect to the value of accumulated FDI, the effect on domestic employment is easily

TABLE 7.3.

Current Effects of Foreign Direct Investment on Domestic Employment (Japan)

	Impact Effect (×1,000)	Steady-state Effect (×1,000)
Agriculture	—	1.3
Mining	—	1.2
Manufacturing	93.4	240.7
Food and tobacco	0.8	1.6
Textiles and clothing	−1.2	−0.1
Chemicals	−0.9	2.5
Metal & metal products	4.3	27.9
Machinery	16.9	50.6
Electric machinery	30.9	80.8
Transport equipment	36.2	45.0
Other manufacturing	6.3	32.4
Construction	—	1.5
Public utilities	—	2.5
Wholesale & retail trade	—	34.0
Banking and insurance	—	10.1
Real estate	—	0.2
Transportation	—	11.4
Service	—	15.7
Garbage processing	—	0.7
Education & health	—	7.5
Public service	—	0.4
Other	—	2.0
Total	93.4	329.3

Source: Author's estimate. See text for details.

obtained. Using this method, estimates were obtained for both the current effects and the future effects of Japanese FDI in the 1980s.

CURRENT IMPACT ON EMPLOYMENT IN JAPAN

First, let us examine the current effect on domestic employment of the acceleration of Japanese FDI in the 1980s. Note that we estimated the effect of *acceleration* of FDI. Since Japanese FDI has been dramatically accelerated since the beginning of the 1980s, we attempted to measure the effects of such acceleration in the 1980s. More specifically, we compared the actual Japanese employment with employment in a hypothetical situation where the growth rate of FDI in 1980–85 remained the same as the growth rate in 1975–80.

Table 7.3 summarizes the result of our estimation. Note that both the impact effects and the steady-state effects are shown. The latter effects include indirect effects from other industries. For example, when

exports of automobiles are contained, the domestic demand for inter-
mediate goods (e.g., steel) is also contained, and the employment level
in the steel industry is indirectly influenced by the outflow of auto plants
through a declined demand for steel by domestic auto plants. Further,
note that the figures in table 7.3 show the change in Japanese employment when the effect of accelerated FDI in 1980–85 is fully realized.
Since there is a time lag of two to three years, the figures in the table
should be interpreted as the effect in 1987–88.

According to our estimate (see table 7.3), the impact effect of accelerated FDI in the 1980s is 93,000 jobs in the manufacturing sector
as a whole. Large effects can be observed in the electronics and the
transport equipment industries, which have been especially active in
transferring their production capabilities to foreign countries in recent
years. When the indirect effect (as explained above) is included, lost
employment opportunities in the manufacturing sector and in the whole
economy are 240,000 and 330,000 jobs, respectively.

FUTURE IMPACT ON EMPLOYMENT IN JAPAN

Estimates of the future impact of Japanese FDI on domestic employment are more interesting. When deindustrialization is discussed in
Japan, very few argue that the Japanese economy has been deindustrialized. Rather, the fear of possible deindustrialization is emphasized.
Therefore, although it is very difficult, it is important to estimate the
magnitude of the employment effect of FDI in the future.

Table 7.4 summarizes the result of our estimation of the future effect.
We assumed (as the MITI assumed) that Japanese FDI will be further
accelerated by 14 percent every year in the future. The figures in table
7.4 show the effect of such a further acceleration in the latter half of
the 1980s. It is estimated that the employment opportunities for the
Japanese workers will be depressed by 320,000 jobs in the early 1990s
due to the acceleration of Japanese FDI. The negative effect on the
electronics industry is especially large, more than 82,000 jobs.

It should be noted, however, that a loss of employment opportunities
does not necessarily mean a decline in the actual number of workers in
these industries. While it is estimated that due to further acceleration
of Japanese FDI about 320,000 employment opportunities will be affected, it should be kept in mind that 3 to 4 million jobs were created
in the Japanese economy in the last few years. In other words, if all
other things are equal, a few million jobs will be created in the few years
to come. Thus, even if the dramatic acceleration of Japanese FDI decreases the job opportunities by 320,000, this is at most 10 percent of
the jobs created. Thus, by our estimate, the recent fears of a possible
deindustrialization of the Japanese economy are not substantiated.

TABLE 7.4.

Future Effects of Foreign Direct Investment on Domestic Employment
(Japan)

	Impact Effect *(×1,000)*	*Steady-state Effect* *(×1,000)*
Agriculture	—	1.9
Mining	—	1.4
Manufacturing	85.2	230.5
Food and tobacco	0.8	1.7
Textiles and clothing	5.2	14.5
Chemicals	2.4	6.8
Metal & metal products	5.8	25.6
Machinery	18.0	50.6
Electric machinery	32.0	82.0
Transport equipment	10.8	14.3
Other manufacturing	10.1	35.1
Construction	—	1.5
Public utilities	—	2.5
Wholesale & retail trade	—	31.6
Banking and insurance	—	10.3
Real estate	—	0.1
Transportation	—	11.2
Service	—	15.4
Garbage processing	—	0.7
Education & health	—	7.0
Public service	—	0.4
Other	—	2.1
Total	85.2	316.6

Source: Author's estimate. See text for details.

CHAPTER EIGHT

Conclusions

ONE OF THE major purposes of this book is to establish a new analytical framework for international trade and its restrictions, which is both rigorous and practical. Since international trade problems have recently become more interrelated with domestic labor problems (see chapters 2 and 3), we attempted to develop a new framework by integrating, at least to some extent, international economics (especially international trade theory) and labor economics. Thus, the new framework might be called labor-oriented international economics.

After establishing a new rigorous general equilibrium trade theory under this framework, we applied the new theory to theoretical and empirical analyses of the U.S.-Japan automobile trade in recent years. Further, because the huge trade imbalance between Japan and the United States (and other major industrialized countries) has brought about a dramatic outflow of Japanese capital through the sharp appreciation of the Japanese yen, we examined the impact of the acceleration of Japanese foreign direct investment on domestic employment now and in the future.

This brief chapter summarizes the major findings in the previous chapters and presents an agenda for future studies.

A NEW FRAMEWORK AND IMPERFECT COMPETITION IN THE LABOR MARKET

Trade Conflict and Domestic Labor Problems

As the national economies of the world are integrated with each other, international trade problems have become more and more closely interrelated with domestic labor problems. For example, faced with growing unemployment after the second oil crisis, many people in major industrialized countries (most notably the United States) came to argue that Japan's hugh trade surplus is responsible for the high unemployment in their countries. At the same time, international trade conflicts are often intensified by pressures from labor unions in the importing country. In spite of a close relationship between international trade problems and domestic labor problems, the discussions of this relationship have been often emotional, in part because of the lack of a firm theory of labor-oriented international economics. There is a great need for such a new framework of analysis.

In chapter 2, important facts underlying trade conflicts between the United States and Japan were discussed. The textile and clothing trade and its restriction were examined in detail as a historical example of trade conflicts between the two countries, and discussions on color television sets and automobiles followed as more recent examples. We found that frequently petitions and lobbying activities of labor unions intensified the trade conflicts.

In chapter 3, the recent labor market and recent labor-management relations were carefully examined. Using data on the U.S. labor market, we showed that strong unions achieved huge wage markup in many industries where trade conflicts with Japan are serious (e.g., the automobile and steel industries) and that the high production costs resulting from these wage markups are a major cause of the weakness of these industries in international competition. Further, we showed that the wage rate in these industries is not only higher but also less flexible than that in other industries and that because of the rigidity of wage rate, adjustment to a decline in production is made largely through a change in employment. This seems to be one of the important reason for the hugh unemployment in these industries in the recessionary years after the second oil crisis.

A New Theory and Orthodoxy

In chapter 4 we developed a rigorous trade model that incorporates the interrelations between trade problems and labor problems, and in chapter 5 this model was used to analyze the U.S.-Japan automobile trade. The model is more suitable than orthodox trade theories for the analysis of intra-industry trade of manufactured goods in general among similar industrialized countries, because the orthodox theories encounter various difficulties when applied to this trade, which has become more and more important in world trade (especially after World War II).

First, according to orthodox trade theories, international trade occurs because of differences in factor endowments, technology, and tastes, and therefore these theories cannot explain intra-industry trade between similar countries at all. Second, generally speaking, the orthodox trade theories are based upon three basic assumptions; (*a*) perfect competition in both the product and the factor markets, (*b*) constant returns to scale technology in production, and (c) a homogeneous product. These assumptions are not very realistic when applied to manufactured goods trade.

The new framework developed in this book is based upon more realistic assumptions: (a) imperfect competition in both the product and the labor markets, (b) increasing return to scale technology due to fixed cost, and (c) product differentiation. After developing the new general equilibrium model, we demonstrated that the new framework is powerful in explaining various aspects of intra-industry trade of manufactured goods (such as automobiles) and that the formal model is readily used in empirical applications concerning real world trade, (such as the U.S.-Japan automobile trade).

This book is intended in no way to deny the importance of orthodox trade theories such as the Heckscher-Ohlin-Samuelson model. The orthodox theories are very powerful in analyzing the international trade of primary products between very different countries, such as trade between a developing country and an industrialized country, while the new theory of international trade under imperfect competition is very useful in analyzing the trade of manufactured goods between similar countries. Therefore, the two frameworks should be considered as supplementary rather than contradictory.

Two Major Extensions

The framework of this theory is an extension of the theories of international trade under imperfect competition that have become very popular in the last few years. Attempts are being made by many distinguished economists to establish a new realistic framework of international trade. But, since such attempts have just started, there is ample room for extension and improvement. This book is intended to contribute to such attempts, in addition to serving for immediate empirical application to analysis of real world trade, such as the U.S.-Japan automobile trade.

First, the model developed in this book has included "variable" elasticity of substitution between various types of differentiated goods, which was often overlooked in previous studies. In addition to the plausibility of the assumption, the model based on variable substitutability has proved to be very powerful in explaining the stylized facts of gains from international trade (discussed in detail in chapter 4).

Second, the model in this book has explicitly incorporated imperfect competition in the labor market in addition to that in the product market. While previous models of international trade under imperfect competition have incorporated the imperfection in the product market, almost all of them still assumed that the factor markets, including labor and capital, are perfectly competitive. According to these models, all workers receive a competitive wage rate equal to marginal productivity and therefore the labor market is always in full employment. In reality, however, the wage rate in some industries (e.g., the automobile and steel industries) is much higher than in other industries, and unemployment is one of the most important issues in discussions of trade restrictions.

In this sense, there has been a big gap between the practical policy makers and the academic economists. This book is intended to fill this gap by explicitly incorporating imperfect competition in the labor market as well as in the product market. By incorporating labor market imperfections into the model, the framework developed here is suitable for the analysis of international trade, unemployment, and labor unions.

Further, we have demonstrated how asymmetry in labor market imperfections creates a competitive edge between trading partners, and additional insights into the effect of trade and its restriction have been presented.

ADDITIONAL INSIGHTS INTO THE EFFECT OF TRADE RESTRICTIONS

Under the new framework developed here, the effect of international trade (and of its restrictions) has been rigorously analyzed in both the long-term and the short-term. After the theoretical analyses in chapters 4 and 5, the magnitude of various effects was estimated in chapter 6 for the U.S.-Japan automobile trade as an example. Note that the framework is general and can be applied to trade of various goods between various countries. The major findings of these analyses are given below.

Long-Run Effect—Quintuple Gains from Trade

In chapter 4, the long-run effect of international trade under imperfect competition was examined theoretically, using the basic model developed there. It was rigorously shown that international trade brings about the following five additional gains beyond the orthodox gains from trade based on the (Baldwin) availability locus.

First, it was found that the opening up of trade in differentiated goods increases consumer welfare by providing increased variety in available goods. For example, thanks to international trade, American consumers can enjoy French and German wines in addition to domestic California wine.

This first gain has been pointed out and analyzed by various authors, including Krugman. But, under most models the gain from trade often stops here because they assume a perfectly competitive labor market and invariant substitutability of differentiated goods without regard to the number of types of goods available to consumers. The model developed in this book gives four additional gains from trade (or losses from trade restrictions).

Second, opening up trade reduces the monopolistic power of domestic producers through increased foreign competition. After the opening up of trade, the number of types of goods available to consumers increases because of the introduction of foreign models, and therefore the goods become closer substitutes than before. Because of the increased substitutability, producers face more elastic demand, and the price markup is decreased.

Third, due to an increase in demand because of the lower price markup and the expansion of market size after trade, the production level of each firm increases. Since technology in the differentiated goods sector is characterized by increasing returns to scale (IRS), the average cost of production is decreased by the increase in the production level. As discussed in chapter 6, this reduction in average cost is substantial: If all the barriers to world automobile trade were removed, the average cost of producing a car would decline by more than $600, in other words, the United States is losing more than $6 billion every year due to various barriers to the automobile trade.

Fourth, at least in the long run international trade reduces structural unemployment through an increase in employment and a decline in the wage markup in the distorted sector (e.g., the American automobile industry). The Hicks-Marshall laws of derived demand state that when the demand for a product becomes more elastic, the derived demand for labor also becomes more elastic. As explained in detail in chapter 4, an increase in the elasticity of derived demand for labor after the opening up of trade contributes to the correction of the imperfect labor market structure caused by union wage markup. Because of the reduction of labor market imperfections, along with the increase in product demand, employment in the distorted sector is increased (and therefore unemployment is decreased) by the opening up of trade in the long run. According to the estimate in chapter 6, structural unemployment in the American automobile industry would be reduced by as much as 14 percent in the long run, if all barriers to automobile trade were removed. Further, we can observe an actual example of the correction of labor market imperfections through international trade. As discussed in chapter 3, faced with severe competition from Japan, a new trend of labor-management cooperation has been emerging in American industries, including the automobile and steel industries.

Finally, international trade contributes to economic growth through the release of capital resources from the distorted sector. As discussed in chapter 4, after the opening up of trade, the number of domestic models declines although the total number of models available to consumers increases due to the introduction of foreign models. Since a (huge) fixed cost is necessary to produce each model, a decrease in the number of domestic models implies a saving in the capital resources used for the fixed cost. Thus, after the opening up of trade, the society can enjoy greater variety with less capital employed in the distorted sector. This released capital may be invested in the rest of the economy, which would contribute to further economic growth.

The Short-Run Effect—Conflict of Interest?

In Chapter 5, the basic model in chapter 4 is extended in two important ways so that the framework can serve for the analysis of the effect of trade (and its restriction) in the short-run asymmetry case. The pattern and effects of the U.S.-Japan automobile trade were examined using the extended model. It was rigorously shown that, even if the relative factor endowments (i.e., economy-wide capital labor ratio) in the two countries are the same, Japan has a strong competitive advantage in automobile trade over the United States because of asymmetry in production technology and labor market imperfections.

It is important to note that, even if the technologies in the two countries are assumed to be the same, the difference in labor market imperfections alone can generate a substantial difference in competitive edge. The wage rate in the American automobile industry is much higher and less flexible than in other industries in the United States partly because (perhaps largely because) of the strong union in that industry. In Japan there is no such wage markup by autoworkers. Thus, it seems that imperfect competition in the labor market is largely responsible for the U.S.-Japan automobile trade conflict.

The effects of trade restrictions were carefully examined using the extended model. In chapter 5, it was rigorously shown that, when asymmetry in labor market imperfections (and/or asymmetry in production technologies) exists, trade restrictions will benefit the producers and workers in the country that is in the weaker position in international competition and will hurt those in the other country, while consumers in both countries will unambiguously lose because of the decreased variety and the higher prices under the restrictions.

After these effects of trade restrictions were rigorously proved, the analysis was applied to the actual automobile trade between the United States and Japan. Specifically, the effect of the VER for the U.S. market in 1984 was estimated, using the extended model that incorporates additional realities of the U.S.-Japan automobile trade, such as asymmetry in economy size and price discrimination (in addition to asymmetry in technology and labor market imperfections). The estimation showed that the American consumers' loss from the Japanese VER was more than $3 billion in 1984, while the number of jobs for American autoworkers increased by 23,800.

Although it is very difficult to compare the loss to consumers with the gain of the autoworkers, simple calculation shows that the cost to consumers per job saved is more than $126,000, which far exceeds the average annual wage of the American autoworker ($37,000). Further, under a continuation of the Japanese VER, all parties, including American autoworkers, lose in the long run through an increase in the degree of imperfect competition in both the product and the labor markets.

In addition to the losses to various parties in the United States, we must consider the losses to the Japanese, including consumers, producers, and workers. As is rigorously shown in chapter 5, trade restrictions hurt all parties in Japan. First, the Japanese producers have a direct effect of the VER in the decline of exports. Although the decline in profits resulting from the reduction of export volume would be partially offset by an increase in price, the net effect is a decline in the profits of Japanese auto producers. Second, the decline in production due to the reduction of exports would hurt Japanese workers through a decline in employment in the Japanese automobile industry. Third, Japanese consumers (as well as American consumers) would suffer an increase in the price of cars.

TOWARD A LABOR-ORIENTED INTERNATIONAL ECONOMICS

Following the detailed examination of the interrelationship of trade and labor, the impact of foreign direct investment (FDI) on domestic labor in Japan was discussed (chapter 7) since the trade conflicts encouraged such FDI from Japan. Japanese FDI has been increasing dramatically in recent years. More and more Japanese firms are building their plants in foreign countries in an attempt to avoid trade conflict and to exploit lower production costs. Faced with the rapid growth of Japanese FDI on a large scale, business and labor in Japan came to express a fear of possible deindustrialization of the Japanese economy. Since, in spite of heated debates on the problem, very few econometric estimates on the effect of FDI on domestic employment are available, we presented estimates of the effect of FDI on domestic employment in Japan, now and in the future. It was suggested that, although the loss of employment opportunities may be substantial (about 300,000 jobs), the Japanese economy is likely to be able to absorb this adverse effect.

Let us briefly discuss what studies are needed in the future to establish a labor-oriented international economics. We have tried to develop a rigorous general equilibrium framework that is based on realistic assumptions and to apply it to the analysis of various problems in the real world. While we have established a rigorous general equilibrium model for the analysis of the effects of trade on the labor market, our estimate on the effects of foreign direct investment (FDI) on domestic labor is based on a rather rough framework. In view of the importance of FDI, a rigorous model should be established for FDI and labor problems. Further, in addition to the international flow of goods and capital, international labor flow is a very important topic for labor-oriented international economics. Obviously, this work is in no way complete, and there is ample room for further extension and improvement. For all that, we hope that this book serves as a stepping stone toward better understanding of interactions between international trade and domestic labor problems in the real world.

BIBLIOGRAPHY

Altshuler, A. et. al. 1984. *The Future of the Automobiles.* Cambridge: MIT Press.

Ashenfelter, O., and G. E. Johnson. 1972. "Unionism, Relative Wages, and Labor Quality in U.S. Manufacturing Industries." *International Economic Review* 13.

Balassa, B. 1967. *Trade Liberalization among Industrial Countries: Objectives and Alternatives.* New York: McGraw-Hill.

Balassa, B., and M. Noland. 1988. *Japan in the World Economy.* Washington, D.C.: Institute for International Economics.

Bhagwati, J. N., ed. 1982. *Import Competition and Response.* Chicago: University of Chicago Press.

Bhagwati, J., and T. N. Srinivasan. 1983. *Lectures on International Trade.* Cambridge: MIT Press.

Blanchard, O. J. 1983. "The Production and Inventory Behavior of the American Automobile Industry." *Journal of Political Economy* 89.

Block, H. 1974. "Prices, Costs, and Profits in Canadian Manufacturing: The Influence of Tariffs and Concentration." *Canadian Journal of Economics* 7.

Blueston, B., and B. Harrison. 1982. *The Deindustrialization of America.* New York: Basic Books.

Brander, J. 1981. "Intra-Industry Trade in Identical Commodities," *Journal of International Economics* 11.

Calvo, G. A. 1978. "Urban Unemployment and Wage Determination in LDCs: Trade Unions in the Harris-Todaro Model." *International Economic Review* 19.

Carlsson, B. 1972. "The Measurement of Efficiency Production: An Application to Swedish Manufacturing Industries, 1968." *Swedish Journal of Economics* 74.

Chamberlin, E. H. 1962. *The Theory of Monopolistic Competition.* Cambridge: Harvard University Press.

Cline, W. R. 1984. *Exports of Manufactures from Developing Countries.* Washington, D.C.: Brookings Institution.

Corden, W. M. 1967. "Monopoly, Tariffs and Subsidies." *Economica* 34.

Cowling, K. J., and J. Cubbin. 1971. "Price, Quality and Advertising Competition: An Econometric Investigation of the United Kingdom Car Market." *Economica* 37.

Crandall, R. W. 1984. "Import Quotas and the Automobile Industry: The Costs of Protectionism." *Brookings Review* (Summer).

Dixit, A. 1979. "A Model of Duopoly Suggesting a Theory of Entry Barriers." *Bell Journal of Economics* 10.

———. 1980. "The Role of Investment in Entry-Deterrence." *Economic Journal* 90.

———. 1982. "Recent Developments in Oligopoly Theory." *American Economic Review* 72.

———. 1984. "International Trade Policy for Oligopolistic Industries." *Economic Journal*. Conference papers.

Dixit, A., and V. Norman. 1980. *Theory of International Trade*. Cambridge: Cambridge University Press.

Dixit, A., and J. Stiglitz. 1977. "Monopolistic Competition and Optimal Product Diversity." *American Economic Review* 67.

Douglas, P. H. 1976. "The Cobb-Douglas Production Function Once Again: Its History, Its Testing, and Some New Empirical Values." *Journal of Political Economy* 85.

Dunlop, J. T. 1944. *Wage Determination under Trade Unions*. New York: Macmillian.

Eaton, J., and A. Panagariya. 1979. "Gains from Trade under Variable Returns to Scale, Commodity Taxation, Tariff and Factor Market Distortions." *Journal of International Economics* 9.

Ethier, W. 1979. "Internationally Decreasing Costs and World Trade." *Journal of International Economics* 9.

———. 1982. "National and International Returns to Scale in the Modern Theory of International Trade." *American Economic Review* 72.

Falvey, R. E., and H. Kierzkowski. 1985. "Product Quality, Intra-Industry Trade and Imperfect Competition." Mimeo.

Farber, H. S. 1978. "Individual Preferences and Union Wage Determination: The Case of the United Mine Workers." *Journal of Political Economy* 86.

Farber, H. S., and D. H. Saks. 1980. "Why Workers Want Unions: The Role of Relative Wages and Job Characteristics." *Journal of Political Economy* 88.

Feenstra, R. C. 1984. "Voluntary Export Restraint in the U.S. Autos, 1980–81: Quality, Employment, and Welfare Effects." In R. Baldwin and A. Krueger, eds., *The Structure and Evolution of Recent U.S. Trade Policy*. Chicago: University of Chicago Press.

Finger, J. M. 1975. "Trade Overlap and Intra-Industry Trade." *Economic Inquiry* 13.

Freeman, R., and J. L. Medoff. 1984. *What Do Unions Do?* New York: Basic Books.

Friedman, J. 1983. *Oligopoly Theory*. Cambridge: Cambridge University Press.

General Agreement on Tariffs and Trade. 1984. *Textiles and Closing in the World Economy*. Geneva.

Gordon, R. J. 1982. "Why U.S. Wage and Employment Behavior Differs from That in Britain and Japan." *Economic Journal* 92.

Goto, J. 1985. "A General Equilibrium Analysis of Trade Restrictions under Imperfect Competition: Theory and Some Evidence for the Automotive Trade." *The World Bank Discussion Paper* (DRD #130).

———. 1986. *A General Equilibrium Analysis of International Trade under*

Imperfect Competition in Both Product and Labor Markets—Theory and Evidence from the Automobile Trade. Ph.D. diss. Yale University.

————. 1988. *Kokusai Rodo Keizaigaku (International Labor Economics)*. Tokyo: The Oriental Economist.

Grossman, G. M. 1982. "The Employment and Wage Effects of Import Competition in the United States." *National Bureau of Economic Research Working Paper*, 1041.

Grubel, H. G., and P. J. Lloyd. 1975. *Intra-Industry Trade: The Theory and Measurement of International Trade in Differentiated Products*. London: Macmillan.

Harris, R. 1984. "Applied General Equilibrium Analysis of Small Open Economies with Scale Economies and Imperfect Competition," *American Economic Review* 74.

Harris, R. G., and D. Cox. 1983. *Trade, Industrial Policy, and Canadian Manufacturing*. Toronto: Ontario Economic Council.

Helpman, E. 1981. "International Trade in the Presence of Product Differentiation, Economies of Scale and Monopolistic Competition." *Journal of International Economics* 11.

————. 1983. "Variable Returns to Scale and International Trade: Two Generalizations." *Economic Letters* 11.

————. 1984. "Increasing Returns, Imperfect Markets, and Trade Theory." In R. W. Jones and P. B. Kenen, eds., *Handbook of International Economics*, Vol. 1. Amsterdam: North-Holland Pub.

Helpman, E., and A. Razin. 1983. "Increasing Returns, Monopolistic Competition, and Factor Movement: A Welfare Analysis." *Journal of International Economics* 14.

Helpman, E., and P. Krugman. 1985. *Market Structure and Foreign Trade*, Cambridge: MIT Press.

Hieser, R. 1970. "Wage Determination with Bilateral Monopoly in the Labor Market: A Theoretical Treatment." *Economic Record* 46.

Hunker, J. A. 1983. *Structural Change in the U.S. Automobile Industry*. Lexington, Mass.: Lexington Books.

Hunsberger, W. S. 1964. *Japan and the United States in the World Economy*. New York: Harper.

Jacquemin, A. 1982. "Imperfect Market Structures and International Trade: Some Recent Research." *Kyklos* 35.

Jacquemin, A., E. De Ghellinck, and C. Huveneers. 1980. "Concentration and Profitability in a Small Open Economy." *Journal of Industrial Economics* 20.

The Japan Institute of Labor. 1984. *Kaigai Chokusetsu Toshi to Koyo Mondai (Foreign Direct Investment and Employment)*. Tokyo.

Johnson, G. E. 1975. "Economic Analysis of Trade Unionism." *American Economic Review*. Papers and Proceedings Vol. 65.

Johnston, J. 1972. "Economic Analysis of Trade Unionism." *Economic Journal* 82.

Jones, R. W. 1971. "A Three-Factor Model in Theory, Trade and History." In

J. Bhagwati, R. Jones, and R. Mundell, eds. *Trade, Balance of Payments and Growth: Papers in International Economics in Honor of Charles P. Kindleberger.* Amsterdam: North-Holland Pub.

Keesing, D., and M. Wolf. 1980. *Textile Quotas against Developing Countries.* London: Trade Policy Research Centre.

Kierzkowski, H., ed. 1984. *Monopolistic Competition in International Trade.* Oxford: Oxford University Press.

Krause, L. B. 1985. *U.S. Economic Policy toward the Association of Southeast Asian Nations: Meeting the Japanese Challenge.* Washington, D. C.: Brookings Institution.

Krishna, K. 1983. "Trade Restrictions as Facilitating Practices." Mimeo. Princeton University.

Krugman, P. R. 1979. "Increasing Returns, Monopolistic Competition, and International Trade." *Journal of International Economics* 9.

——— . 1980. "Scale Economies, Product Differentiation, and the Pattern of Trade." *American Economic Review* 70.

——— . 1981. "Intraindustry Specialization and the Gains from Trade." *Journal of Political Economy* 89.

——— . 1982. "Trade in Differentiated Products and the Political Economy of Trade Liberalization." In J. Bhagwati, ed. *Import Competition and Response.* Chicago: University of Chicago Press.

Lancaster, K. 1978. *Variety, Equity, and Efficiency.* New York: Norton.

——— . 1980. "Intra-industry Trade under Perfect Monopolistic Competition." *Journal of International Economics* 10.

——— . 1982. "Protection and Product Differentiation." Mimeo.

Lawrence, C., and P. T. Spiller. 1983. "Product Diversity, Economies of Scale and International Trade." *Quarterly Journal of Economics* 97.

Lawrence, R. 1984. *Can America Compete?* Washington, D.C.: Brookings Institution.

Leamer, E. E. 1984. *Sources of International Comparative Advantage.* Cambridge: MIT Press.

Lewis, H. G. 1963. *Unionism and Relative Wages in the United States.* Chicago: University of Chicago Press.

Linder, S. B. 1961. *An Essay on Trade and Transformation.* New York: John Wiley & Sons.

Markusen, J. R. 1981. "Trade and Gains from Trade with Imperfect Competition." *Journal of International Economics* 11.

——— . 1984. "Multinationals, Multi-Plant Economies, and the Gains from Trade." *Journal of International Economics* 16.

Ministry of Labour, Japan. *Yearbook of Labour Statistic.* Tokyo. Various issues.

Mitchell, J. B. 1980. *Unions, Wages, and Inflation.* Washington, D.C.: Brookings Institution.

Motor Vehicle Manufacturing Association of the United States. 1985. *World Motor Vehicle Data.* Detroit.

Mussa, M. 1974. "Tariffs and the Distribution of Income: The Importance of

Factor Specificity, Substitutability, and Intensity in the Short and Long Run." *Journal of Political Economy* 82.

―――. 1978. "Dynamic Adjustment in the Heckscher-Ohlin-Samuelson Model." *Journal of Political Economy* 86.

―――. 1979. "The Two-Sector Model in Terms of Its Dual." *Journal of International Economics* 9.

Oswald, A. J. 1982. "The Microeconomic Theory of the Trade Union." *Economic Journal* 92.

Petri, P. A. 1984. *Modeling Japanese-American Trade: A Study of Asymmetric Interdependence*. Cambridge: Harvard University Press.

Rosen, S. 1970. "Unionism and the Occupational Wage Structure in the United States." *International Economic Review* 11.

Sampson, G., and W. Takacs. 1988. "Return Textile Trade to the Normal Workings of GATT." Mimeo. Stockholm.

Scherer, M. 1980. *Industrial Market Structure and Economic Performance*. Boston: Houghton Mifflin.

Scherer, M. 1975. *The Economics of Multi-Plant Operations: An International Comparison Study*. Cambridge: Harvard University Press.

Schmidt, P., and R. P. Strauss. 1976. "The Effect of Unions on Earnings and Earnings on Unions: A Mixed Logit Approach." *International Economic Review* 17.

Spence, M. E. 1976. "Product Selection, Fixed Costs, and Monopolistic Competition." *Review of Economic Studies* 43.

Spencer, B. J., and J. A. Brander. 1983. "International R & D Rivalry and Industrial Strategy." *Review of Economic Studies* 50.

Statistics Bureau, Japanese Management and Coordination Agency. 1985. *Japan Statistical Yearbook*. Tokyo.

Tarr, D. G., and R. Morkre. 1984. *Aggregate Costs to the United States of Tariffs and Quotas on Imports*. Washington, D. C.: Federal Trade Commission.

Toder, E. J. 1978. *Trade Policy and the U.S. Automobile Industry*. New York: Praeger Publishers.

U.S. Congress House of Representatives, Committee on Energy and Commerce. 1984. *Hearings on General Trade Policy*. Committee serial no. 98—55.

―――, Committee on Ways and Means. 1983. *Hearings on Reciprocal Trade and Market Access Legislation*. Committee serial no. 97–77.

U.S. Department of Commerce. 1984. *The U.S. Automobile Industry, 1983*. Washington, D.C.

―――. 1985. *Statistical Abrastract of the United States*. Washington, D.C.

―――. *Survey of Current Business*. Washington, D.C. Various issues.

U.S. Department of Labor, Bureau of Labor Statistics. *Employment and Earnings*. Washington, D.C. Various, issues.

United States International Trade Commission. 1985. *A Review of Recent Developments in the U.S. Automobile Industry Including an Assessment of the Japanese Voluntary Restraint Agreement*. Washington, D.C.

Varian, H. R. 1978. *Microeconomic Analysis*. New York: Norton.

Venables, A. J. 1982. "Optimal Tariffs for Trade in Monopolistically Competitive Commodities." *Journal of International Economics* 12.

Vernon, R. 1966. "International Investment and International Trade in the Product Cycle." *Quarterly Journal of Economics* 80.

Ward's Communications Incorporated. 1985. *Ward's Automotive Yearbook*. Detroit.

Weiss, L. W. 1985. "The Economic Rents Accruing to Union Workers by Industry." Mimeo.

White, L. J. 1971. *The Automobile Industry since 1945*. Cambridge: Harvard University Press.

Zysman, J., and L. Tyson, eds. 1983. *American Industry in International Competition*. Ithaca, N.Y.: Cornell University Press.